LABOUR IN BRITISH SOC

Social History in Perspective

General Editor: Jeremy Black

Social History in Perspective is a series of in-depth studies of the many topics in social, cultural and religious history for students. They also give the student clear surveys of the subject and present the most recent research in an accessible way.

Labour in British Society, 1830–1914

Donald M. MacRaild
and
David E. Martin

First published in Great Britain 2000 by
MACMILLAN PRESS LTD
Houndmills, Basingstoke, Hampshire RG21 6XS and London
Companies and representatives throughout the world

A Catalogue record for this book is available from the British Library.

ISBN 0–333–73158–1 hardcover
ISBN 0–333–73159–X paperback

First published in the United States of America 2000 by
ST. MARTIN'S PRESS, INC.,
Scholarly and Reference Division,
175 Fifth Avenue, New York, N.Y. 10010

ISBN 0–312–23313–2 (cloth)

Library of Congress Cataloging-in-Publication Data
MacRaild, Donald M.
Labour in British Society, 1830–1914 / Donald M. MacRaild and
David E. Martin.
p. cm. — (Social history in perspective)
Includes bibliographical references and index.
ISBN 0–312–23313–2
1. Labor movement—Great Britain—History. 2. Labor unions—Great
Britain—History. 3. Social conflict—Great Britain—History. 4. Great
Britain—Social conditions. I. Martin, David E., 1944– II.Title.
III. Series.
HD8390.M175 2000
331.88'0941'09034—dc21   99–045253

This book is printed on paper suitable for recycling and made from fully managed
and sustained forest sources.

10   9   8   7   6   5   4   3   2   1
09 08 07 06 05 04 03 02 01 00

Printed in China

For Lisa and Ann

CONTENTS

LIST OF TABLES

PREFACE

In his essay of 1941, *The Lion and the Unicorn*, George Orwell asked: 'What can the England of 1940 have in common with the England of 1840?' We have similarly inquired about the condition of the British working class in 1830 and 1914. Orwell answered his own question with another – 'what have you in common with the child of five whose photograph your mother keeps on the mantelpiece?' – and with a characteristic flourish added: 'Nothing, except that you happen to be the same person.' Though mindful of the problem of giving due weight to continuity as well as change, our answer to the question is more prosaic. In approaching almost a century's history of labour, we have two main aims.

The first is to provide in a fairly brief form an account of the key elements of labour's experiences between about 1830 and 1914. By 'labour' we understand not only the economist's 'factor of production' – although the workplace will be given particular attention – but also the wider experience of the working class. This, latter, includes the relationship between workers and other social and economic interests. In examining these themes, our supporting evidence draws frequently on primary sources, with the intention that the reader will gain some sense of the issues involved. We have tried to incorporate the findings of other historians and to indicate the substance of some principal debates, without, however, merely summarising the work of others. In the 40 years since the foundation of the Society for the Study of Labour History, the literature has burgeoned considerably (as the annual bibliographies of the Society's journal, the *Labour History Review*, comprehensively demonstrate). An attempt to include all contributions to the labour historiography of a particularly vibrant and debated period would absorb more space than we have. Besides, the field of labour history already contains many historiographic studies, as our bibliographical essay demonstrates. Nevertheless, if our main text has passed over or treated briefly some issues, the references in footnotes and the bibliographical essay should allow the student of the period to embark on a more detailed inquiry.

At the same time, we have aimed to interpret the experience of labour, without allowing our views to drown those of other historians. The process of social class formation during a period of extensive economic change was, in our view, the principal feature of the years from 1830 to 1914. In seeking to explain the character of that period, we lean towards the view that industrial capitalism brought workers more burdens than blessings, that the state privileged the interests of those with property at the expense of those without, and that political change was primarily the result of conflict, not conciliation. However, in holding these positions we hope we do so with more subtlety than in the form we have just stated them, while paying due respect to evidence on the other side of the argument.

In writing even such a short book as this, several debts have been incurred. We should like to acknowledge the advice and encouragement of the editorial staff at the publishers. Our copy editor, Juanita Bullough, made numerous suggestions for improving the text, which are much appreciated. A particular debt of gratitude is owed to our series editor, Jeremy Black, and to three scholars – Keith Laybourn, Matt Perry and Bill Purdue – who kindly read earlier drafts of the book. Each of them made numerous useful comments that have helped us to improve the following text. However, as we declined to follow all of their counsels, the usual caveat – acquitting them of responsibility for the faults that remain – must be entered. Although the gesture is an adequate measure of our appreciation of the support they have given to us, this book is dedicated to our wives, Lisa and Ann.

D.M.M.
D.E.M.

NOTE ON CURRENCY

In our period, Britain had a currency comprising pounds (£), shillings (s) and pence (d). There were 20 shillings to the pound, and 12 pence to the shilling. The Victorians used two different ways of writing out their currencies. Sixteen shillings and seven pence might be denoted as 16s 7d or as 16/7. A larger sum, such as forty-one shillings and four pence, could be written in four different ways: 41/4 or 41s 4d and £2 1s 4d or 2/1/4.

Throughout the text we refer to money values in this old currency. To do otherwise – to translate the agricultural labourer's wages from 8s to 40p (in new money) – would obscure values as they were.

INTRODUCTION: THEMES IN BRITISH LABOUR HISTORY, 1830–1914

The Early 1830s: A Watershed in Labour History?

The early 1830s are among the most decisive years in British labour history. They may lack the great symbolic importance of a number of other years and periods – 1848, the year of revolutions and effective end-point of Chartism as a mass movement; 1851, the birth-date of 'New Model Unionism' with the formation of the Amalgamated Society of Engineers; 1889, the year of 'New Unionism', and so on. But in the early 1830s a series of events, a conflation of forces and processes, presaged much of what happened in later labour history. The 'Swing Riots' of 1830–1, the 1830–2 reform crisis and the Poor Law Amendment Act of 1834 each in their own way made this age one of upheaval and change. In a number of respects, the year 1830 marked a crucial turning point – a watershed – in British history. Although the traditional handicraft workers were far from defunct, there was, nevertheless, a sense in which the crises of these years marked the coming of age in so many spheres.[1] For ordinary labouring people, new modes of production and new modes of work – not least, but by no means exclusively, in the mills of northern England – were coming to great prominence. Industrialism seemed to be triumphant and the political survival of the establishment was wrested from the jaws of civil unrest. And while industrialism seemed to hold out the prospect of dislocation rather than prosperity, the reform settlement of 1832 ended the immediate political crisis.

The sound of change rung loud and long in post-Napoleonic Britain. The population may have remained predominantly rural-dwelling in the early 1830s, but the progress of industrial and urban development decreased daily the relative importance of the rustic world lamented by

Cobbettite radicals and romantic idealists alike. The pressure of subsistence living standards on rural workers made them restive at the same
time as the growth of towns and factory production created new spheres
for social conflict among the expanding industrial proletariat. Bringing
the population together into larger units inevitably increased the potential for collective action – a potential noted, and much feared, in the early
days when effective policing remained a middle-class wish-fantasy. Activity could, and often did, occur without formal organisation, though more
workers were forming trade unions. For John Doherty, the cotton trades'
organiser, the union provided a key to unlock the capitalist world.
Doherty's view was shared, from a somewhat different perspective, by the
prime minister, Earl Grey (1830–4), who noted that workers were coming
to see their salvation, not in small local amalgams of kindred craftsmen,
but in consolidated national trade unions. For Doherty, Robert Owen
(the utopian socialist) and others like them, grand unions of all workers
were considered to be the best way to protect wages and to resist the pauperism that accompanied 'the fearful change, which the workings of the
last few years have produced in the condition of every class of labourers'.[2]

Doherty's language was neither acquiescent nor revolutionary. Yet
revolution was not beyond the realms of possibility; neither in 1830 nor
at points in the next two decades. In the early 1830s the authorities were
facing a crisis – not simply because men such as Doherty were issuing
exhortations for working men and women to join trade unions, but
because of two more noticeable problems. While the clamour for parliamentary reform deafened the towns, burning haystacks illuminated the
skies over England's southern shires. The reform crisis, which pulsated
for much of 1830–2, and the 'Swing' riots, which convulsed the rural
south and east of England in 1831–2, presented national government
and local officials alike with a frightening combination of forces. The
bravery of rural protesters grew as their plight worsened. After the general election of 1830, Grey's government came to power with a strong
commitment to parliamentary reform, in contrast to its predecessor
under the Duke of Wellington; but, as Brian Inglis once reminded us,
'the promise of it could do little to pacify the labourers, who stood no
chance of gaining the vote'.[3]

The 'Swing' riots never approached a national movement. They consisted of 1400 or more incidents of rick-burning, cattle-houghing and
other methods of rural persuasion, committed by agricultural workers
under the leadership of the imaginary 'Captain Swing'. As Cobbett's
Political Register, 20 November 1830, reported:

threatening letters have been sent to . . . farmers and gentlemen who have estates upon which they have for some time used machinery instead of hand labour. . . . The threatening letters are signed, as they are in Kent, by the name 'Swing', and they are to the same purport. About a fortnight since, one of them was sent to Mr Sherwin, at Bedfont, declaring that unless he immediately dispensed with his threshing machines his barns should be razed to the ground. Mr Sherwin took no notice of the threat . . . his two barns, several outhouses, and stabling were discovered to be on fire.

The turbulence of the southern counties in the early 1830s emanated from an accumulation of local and regional problems which together constituted a tension of national significance. In counties where wages were already desperately low, the spread of threshing machines, and other agricultural technology, threatened the livelihoods of already impoverished labourers. Yet for farmers, landlords and magistrates, the 'Swing' protesters were very much more than a mere nuisance; their threats were sinister, and the deeds more terrifying still. To the propertied classes, incendiarism was akin to the events of the French Revolution, although most workers would have been satisfied with wages of a few more pence.

The government's slowness to move against this widespread and disruptive show of solidarity can be explained partly by the nervous state already created by reform riots. When they did act, however, it was with a savage firmness. In all, nearly 2000 alleged perpetrators were tried in almost 100 courts and – after the new Home Secretary, Lord Melbourne, had declared the magistrates too soft – special commissions, across 34 counties. Some 600 imprisonments, 500 transportations and 19 executions were the result, even though no one had died at the hands of a 'Swing' rioter. Indeed, the incendiaries who burned Sherwin's stables to the ground had the humanity to remove all the horses first.[4]

Of even greater effect than the brutal sentences meted out to the 'Swing' rioters, and more pervasively callous, was the official commitment to poor law reform. The 'Swing' riots made it clear, to government at least, that existing poor law arrangements, including the much-maligned and exaggeratedly pervasive Speenhamland system, was no guarantee of rural tranquillity. 'Swing' provided the excuse, and, if it were needed, the political will to drive through the harsh utilitarian orthodoxies that became the Poor Law Amendment Act (1834). This piece of legislation helped to colour social attitudes for the remainder of the century and beyond, providing workers with a clear image of how they were regarded by the bourgeoisie.

The first Reform Act (1832), too, confirmed the subordinate status of the working class. It was slow in coming and its final manifestation was a huge disappointment for working men whose alliance with middle-class reformers had frightened Westminster. Earl Grey's ministry, formed during at the height of the 'Swing' crisis, was committed to reform of some sort. Framing a bill for reform proved to be much easier than pushing it through the Commons and, especially, the Lords. The first bill sparked a political storm in March 1831 which did not really subside until a watered-down version finally became law on 7 June 1832. Inside parliament, alliances were forged and broken; outside, there were serious riots in Bristol, Nottingham and Derby, with lesser outbursts elsewhere. Labour unrest, such as the miners' strike of 1831–2, added greatly to the ferment. It may have been that the striking miners of Merthyr Tydfil, a particularly fractious town, had no idea that the reform crisis involved them, but, as one observer recollected, 'it was natural that a suffering people should attribute their condition to many causes and think that "Reform" would bring them better times'.[5] This was a common view, even if the provisions of the Reform Act left many people desperately disillusioned. O'Gorman has shown how the act enfranchised far fewer voters than once was thought, and the loss of 'potwalloper' and 'scot and lot' boroughs denied certain groups of people – working men and some of the lower middle classes – the votes they had previously enjoyed.[6] The act did not deliver a universal middle-class franchise, although it did purge the constitution of some of its increasingly indefensible electoral anomalies.

The early 1830s offered the workers of Britain clear evidence of the hardship of life under the emerging system of capitalism. In some ways, the Poor Law Amendment Act (1834) symbolised the passing of the old age more effectively than did the Reform Act. The question of the poor laws had long exercised politicians and taxpayers alike, but no one possessed the political will to overhaul the system so long as the revolutionary spirit burned in France. In the post-war period, however, several attempts at reform, as well as outpourings of numerous committees, commissions and reports, suggested that wholesale change was necessary. The increasing costs of relief provided ample evidence for utilitarian philosophers and political economists to support their cold calculations.

The 'Swing' incidents provided the governing classes with a stark illustration that a softline approach towards the poor had failed to deliver peace and harmony, and the old and much-used adage about the ingrate poor surfaced time and again. The Poor Law Amendment Act (1834), which despite its utilitarian logic was only patchily adopted, had no real application in the industrialising northern regions of Britain. The act attempted to solve a problem, caused by chronic underemployment in the shires, with a philosophy that simply pinched those already suffering want. This legislation certainly did not address directly the causes of poverty. The architects of reform may have reinforced the poor person's fear of poverty, but, by threatening the poor with the 'workhouse test' and the 'principle of less eligibility', they ignored the fact that no amount of self-denial could help the poor to make an honest living from the land. Discontent, poverty and migration continued to be persistent themes in the shires throughout the century, and the act increased all three. The utilitarian aspects of the act, with its unevenly implemented and partially mythical 'cruel bastilles', lived long in the minds of the working class. Internment in a poorhouse was one thing, but separating women and children was quite another. In 1838, the firebrand Methodist minister J. R. Stephens demanded of an angry Newcastle crowd: 'Let the men with a torch in one hand and a dagger in the other, put to death any and all who attempted to sever man and wife.'[7] Even today old people quake at the thought of spending their last days in hospitals that were once workhouses. There was a fierce backlash against the authorities in the winter of 1837–8 when the northern poor law unions (the geographic and administrative bodies charged with adminstering poor relief) were faced with an extension of the 1834 legislation. The resistance of urban workers fed directly into the emerging Chartist movement, and riots erupted in a number of towns in east Lancashire and west Yorkshire, including Rochdale and Bradford.[8] Indeed, the New Poor Law remained partial and ineffective in the northern towns until the 1860s and 1870s.[9] Thus, from the maelstrom of the early 1830s came the mass movement that shaped the language of popular politics in the mid-to-late nineteenth century.

These momentous events attest to the importance of the early 1830s. They also suggest that the struggles of the 1840s, which focused so much on Chartism, are best seen as an outgrowth of previous forms of protest and discontentment. Without the 'divide-and-rule' effect of what would subsequently be dubbed the 'great' Reform Act, militant working-class agitators may have won their revolution. But the reform of parliament – however bitter a blow it was at the time to the hopes and ambitions of radicals of London, Birmingham and other urban centres – still opened up the possibility of further reform. For instance, an upper-class figure admired by many political acitivists, 'Radical Jack' Durham, clearly viewed an act he had driven through parliament as the thin end of the wedge. With widespread agitation, and a growing sense that people were rejecting 'their' parliament and denigrating the ancient constitution that so many Tories wished to preserve, Durham was correct to sound a terrible warning. During the heated Lords debate on 9–13 April 1832, the last in a tortuous series about the scale and nature of reform, Durham struck fear into their lordships. Alluding to a world of class turmoil he pertinently asked: 'are you prepared to live in solitude in the midst of multitudes – your mansions fortified with cannon ... and protected by troops of faithful, perhaps, but if the hour of danger come, useless retainers?' Peel had thought the reform bill, which threatened the removal of votes from working men, was too elitist. He feared it 'severed all communication between the legislature and that class of voters above pauperism'. Peel also echoed Durham's view; once reform had been granted, he felt, pressure for change would reoccur.[10] At the same time, such observations indicate the formidable staying power of the British elite. Despite its limitations, the reform of 1832 confirmed the ability of Britain's open aristocracy – an institution that beguiled foreign commentators such as de Tocqueville[11] – to maintain equilibrium with limited change. By acceding to popular pressure, Lords, Commoners and the King gave new meaning to the word 'reform'. Were it not for their instinct for self-preservation by reform it may have been Lord John Russell, the then British Prime Minister, and Queen Victoria, rather than Louis Philippe, the King of France, who in 1848 succumbed to the people of the barricades.

Industrialisation and Social Change

By 1830, industrialism had made significant and irreversible progress. Yet many aspects of life would change even more dramatically in the following 80 years. Pastoral Britain was giving way to the towns and industrial villages that came to typify early Victorian society. Although urban dwellers were not quite a majority of the population in 1830, and the decline of the rural world was relative rather than absolute, large towns, such as Birmingham and Bradford, and the great industrial and commercial cities of Glasgow and Manchester, achieved a psychological dominance which complemented their preponderant role in the nation's prosperity. In a sense, industrialisation and urbanisation had cultural as well as socio-economic dimensions: they altered people's perceptual horizons, and became ingrained in their mental structures, as well as affecting the way they lived.

Work patterns and the nature of daily toil changed in many ways between 1830 and 1914. At the beginning of our period, thousands of traditional handicraft trades had yet to die out, and handwork still provided most workers with their livelihood.[12] The archetypal new labour processes of Lancashire 'machinofacture' were far from completely dominant, even in that county: spinning was mechanised long before weaving, and the latter was not fully integrated into the factory system until the second half of the century. Thus, in 1815 weaving remained a handicraft trade, and the average cotton mill employed no more than a couple of hundred workers. The technological gap between spinning and weaving was such that hundreds of thousands of handloom weavers continued to ply their trade long after the first Lancashire textile sheds appeared. What is more, fancy work – as intricate embroidery and lacemaking, and so on, were called – was still being done on handlooms in the 1830s and beyond, because weaving machines were too crude to work the required fine threads. Nevertheless, the average wage of a handloom weaver had fallen from 30s per week in 1800 to 5s or so in the 1830s. The coming decades would see further transformations in weaving, with mechanisation spreading to such an extent that the impoverishment of the handloom weavers was a major social concern of the 1840s.[13] Even if they swam against the tide of social and economic change, men and women continued to protest against the demise of their way of life. It is notable, for example, that so many weavers clung on to their trade rather than seeking out more remunerative unskilled work as general labourers. No doubt some hoped the good times would return, but to have a trade was a matter of pride, not merely a source of income, and small-scale domestic cloth production was intimately tied up with the wider family economy. It was common, for example, for male weavers to have wives who were spinners, thus restricting their geographical and occupational mobility.

There was an inevitability about the process of industrialisation, but the changes wrought in this period were neither evenly-paced nor all-enveloping. This explains why workers were sometimes resistant to the changes wrought by industrialisation, but also why their exertions, in the form of strikes, machine-breaking and so on, were uneven. For every sector of the economy – agricultural labour, hawking or brushmaking – where workers might have earnt as little as 3s or 4s per week, there were others – such as coal mining, engineering and shipbuilding – which paid workers over 20s per week. In times of prosperity, unskilled labourers in the big towns could earn 15s. Yet even in well-paid labour, struggles occurred regularly. The desire to continue particular work rhythms or to enjoy what employers regarded as specific forms of labour privilege often outlived the macroeconomic transformation of sectors of the economy. The North-East miners' resistance to changes in the nature of contracts and payment provides an example of the sort of grievance that regularly resulted in industrial conflict. Moreover, as we see in Chapter 2, resentment at new time disciplines and a desire to celebrate 'St Monday' continued long after 1830.

The establishment of the factory system required innovations in industries other than cotton and wool, for these were largely regionalised and made almost no impression on other great industrial centres such as the North-East and Midlands. Indeed, an Industrial Revolution cannot occur if only a 'leading sector' experiences 'take-off'.[14] The most widespread changes in the nature of productive units really occurred in the 1860s and 1870s, when new iron and steel manufacturing technologies led to the erection of huge iron and steel mills. This development, in turn, led to the manufacture of engines and railways, much of this volume for export around the world, at a hitherto unknown rate. Perhaps the most striking result was, however, the advent of the iron ship. The production of unprecedentedly large vessels utterly transformed the shipbuilding regions, such as Clydeside and Tyne and Wear; it brought to prominence new or previously little-known centres of production, such as Belfast, the Hartlepools and Birkenhead; and led to renewed growth in the long-established naval dockyards of the south of England.

It is important not to exaggerate the proportion of the workforce engaged in large units of production. Apart from cotton, ships and steel, few enterprises benefited from concentrated production methods. Far more men were employed in mines than in almost any other single sector of the economy. There were more agricultural labourers in 1850 than there were textile mill operatives. The shift from handwork to machinofacture has often been overstated. Indeed, hand labour, not machine work, constituted the pervasive labour experience in this period. New levels of productivity in small productive units – the product of sweating and exploitation – are as much a feature of the late Victorian economy as are the rolling mill or the wire works. Production lines, though developed in our period, did not constitute a widespread experience for workers until the twentieth century. There can be no doubting the huge strides made in both scale and nature of operation in areas such as shipbuilding and rolling-stock manufacture; but a mixed economy of varied labour processes and innumerable work experiences was the reality and so must be seen as providing a backdrop to the discussion that follows.

None of this is meant to compromise the idea of an Industrial Revolution. Although Britain's Industrial Revolution, which occurred between 1750 and 1850, was not rapid, it was thorough. The world of 1750 had been transformed beyond recognition by 1850.[15] There were, for example, incidents of massive changes in labour and work, which we discuss at length in the first two chapters. Such changes were bound to impact on individuals, families, communities, and on the way in which they saw the world. Even coal mining, long established as a proletarianised industry, with a traditional emphasis on the export trade, showed a remarkable expansion in productivity and the numbers of men employed after that date. In 1830, the industry produced 504000 tons of coal for export; by 1870 the figure was 11162000; and in 1913 the level had reached a staggering 73400000 tons. Data on employment, as we shall see in Chapter 2, are notoriously difficult to interpret, and are in any case sketchy for the pre-1850 period; however, we can ascertain that in 1865 there were more than 315000 men working in Britain's mines and that by 1914 – the peak year – these numbered a huge total of 1.13 million. The picture was similar in iron and steel. In 1830, Britain exported 118000 tons; in 1870 the figure had climbed to 2826000; but by 1913 the total had reached 4969000 tons.[16]

Although the changing structure of the labour market exerted its impact on workers' consciousness, it also involved many individuals and families in significant geographical movements. Thus, expanded horizons were 'real' as well as 'imagined'. People who left the land, or who migrated in 'step' or 'chain' patterns from villages to towns, from towns to cities, or from Britain to America, were fundamentally pushed or pulled by a vision of social improvement and increased life-chances for their families. Not all migrating people fled such shocking circumstances as those Irish migrants who sought to escape the death pall of the Great Famine (1845–51); but all migrants were attempting to benefit economically from their own rational choices. Whatever the explanation of migration, there can be no doubt that population movement was absolutely vital in reshaping the physical and cultural terrain of the British Isles in the period under consideration. These issues are discussed in detail in Chapter 3.

Continuity and Change: Labour and the Working Class

History is a multi-layered series of processes, with time seeming to pass over different phenomena at varying speeds. Much of the early writing on working-class history focused on the discontinuities, the breaks, in historical development. 'Watersheds', moments of transformation, were stressed at the expense of uncovering the relatively unchanged elements of economic life and social relations. The Webbs, pioneers of a still strong institutional approach to labour history, took the birth of the Amalgamated Society of Engineers, in 1851, as the beginning of the forward march of labour, and, thus, a break with the radical tradition that ended with the defeat of Chartism.[17]

The traditional importance of Marxist theory to labour history has also ensured that momentous periods of upheaval, and incidents of class struggle and repression, achieve predominance over a more *Annales*-type 'history of everyday life'.[18] Even after historians such as Cole and Postgate – who were both active in the labour movement – had laid greater importance upon ordinary workers' daily lives, labour history nevertheless continued to be divided into grand epochs. Such a schematic division is one shared, if for different reasons, by many Marxist writers as well as by the founders of institutional labour history, Sidney and Beatrice Webb.[19] The chronological (and mental) framework of labour history remains thus divided, with many of the key punctuation points inserted to illustrate a change from a previous mode of operation or to announce the beginning of a new mode: 1789–1848, the age of radicalism; 1848–1889, the age of acquiescence; 1889–1914, the age of New Unionism and independent labour politics, and so on. Historians may tweak the years and modify the labels to suit their particular ends, but the language of 'revolution or reform', 'acquiescence or reformism', 'socialism or labourism', and so on, has remained, for the most part, constant. Indeed, one recent analysis of the theory and historiography of labour suggests an even starker chronological division between two periods: 1780–1848, when (in the style of the cultural Marxist, E. P. Thompson) the working class was 'made', and 1848–1870s, when it was 'unmade'.[20] The first phase was heroic and confrontational, a period when revolution might have occurred; the second was, by contrast, an age of accommodation and integration, when the fires of rebellion were doused.

Since various nineteenth-century writers emphasised momentous change as a determining feature of working-class life, the mood has altered. In the first half of the twentieth century the growth of trade unionism and the Labour Party coloured the writings of historians. After 1979 the fall in trade union membership and Labour's four consecutive general election defeats altered the perspective of many authors, especially those who played some part in the labour movement of which they wrote. More recent approaches, especially those influenced by what is broadly termed the postmodernist 'school' or 'style', have placed much greater emphasis upon the idea of continuity. There has been considerable debate between the two camps, focusing particularly on the concepts of class and class-consciousness. Nowhere, perhaps, was the suggestion of change – often violent or sudden change – more apparent than in the work of a long line of British Marxist historians whose work has been so influential in British labour history.[21] Conversely, a feature of postmodernist writing has been the rejection of class, or at least the significant downplaying of its usefulness.[22]

Our study attempts to balance incidents of continuity and of change. However, where continuity is emphasised our intention is not to iron out the contours of history, to ignore apparently momentous periods of change, nor to overlook the essential dynamics of struggle as they influenced ordinary lives. Our purpose is not to show why revolution did not occur in Britain in spite of the prophesies of Karl Marx and others; neither is to say that the revolution could never have happened. Many of the continuities that we see in labour history are not acquiescent or benign; they were resistant and aggressive. The history of labour is full of stories of near-misses: John Frost's failed rising at Newport in 1839; the year of revolutions, 1848; and a plethora of Irish insurrections. These are usually discounted, quite correctly, as partial mobilisations. Yet resistance and struggle marked out the day-to-day lives of ordinary men and women, just as their experiences were coloured by employers' philanthropy. The creation of 'model industrial villages' or the buying-off of a 'labour aristocracy' are just two examples of how employers attempted to divide the elements of the working class.[23] Without discussing the 'Whig' histories of trade union development and the emergence of the Labour Party, there is still room for the struggles of ordinary men and women to control their crafts, regulate their wages and improve their diet. The umbrella of labour's institutions covered but a small fraction of the working people of Britain in the nineteenth century, and official negotiations between trade unionists and employers were often painfully out of kilter with the workers' perception of the world of work.

There is an enduring myth concerning the Amalgamated Society of Engineers (ASE) which illustrates this tendency quite well. In their study of British trade unionism, Sidney and Beatrice Webb explained that the 'new model unions' of the late 1840s and 1850s gained a reputation as opponents of strike action. For the Webbs, the emergence of conservative-minded trade unions which emphasised friendly society benefits and central organisation marked the 'substitution wherever possible of Industrial Diplomacy for the ruder methods of the Class War'.[24] But more recent writings have suggested that, while the executives of unions of skilled men, such as the flint glassmakers, ironmoulders and engineers, only reluctantly endorsed strikes, and did not provide strike pay, this did not mean that ordinary workers never withdrew their labour in times of struggle. They and other workers never abandoned the strike weapon. There has always been a gulf between the perceptions of union leaders and the realities of rank-and-file activity.

The debate is much older and deeper than discussions of class and working-class politics might suggest. The intellectual differences might be characterised as those separating idealist (often Hegelian) and materialist (usually Marxist) interpretations of social change. Such a dichotomy, between those who stress the primacy of language and ideas, and those who emphasise material conditions, has been at least implicitly influential for over a century. In the field of British labour history, however, an emphasis upon dramatic, revolutionary change dates back to the mid-nineteenth century when commentators were assessing the first phases of industrialism. Contemporaries recognised the significance of the Industrial Revolution and its transforming effects on British social and economic life. An apocalyptic vision of Britain in turmoil was influential during the crisis years of the 1830s and 1840s; moreover, this spirit was rejuvenated (in the 1880s, at a time when Britain's industrial hegemony was being challenged) under the auspices of a new generation of writers who offered a devastating critique of the limited gains made by working men and women under the capitalist system. For Arnold Toynbee, the Industrial Revolution was

> a period as disastrous and as terrible as any through which a nation ever passed; disastrous and terrible, because side by side with a great increase of wealth was seen an enormous increase of pauperism; and production on a vast scale, the result of free competition, led to a rapid alienation of the classes and to the degradation of a large body of producers.[25]

The writings of Toynbee, Sidney and Beatrice Webb, J. L. and Barbara Hammond helped to bring socially orientated labour history to the attention of both the academy and a wider audience. Indeed, as the century was drawing to a close, a debate raged over the question of whether or not the Industrial Revolution had a positive effect on the British working class, particularly on their standards of living. In some respects it represented a more systematic attempt to examine questions about the impact of economic change that had been discussed for several decades. While this is not the place to go into the massive literature of the standard of living debate,[26] it is nevertheless important to acknowledge that visions such as those of Toynbee, cast as they were at the end of Britain's economic pre-eminence, remain deeply embedded in the historiography of labour.

If acquiescence largely replaced turbulence as the orthodoxy of British labour in the middle of the nineteenth century, we must also acknowledge the experiences of those whose accommodation with capitalism was grudging. This point is captured well by R. J. Morris in his trenchantly argued claim that by the 1890s the British working class had been 'remade' on three crucial levels. First, on account of there being a much greater acceptance of capitalism. Secondly, because new commercial and leisure opportunities came with the improved standards of living enjoyed by a substantial part of the working class. Morris's third contention, however, was that in the consciousness of the working class there remained a sense of disaffection, albeit in a less protean form than had been the case under the Chartists. Such an attitude, Morris noted, caused 'the production of a vast infrastructure of Socialism, fragments of organisation within which groups and individuals not only began to question the subordinations and poverty they experienced but sought to puzzle out ways of reorganising social and economic relationships which seemed unsatisfactory'.[27]

Class

The role of class is a common preoccupation of labour historians, though few define it. It is important that students of labour history demonstrate a willingness and an ability to wrestle with the complexities of the term 'class' and to apply it, and the alternative models offered by its critics, to the social, economic and political lives of ordinary people in the past.

Class has always been a controversial term – receiving far more slavish or acrimonious attention than similar concepts, such as community, which have largely gone without significant criticism. The validity of class, as a descriptor of an individual's or a group's economic status, is still largely accepted. We still talk of class as though it exists, yet a recent empirical study of Britain's historical attitude to class suggests the term is only useful as a prism through which other images are refracted.[28] As an objective reality (in the classic Marxist sense), as an organic sense of being and as a determinant of the individual or group's political action, class is much more contested.

There has always been a more than residual aversion to the term 'class'; and its opponents are not purely of the postmodernist 'school' (a philosophical 'style' which questions our ability to know the past because it has gone and is unobservable[29]). For example, John Benson's study of the working class in Britain, a book written more than a decade ago, noticeably rejects a class-centred approach to status issues. Benson suggests diversity – in terms of experience and outlook – as an antidote to the once prevalent idea that working families in Britain formed a homogenous singular class.[30] Recent postmodernist writings have placed the concept of class under further close epistemological scrutiny. Even within the confines of a labour historiography that is more sympathetic towards class, there is now a much more emphatic embrace of poststructuralist (with its centrality of language) interpretations of social relations.[31] Yet writers such as John Belchem, who has sought to engage both with Marxist approaches and the more recent 'linguistic turn' (an umbrella term for postmodernist approaches that stress language in criticism of the materialist emphasis of modernism) still finds evidence to suggest that class is a valid term. The 'culturalist' approach, originated by E. P. Thompson and developed by his disciples, offers a challenging intermixing of perspectives on the issue of class. Thompson's language of cultural 'lags' and 'cultural superstructure' (wherein culture is ascribed a degree of independence from the material world) in some ways breaks with classical Marxism.[32] Thompson was always willing to consider that factors such as cultural tradition or ethnic rivalries might modify any straightforward or inexorable movement towards class consciousness and thus to revolution.

There is today an even more fundamental assertion of the role of fractured and multiple identities in the formation of working-class experience. Indeed, there is now a willingness on the part of labour historians to embrace a broader appreciation of social relations; claims can be made for the role of ethnicity or gender over class, of regional distinctiveness over the idea of an homogenous nation. Although the picture is in fact more complicated and more varied than we imply here, important common themes – culture over economic or material factors, identities over identity – can nevertheless be suggested. One of the aims of this book is to consider the impact of these tensions.

Much of the old language of class has been modified to take account of the 'linguistic turn' (the emphasis upon, for example, language rather than economics as constitutive of identity) and the overall trend against class. This engagement with class, as with its wider contestation of 'old' social history, is based upon the classic postmodernist nostrum, derived from Roland Barthes, Jacques Derrida and Michel Foucault, that knowledge, rather than 'a reflection of some external reality', is in fact 'a discourse created by language'.[33] Recent influential writings by cultural historians, such as Gareth Stedman Jones (often apostates from an earlier Marxisant mode of labour history writing), have asserted that continuities of tradition might be more useful in explaining the experience of the working class than any idea of revolutionary change. A notion of graduated, organic social relations and political expression is noticeable in Patrick Joyce's relatively recently declared preference (one shared by James Vernon) for the word 'people' as opposed to 'class' – for the 'people' not only represented a wide and disparate range of groupings under its broad banner, but also supposedly harboured greater appeal for the men and women of the time.

Many of the postmodernists' observations on class are valid. If 'linear notions of economic development seem untenable' (and we argue as much here), then 'so too do linear notions of class development'.[34] As Joyce goes on to explain, traditional centres of labour organisation, regional coherence and class solidarity – such as the mining centres of south Wales – were actually late developers in terms of class cohesion. Even in the North-East of England, where mining was a much older tradition than in those valleys to the north of Cardiff, the miners' organisation was Liberal rather than Labourist for much of the nineteenth century. It was only from the late 1890s that these two great areas of 'red' resistance began to press themselves behind the political cause of the labour movement. Even between 1911 and 1914, when syndicalism (exerting political pressure through industrial action) reached its pre-war high point, coal leaders were exercising the sort of influence we might expect from the representatives of the largest body of workmen in the country, but the militancy of their mood has been questioned.[35]

There can be little doubt that class was but one of a multitude of identities affecting workers, although the presence of other factors in their consciousness does not preclude it from primacy. But neither does it necessarily follow that language enjoyed a constitutive power over the consciousness of those same workers. It is difficult to argue only, or completely, that the material base was directly responsible for all immediate forms of identity and experience. It is equally apparent that when we seek to determine the character of longer-run social change – the 'idea of history' – then economic considerations, and those of class, allied to modes and languages of expression, should share the privilege of explanatory force.

One of the problems faced by those who oppose the validity of class-centred explanations of working-class action is that the evidence sometimes appears to confound their viewpoint. Studies which suggest the importance of ethnicity over class sometimes seem inadvertently to present a contrary case, or to suggest that class and ethnicity are aligned. The Irish workers of Victorian Britain provide a case in point.[36] Initially presented as a group whose influence upon the wider working class was negative, the role of Irish migrants has recently been reinterpreted. Even Friedrich Engels, perhaps the single greatest influence on historical opinion of labour experience of the 1840s, fluctuated in his view of Irish migrant labour. His political tract on the working class of Manchester considered the Irish as the worst evil the native worker had to strive against. On other occasions, however, Engels felt that he could overthrow the British Empire if he stood at the head of an army of Irish labourers.[37] This Janus-faced view is common. With their affiliation to an alien Catholic religion, or else their introduction of ultra-loyalist organisations, such as the Orange Order, Irish migrants were viewed as different or 'apart'. It stood to reason, therefore, that they were unlikely to be defenders of class solidarity. Contemporary commentators dismissed them as primitive and uncivilised drones whose principal class utility was to employers. Yet the army of Irish migrants who fell in with the radical projects of Thomas Spence, Robert Wedderburn, Henry Hunt, the Chartists and, later, trade unionists and the pioneers of the Labour Party, suggests that ethnicity was not, in fact, a bar to class-inspired activity. Rather, it might be suggested that the development of ethnic attachments – Ribbonism, the Catholic Church, the pub, club or society – strengthened the Irish migrants' confidence, empowered their group's position, and helped them to formulate ideas of collective action that would come to benefit labour. The suggestion that Irishmen were ethnically aligned rather than class-orientated is as much a measure of external 'myth' as of internal 'reality'. It must be remembered, too, that the 'linguistic turn' can 'turn' both ways; language, rather than economic experience, may well have constituted the visions of the people; but surely ethnic experiences – of being downtrodden, outcast and necessarily solidary – could yield a cultural superstructure from language which suited class as much as ethnic imperatives.[38]

There remain strong arguments for maintaining a Marxist presentation of class as an important aspect of the history of labour in our period. Indeed, there is more than a hint in the most recent postmodernist writings that we need to re-emphasise 'practice' (the actual 'doing' of history) – presumably at the expense of 'language'.[39] There did exist in Victorian Britain a deep-seated, we might even say brooding, sense of inequality, of 'them and us'. As Hobsbawm argued, in a series of careful empirical studies, the feeling that manual labour was different was both intense and long-living.[40] Those who seek evidence of real improvements in the standards of living of the working class have anguished over a few pennies; but the conclusion that there were gains for some from the 1870s, with other groups having to wait until after 1914, seems inescapable. Even then, it appears much safer to focus on the post-1945 period – the age of 'cradle to the grave' welfarism and of a genuinely widespread consumerism – before announcing that the working class had become better nourished and healthier. Before 1945, and much more before 1914, although certain sections of the working class enjoyed greater benefits than in 1830, the greater part of the working class was just one downturn of the trade cycle away from acute hardship. The problem for the historians of living standards is that no one has ever been able adequately to represent the impact of unemployment upon the working family. Yet we know from Booth's and Rowntree's investigations of the 1890s and early 1900s that at least one-third of the working class of London's East End and York slipped at various times below these investigators' harshly defined poverty lines. Yet, in Britain, which relied so heavily on trade, the golden years of boom and plenty were much less frequent than those of depression and want.

To say this is not to place historians' observations ahead of the experience of those who lived through the conditions described. Nevertheless, it has always been difficult (and it remains so, notwithstanding the interventions of postmodernists) to view the workers of the past as motionless sites of linguistic formation, empty vessels waiting dumbly to be filled with the noise of jargon and rhetoric. The language of class was the creation of economic certainties – of the reality of living, day by day, in this way or that. Language did not invent the lives of ordinary people, but it did articulate visions of their world.

The End of an Era?

Against a backdrop of economic growth, uncertain trade and the threat of overseas competition, a social transformation did occur. By 1914, Britain had become a very different place. Dangerfield's 'Liberal England' purportedly met its end; the old confidence of the Victorian age was beginning to ebb. Britain stood on the brink of disaster – a war so terrible that no one alive in 1914 could begin to imagine its destructiveness; a hollow, pyrrhic victory that required more than four years of struggle by more than five million men at arms. If the politicians of 1914 could have looked into the future they would have seen that, from the perspective of the ruling class, Britain's best years had passed. But, in truth, many already realised this; for in just 50 short years 'the first industrial nation', the world's workshop, had been left trailing in the wake of the United States and German producers. The Empire, too, stood in its sunset hour. The costs of the Boer War (1899–1902) probably started the imperial rot, while, much closer to home, the brittle union with Ireland compounded the paradoxes of holding overseas possessions. In the post-1918 years a full-scale repudiation of world conquest was beginning to emerge. There was an 'end-of-era' feel about 1914 – but it was of course part of the wider anxieties of office holders, rent receivers, property owners and privileged elites, about the age of mass democracy. Liberal England was dying if not dead; Liberalism, the credo of high Victorian politics, was being shrugged from the nation's shoulders, George Dangerfield argued, like 'a venerable burden, a kind of sack'.[41]

In many respects, from the social point of view too, the people of Britain in 1914 faced altered horizons. Throughout the nineteenth century, economic wealth far outstripped the proportion of it that accrued to wage earners. In response, workers and those who identified with their interests formulated a new social compact. In the twentieth century this began to replace the older shibboleths of self-help individualism and laissez-faire political economy. It was in principle a compact based on universal welfare and social democracy, with ordinary people, both men and women, realising the old Chartist dream of a society shaped by economic justice and democractic citizenship. Although what has happened in fact fell far short of these ideals, it provides a perspective on the years 1830 to 1914.

1
VARIETIES OF WORK

Categories and Numbers

The officials of the General Register Office who compiled the returns of the population census of 1841 had been faced with a problem. A decade earlier, the enumerators who went forth to conduct the census of 1831 were provided with lists of occupations, but found 'there was a want of uniformity' in the way those in employment described the work they did. The enumerators of 1841 were instructed to take 'each man's description of himself' (as for women, their occupations were recorded, though then and for the rest of the century the numbers in paid employment were understated). This had resulted in a mass of detail that was overwhelming and bewildering. It would be necessary, it was noted, to have a scientific knowledge of industry to understand the minute subdivisions of labour that had been recorded: in the Lancashire cotton industry, for instance, 1255 different terms had been used. The officials' solution, 'for the convenience of publication' and to make such detail 'accessible to the ordinary enquirer', was to simplify; in Lancashire, the 1255 occupations were reduced to 'cotton manufacture, all branches'.[1]

Before the next census was taken, the shortcomings that had affected the occupational returns were to some extent remedied. However, when using information drawn from nineteenth-century censuses, an element of caution is necessary. The undercounting of women in paid employment, for example, remained a feature of the enumerators' returns. Certain groups were treated inconsistently: in the case of domestic servants, to cite one instance, in Scotland nurses were classified as such in

19

1841 and in 1891 female relatives of heads of households were counted among the number of those in domestic service. Until 1881 retired people were assigned to their former occupations.[2]

In 1851 an elaborate system of occupational classification was introduced. It consisted of 17 classes, and numerous sub-classes, and reflected some of the conventions of the time ('At the head of the FIRST CLASS stands HER MAJESTY THE QUEEN'). However, this schema also attempted to classify together persons similarly occupied, rather than being employed in the same industry. To some extent this did provide a measure of the extent to which work required particular skills, but criticisms of the inaccuracies and inconsistencies to be found in the censuses continued. Those responsible for the 1891 census, for example, deplored 'the extremely inaccurate manner in which uneducated, and often, indeed, educated persons, describe their calling'. The problem was partly insufficient ability or inclination to make accurate returns, and also 'the foolish but very common desire of persons to magnify the importance of their occupational condition'.[3]

Nevertheless, the censuses remain, in spite of deficiencies both on the part of those who did the counting and who were counted, the historian's main source for the structure of the labour force. Indeed, other records, such as those made by trade unions and the street and trade directories that were compiled for most Victorian cities, are in comparison of very limited value. The reports of inspectors of factories and mines, however, especially for the later nineteenth century, are useful. Nevertheless, bearing in mind the inaccuracies that occur in the census figures, Table 1.1 broadly indicates the pattern of employment in Great Britain between 1841 and 1911. The numbers of male workers in each occupational group are given first, followed by those of females.[4]

Between 1841 and 1914 the occupied population increased from about seven million (5.1m men, 1.8m women) to almost eighteen and a half million (12.9m men, 5.4m women). Over this period, therefore, it is evident that with regard to both gender and occupation major shifts took place. The remainder of this chapter seeks to identify the main changes that occurred, as well as giving some indication of the characteristics of the principal groups of workers involved. Such a discussion should help to resolve an apparent paradox: how so varied a labour force can nevertheless be regarded as a social class. Observers from the bourgeoisie, whose own class-consciousness served to remind workers of their own, inferior, standing tended to overlook the complexities of

Table 1.1 Employment in Britain, 1841–1911 ('000s)

Occupations	1841	1851	1861	1871	1881	1891	1901	1911
Agriculture,	1434	1788	1779	1634	1517	1422	1339	1436
horticulture, forestry	81	229	163	135	116	80	86	117
Mining, quarrying	218	383	457	517	604	751	931	1202
	7	11	6	11	8	7	6	8
Textiles	525	661	612	584	554	593	557	639
	358	635	676	726	745	795	795	870
Clothing	358	418	413	390	379	409	423	432
	200	491	596	594	667	759	792	825
Domestic service	255	193	195	230	238	293	341	456
	989	1135	1407	1678	1756	2036	2003	2127
Transport	196	433	579	654	870	1104	1409	1571
	4	13	11	16	15	20	27	38
Metal manufacture,	396	536	747	869	977	1151	1485	1795
machines, etc.	14	36	45	46	49	59	84	128
Building,	376	496	593	712	875	899	1216	1140
construction	1	1	1	4	2	3	3	5
Wood, furniture,	107	152	171	186	185	206	267	287
fittings, decorations	5	8	15	26	21	25	30	35
Bricks, cement, glass,	48	75	93	97	111	119	152	145
pottery	10	15	19	25	27	32	37	42
Paper, printing, books,	44	62	79	94	134	178	212	253
stationery	6	16	23	31	53	78	111	144
Food, drink, tobacco	268	348	386	448	494	597	701	806
	42	53	71	78	98	163	216	308
Other (fishing,	570	578	670	1166	1089	1269	1203	1125
chemicals, leather,	45	85	92	122	106	127	133	176
gas supply, etc.)								
Professions, etc.	298	380	499	646	829	1016	1312	1644
(incl. commerce,	53	106	132	164	223	307	431	590
armed forces, civil								
service)								

Source: *Census of England and Wales: Reports, 1921–51.*

working-class life. Although there were many types of work, and though the multitude of trades and practices suggested differences between workers, all employees were linked by the fact that the need for work structured their lives. Moreover, as we go on to argue in the later chapters, there are also many other reasons why we emphasise the importance of social class for an understanding of the labour experience in these years.

The Question of Skill

Though the census takers were long aware that manual work might be highly skilled, it was not until 1911 that sufficient information was given to allow detailed research into such occupations.[5] This deficiency in the census might be one reason why historians have disagreed about the impact of industrialisation on the skills of workers. Studies of particular industries have tended to conclude that the best-paid men possessed abilities that were scarce, and therefore well rewarded. However, it has been argued that an employer who wanted to exert a stronger control over his workforce would seek to employ technology in a way that minimised the power conferred by the possession of skill. The influential work of Harry Braverman has developed this approach, although critics suggest that it is stronger on hypotheses than empirical research.[6] The debate has also been complicated by historians' understanding of the Industrial Revolution. Those who emphasise the factory system as the central feature tend to see the use of steam as the new way of powering machines that replaced hand labour. In the words of Landes, the 'heart of the Industrial Revolution was an interrelated succession of technological changes….a substitution of mechanical devices for human skills'.[7] Others, however, have shown how industrial capitalism expanded in a variety of ways, which sometimes did lead to deskilling but at other times gave workers the opportunity to develop new skills. Raphael Samuel, for example, examined this 'machinery question' from the perspective of a labour historian more concerned with the human factor than with the impact of industrialisation in more general terms.[8]

This matter of skill was also both widely noted and misunderstood by middle-class commentators in the century before 1914. To some, the toilers in the cities of Victorian Britain were 'the masses', as when the Tory leader, Benjamin Disraeli, wrote of 'the mighty mysterious masses of the swollen towns'.[9] Yet such phrases missed the workers' sense of their place within 'the masses'. On the Liverpool docks, for instance, there was 'a caste system quite as powerful as India's', not so much based on religious divisions as on the skill and therefore status associated with different forms of work.[10] Such attitudes extended to the workers' spouses; in the words of one commentator, 'artisans' wives hold the wives of labourers to be of a lower social grade, and very often either will not "neighbour" with them at all, or else only in a patronising way'.[11] Numerous other instances might be given of the differences perceived by workers, both within and between occupations. Moreover, these perceptions remained pronounced, though possibly less so, until 1914 and beyond. In a letter of 1915 from the Western Front, for example, the Fabian socialist Frederic Keeling wrote: 'I talked long this evening with my two Yorkshire corporals, who come from the G. N. R. plant at Doncaster, where they work as skilled engineers. There is less of a gap between the upper middle class and them than between them and their labourers.'[12]

Even allowing for some exaggeration, Keeling's statement does point to the relative position of the skilled and unskilled worker. The worker who entered a skilled trade as an apprentice could expect to obtain regular and higher wages; as well as a trade union, he might belong to a friendly society; and he would be more likely to take an interest in social and political questions. Then and subsequently he would be dignified by the term 'labour aristocrat'. The role of this stratum of society has been discussed at length by historians of nineteenth-century labour. Some have found the term unhelpful, in part because of the difficulties of precise definition – 'skill' was not, as this chapter will try to show, the exclusive preserve of the aristocrat. Moreover, the concept of the labour aristocracy involves a political dimension that has proved even more contentious. Some historians have characterised the labour aristocrat as someone prepared to compromise with the owners of capital, and thus act as a drag on the revolutionary potential of the working class. Such an approach follows that taken by Marx and Engels; the latter, for example, complained in December 1889, after a year of industrial militancy, that:

> The most repulsive thing here is the bourgeois 'respectability' bred into the bones of the workers. The social division of society into innumerable gradations, each recognised without question, each its own pride but also its inborn respect for its 'betters' and 'superiors', is so old and firmly established that the bourgeois still find it pretty easy to get their bait accepted.[13]

Other historians, more comfortable with the Fabian tradition of the Webbs, whose history of trade unionism delineated the 'new model unionism' of engineers, carpenters, boilermakers, and so on, have found the labour aristocrat at the forefront of such progressive movements as parliamentary reform, republicanism, free thought, land radicalism, co-operative societies and independent labour representation. Although one recent contributor to the debate has concluded 'that the concept of the labour aristocracy is so seriously flawed that it should be modified or superseded',[14] the term, nevertheless, has its place when discussing elements of the skilled working class between 1830 and 1914.

On the other hand it should also be emphasised that the term 'unskilled' does an injustice to those so described. Not many occupations were characterised by an absence of skill. A few examples should make the point. In agriculture, the wretchedly paid farm labourer would probably be practised at ploughing or hedge-cutting – competitions were organised to encourage these skills – or in rearing various forms of livestock. Miners needed a variety of tools when winning coal, in order to hole and shear the coalface efficiently; a lack of dexterity could produce dross instead of the coal desired. Miners also had to be able to decide how and when pit props should be used and the best means of following faulted seams. In cotton textiles, the predominantly female workforce, though having no formal qualifications and not conventionally regarded as skilled, needed a range of abilities, especially in those factories where better quality items were produced. In Bolton in 1927 the time was recalled 'when a plain weaver would have stood as much chance of obtaining work in a fancy mill as she would have of being made the manager of it'.[15]

Entry into these and similar occupations was relatively straightforward. The main qualification was often geographical – boys in mining villages, for example, were expected to enter the pit. But the father's occupation was also an important influence on a boy's work, and working-class autobiographies offer many accounts of boys entering for the first time mill, mine and workshop in the company of their fathers. Young people would begin work at an early age, often long before they reached their teens. In the 1840s legislation sought to keep children under the age of eight out of textile factories; in the coal industry boys below ten were not to work underground. Minimum age legislation was slowly extended to other forms of employment, though sometimes it was flouted: in 1872, 1873 and 1875 illegally employed 'climbing boys' were suffocated in chimney flues in Staffordshire, Durham and Cambridge (an outcry after this last case led to the Chimney Sweepers' Act of 1875). Not until 1891 was it made illegal to employ children under the age of 11 in factories, and only in 1900 were boys under 13 barred from coal mines.[16]

For most of the nineteenth century, school attendance was not compulsory; as late as 1899 the school-leaving age was raised to 12, at which age it remained until 1918. Those working-class children who received an education went to work with little more than the basics of reading and writing (although a strong autodidactic tradition ensured that some workers were familiar with such authors as Bunyan, Burns, Paine, Shelley and, later, Dickens, Ruskin and Carlyle). Towards the turn of the century, in part due to concern about the rise of foreign competition, more attention was paid to the training of the working-class child. The need for technical instruction received particular emphasis, which gradually led to the creation of scholarships. Yet while education did offer a ladder to some working-class children, those from better-off homes were most likely to climb it. Not untypical were the findings of an investigator into the parental occupations of 100 east London scholarship boys in the 1890s:[17]

Architect	1
Retail tradesmen	43
Licensed victuallers	6
Clerks	4
Commercial travellers and agents	3
Warehousemen	2
Managers and foremen	11
Artisans	26
Policeman	1
Street-seller	1
Labourers	2

For most young people, the skills necessary to carry out a job were acquired gradually, by doing menial tasks while picking up the essentials of the work in a mostly informal way. Some boys left school for what became known as blind-alley or dead-end jobs, though only in the Edwardian period did disquiet about their fate become widely expressed. After a few years as an errand- or messenger-boy, according to a report minuted by the education committee of the London County Council in 1909:

> the lad is a distinctly less valuable item in the labour market than he was when he left school. . . . He has lost the intelligence and aptitude of the boy, and remains a clumsy and unintelligent man, fitted for nothing but unskilled labour, and likely to become sooner or later one of the unemployed.[18]

Such opinions, however, were probably not so much an analysis about what was happening in the labour market than expressions of anxiety about national efficiency in a period of economic and social change.

As well as young people, women workers too were especially subject to the attitudes bound up with a patriarchal society. Some investigators were evidently oblivious of the extent of women's labour. Reference has already been made to their neglect in the census – probably the most striking instance of this occurred in 1841 when the figure for occupied females was 1.8 million. Ten years later it was 2.8 million. Perhaps half of the difference between the two figures can be explained by the failure of the earlier enumerators to recognise the numbers working in, particularly, domestic service, textiles and clothing. Paid work undertaken at home by women who were seamstresses, jewellery-makers, takers-in of laundry, and so on, tended to be unrecorded. Moreover, the modern concept of women undertaking unpaid employment in the home was unrecognised, other than in the form that the domestic sphere was regarded as the woman's most suitable place.

In general, working-class men were reluctant to see their wives going out to work. This has sometimes been understood as an example of a dominant, bourgeois morality being accepted by the working class. As in the middle class, there was an element of social status involved in the male demonstrating his ability to support his wife economically. However, many workers depended on their wives to maintain their efficiency as family breadwinners. A miner's wife, for example, would be relied upon not only to have a supply of hot water awaiting her husband's return but also to help him to take a bath, and to provide a cooked meal afterwards. Where large numbers of women did go out to work, as in textile areas, the wages of men tended to be lower. Drawing on what were taken to be the laws of the dominant political economy of the period, the better organised workers argued that any addition to the supply of labour would reduce its price. In industries where there was a degree of trade unionism, vigorous efforts were made to exclude women from work to which men had traditionally laid claim. Often these efforts were successful; the Amalgamated Engineering Union until 1943 did not allow members who were women, and then admittance was only granted in part as a reaction to their recruitment by other unions.

Such discrimination did have adverse consequences for women. Many, who could not financially depend on a father or husband, were prevented from getting work that was better paid and which they were capable of doing. Often they had to be satisfied with employment in unskilled and even sweated occupations. Moreover, where women did similar work to men, pay rates were generally lower, frequently by as much as fifty per cent. Frugality had to be the rule of the older unmarried woman or widow who could not rely on help from her relatives. To live on a wage of a few shillings a week, she might rent a room in the house of another family. More independent single women, who because they had the responsibility of talking to the enumerators themselves, tend to be better represented in census returns, could make a living as keepers of lodging houses, laundresses and seamstresses and dressmakers – descriptions sometimes taken as euphemisms for prostitutes, the numbers of which can only be guessed at.[19]

Although very often male workers preferred to keep their wives at home, the poor wages of many men resulted in substantial numbers of married women taking paid employment. A survey conducted in 1909 and 1910 by the Women's Industrial Council did identify a small proportion of wives who chose to work and said they liked it. However, the survey confirmed that the main reason for married women working was the inadequacy of their husbands' wages. In a few cases, the husband was infirm or unemployed, while there were probably some – as hinted at by the woman who remarked 'A shilling of your own is worth two that *he* gives you' – who kept back a selfishly large part of their wages while expecting much to be done with what was handed over.[20] Women with small children often depended on 'homework'; classically this consisted of sewing, though many other types of labour were undertaken too. The *Daily News* exhibition of 1906, for example, which was mounted to publicise the abuses of the system, showed the variety of work done by homeworkers. Very often, various types of tailoring were undertaken, but other tasks, such as matchbox making, sewing buttons and hooks and eyes on to cards, book folding and artificial flower making, were also performed in the rooms in which workers lived. A variant form of sweated labour occurred in the Black Country, where, in small sheds next to workers' houses, nail and chain making could be found. All these workers were paid on a piece-rate basis, on terms that typically involved long hours and small wages. The organising secretary of the *Daily News* exhibition roundly condemned the selfishness of the competitive system, writing that 'Sweating follows unrestricted competition as naturally and inevitably as pain follows disease.'[21]

Not all homeworkers were women, though the majority probably were. Indeed, some of the Edwardian reformers tended, as a way of rousing public opinion, to present the victims of sweating as hapless women who deserved the protection of the state.[22] Nor was the phenomenon a feature of the thirty or so years prior to 1914; it was in that period that reformers were most vigorous in their attempts to improve or even end the system. As early as 1843, Thomas Hood's vivid poem, 'The Song of the Shirt', had caused great interest when it appeared in *Punch*, and Charles Kingsley's novel *Alton Locke* again raised public awareness of the plight of tailors on its publication in 1850. However, non-interventionist attitudes were slow to alter. The case of the handloom weavers, once relatively prosperous until their living standards fell with the advent of factory production, suggested that economic change had to follow its own course. Thus, by 1914 and in spite of much pressure from reformers, only a small proportion of sweated trades were covered by minimum wage legislation.

Regions and Industries

A theme of many who wrote in the nineteenth century on British society and politics was the tendency towards greater centralisation. By the second quarter of the century, it appeared that the functions of central government were becoming more pervasive. Such a process involved a complexity of forces – for example, the growth of the railways, the development of a national press, the operation of the New Poor Law of 1834, the spread, with the encouragement of the state, of elementary education – which combined to make local variations seem less significant. Similar changes occurred in the labour market between 1830 and 1914. By the later date, organised labour, in the form of the trade unions, had a national character. The annual Trades Union Congress had been held since 1868; the Labour Representation Committee was formed, largely by trade unionists, in 1900 and became the Labour Party in 1906; and some of the best-known trade unions recruited members from all parts of the country and had elaborate administrative structures linking the full-time officials at headquarters to local branches. Yet questions of national identity are still grappled with by historians, in connection with the concept of nationhood (of 'Englishness' and 'Britishness') as well as with the characteristics of the working class. Without at this point engaging in these debates, some writers, it is now usually accepted, have too freely assumed that with the advent of capitalism a fairly homogeneous working class was created. Not only have some Marxists been over-ready in their discovery of a cohesive 'proletariat', but commentators adopting neoclassical models have also tended to assume that all those who depended on selling their labour for wages belonged in the same broad category. It is, however, possible, as in the following brief case studies, to point to forces making for a more integrated working class while recognising the continuance of variations within both local and national labour markets. Britain's many distinctive geographical areas also ensured marked differences which continued long after 1914.[23]

Coal miners

Some of these points can be discussed with reference to coal mining, the occupation which, on the eve of the Great War, had the largest number of trade unionists. These continued to be organised on a regional basis. Moreover, within the trade, miners' pay and conditions were by no means uniform. The explanation of these characteristics lies mainly in the separate location of coalfields, the larger of which employed men on a scale that made unions viable. Moreover, as the demand for coal increased, which with industrialisation it did steadily, the workforce increased proportionately. Mining was essentially a pick-and-shovel industry, with limited mechanisation, so that higher output could be achieved only by employing more men. Indeed, as for much of the period output per miner was falling, in part due to the reduction in the length of the working day and the need to open more inaccessible seams of coal, disproportionately more men were employed to keep up with the demand for coal. The figures in Table 1.2 illustrate this trend.[24]

There were attempts to bring together the various miners' trade unions. In Wakefield in November 1842 the Miners' Association of Great Britain was formally established, only to collapse by the end of the decade. Twenty-one years later, at Leeds in November 1863, 53 delegates from the principal British coalfields met and agreed to form the Miners' National Association. This body faced a rival in 1869, the Amalgamated Association of Miners, a more militant organisation which, however, was broken by the fall in prices in 1874. In the following year it was dissolved and those members who remained were encouraged to join the Miners' National Union (as the Miners' National Association then became known). At a conference held in Newport in November 1889 the Miners' Federation of Great Britain was formed, with affiliations that allowed it to claim to represent about half the unionised miners in the coal industry (although most miners were not in trade unions). Of the coalfields affiliated to the Federation, the most important were the Yorkshire Miners' Association, the Lancashire and Cheshire Miners' Federation and unions in the Notts–Derby coalfield. Outside it was the union in the largest coalfield, the Durham Miners' Association, which joined in 1892.

Table 1.2   Employment and output in UK coal mines, 1864–1914

Year	UK coal output (m. tons)	Numbers employed ('000s)
1864	92.8	307.5
1874	126.6	538.8
1884	160.8	520.4
1894	188.3	705.2
1904	232.4	847.6
1914	265.7	1133.7

Source: B. R. Mitchell and P. Deane, *Abstract of British Historical Statistics* (Cambridge, 1962), pp. 115, 118–19.

This association, fiercely independent and aware of its region's powerful position, had a turbulent relationship with the national association, and was expelled in 1893 before becoming reaffiliated by 1908.[25]

Just as the regional unions were largely autonomous and jealous of their independence, so too, it has been widely maintained, were the pitmen of coal-mining villages. Physically dominated by spoil heaps and the winding gear of the pithead, with a large majority of the population economically dependent on coal production, these communities, which were also often fairly remotely located, have been seen as qualitatively different from working-class populations in other parts of the country. The coal miner, in a well-known phrase, was 'the archetypal proletarian'.[26] Certainly, men who worked together underground, in harsh conditions and frequently resentful of their treatment by the mine owners, forged close ties. In a dangerous occupation, men were closely dependent on each other for their safety and even their lives. Moreover, in the more isolated mining areas, patterns of kinship were often such that miners worked closely with members of their extended families. In those villages where other occupations hardly existed, men tended to associate with each other during their leisure time. This might involve the chapel, pigeon-racing, brass bands or, very commonly, the public house, where it was widely said that mining so dominated conversation that more coal was dug on a Saturday night in the pub than all week in the pit. When strikes and lockouts occurred, communal solidarity meant there were few local blacklegs, and the mine owners hesitated to bring into a hostile village 'scab' workers who would have to face violent picketing to get into the pit and then work in an unfamiliar coal mine. Similarly, with the extension of the franchise, miners were able to dominate several constituencies. Their leaders were mostly Liberals, and their ability to win seats in the House of Commons and on local councils is one reason why most miners' unions came late to the principle of independent labour representation.

However, the social and political cohesiveness of coal miners, compared with other occupational groups, has sometimes been overstated. Not all coalfields were isolated from other centres of population. Moreover, the use in some coalfields of the butty system, a form of subcontracting, could divide the workforce and encourage the 'buttymen' – those who employed other miners – to identify with the owners' interests. Underground, the hewers made up an elite who received the highest wages. However, such were the physical demands of the work that few could work productively beyond middle age. The older miner would expect to do work that was less strenuous, and less well paid, and therefore was content to be a member of a trade union that catered for all men in the industry. There were, additionally, divisions between coalfields, and sometimes strikes in one area were compromised when coal dug in other parts of the country was brought in. Nor can all miners be regarded as having similar industrial attitudes. Rank-and-file workers were often at odds with their leaders who followed conciliatory policies such as sliding-scale agreements, which linked wages to the price of coal. On the eve of the war, syndicalist ideas had affected a section of the labour force and in south Wales were articulated in the form of *The Miners' Next Step*. This pamphlet pressed the case for the control of industry by workers and outlined the problems associated with the leadership of trade unions.

Cotton textile workers

Numerically, the textile industries employed more than did coal mining, with women comprising an increasingly important part of this body of workers. The main areas of activity were, however, fewer. Cotton was concentrated in south-east Lancashire and wool in the West Riding of Yorkshire, with lesser, and increasingly insignificant, centres in parts of Scotland and the Midlands. Though remnants of the once-dominant domestic system with its multiplicity of handloom weavers survived into the second half of the nineteenth century, textile production based on the large-scale use of water- and then steam-powered machinery which made possible a rapid growth of output was widely regarded as characteristic of what became known as the Industrial Revolution. The factory symbolised the growth of towns on both sides of the Pennines, the rise of a wealthy and influential class of manufacturers, and the emergence of an industrial proletariat. Writers sympathetic to the factory workers, of whom Friedrich Engels was perhaps pre-eminent in the 1840s, were inclined to see them as a single entity, just as the census officials of 1841 had simplified the 1255 occupations stated by workers into 'cotton manufacture, all branches'. Work determined by machines seemed to reduce workers to 'hands'; an attitude Charles Dickens sardonically commented on when he wrote of 'the multitude of Coketown – generically called "The Hands" – a race who would have found more favour with some people, if Providence had seen fit to make them only hands'.[27]

Yet, as Marx and Engels had perceived in the *Communist Manifesto* of 1848, bringing together large numbers of workers in factories stimulated an awareness of their shared conditions. This consciousness did not help to lead to the overthrow of capitalist production, as Marx and Engels had also predicted, but it did underpin the organisation of trade unions. In cotton, which by 1851 employed twice as many workers as wool textiles, trade unions tended to be localised organisations. Moreover, though not without skill, those employed in cotton mills did not serve apprenticeships. It was through experience gained at an early age and picking up the knowledge needed to do the work from other workers that the operative became qualified. Nevertheless, by the 1800s spinners and weavers had their societies, which were similar to the organisations of craft workers.

In spite of the sort of vicissitudes experienced by most trade unions in the 1830s and 1840s, collective bargaining continued to take place. By the end of the third quarter of the century, the cotton unions could boast of financial reserves, size of membership and negotiating clout comparable with those of the 'new model' unions of time-served craftsmen. These unions, however, reflected the specialisation that was characteristic of the cotton industry. The towns of south-east Lancashire were noted for different types of work. As a broad generalisation, weaving predominated around Preston, Blackburn and Burnley, with spinning to the south, notably in Bolton, Oldham and Rochdale. Moreover, within each town, there tended to be further specialisation; Bolton's mills, for example, were noted for fine spinning, while Rochdale's specialised in coarse. Lists of prices, showing the rates paid by employers, determined wages, and a vital requirement for the trade union official was the ability to understand the details of how wages were calculated. Although accident and chance played a part in the way Lancashire textile workers were organised, the existence of dozens of unions, catering for different areas and branches of the industry, reflected the structure of cotton manufacturing. Gradually, as with coal miners, the movement to amalgamate grew stronger, although in both the weaving and spinning areas less successful bodies were formed before the creation of the Amalgamated Association of Operative Cotton Spinners, Self-Actor Minders, Twiners and Rovers in 1870 and the Northern Counties Amalgamated Association of Weavers in 1884.[28]

Workers in the wool industry

In a comparable way, parts of Yorkshire's West Riding were dominated by different branches of the wool trade. Bradford and Halifax tended to produce worsteds, Leeds and Huddersfield woollens. In addition, there was much product diversity, for example, the manufacture of cheap woollen goods in Batley, blankets and 'shoddy' in Dewsbury and carpets in Halifax and Brighouse. Titus Salt devised a means of weaving alpaca wool and, in a spirit of autocratic paternalism, founded the model village of Saltaire, a few miles north-west of Bradford, in the 1850s.

Weaving sheds, as the name implies, tended to be fairly small-scale at first, to some extent growing out of the domestic system, which survived in remoter villages until mid-century. However, large factories were established by the later part of the century. For example, in Bradford some 5000 workers were employed in the Manningham Mills in 1890–1, when a bitter dispute helped to pave the way for the establishment of the Independent Labour Party.[29] Although in Lancashire large numbers of women cotton workers were trade union members, in the West Riding the similarly localised unions tended to explain their relative weakness by referring to the scale of women's employment in the woollen and worsted mills. Indeed, E. P. Thompson took this position when writing of the way in which the 'high proportion of women and juvenile workers, and the variations and jealousies between town and town, mill and mill, and even shed and shed, placed almost insuperable difficulties in the way of trade union organisation'.[30]

Agricultural workers

Although it expanded in the nineteenth century, wool was an older staple industry, rapidly overtaken by the new staple, cotton. To meet the demand for woollen goods, there was a greater need to import raw materials – just as the cotton industry drew its supplies from overseas (in both cases, however, the need for powered machinery stimulated the coalfields of Lancashire and Yorkshire). The production of raw wool was an important aspect of British farming. In the early 1830s the domestic wool clip totalled about 120 million pounds per year, and some 30 million pounds were imported (by the Great War, home output was about the same, with net imports of 500 million pounds).[31] Shepherds enjoyed a higher status than most other farmworkers. Their work was carried out with little day-to-day supervision and entailed specialist skills, especially during lambing. The shepherd's cottage was often better than the labourer's, while his wages were higher and more regular. However, because of the practice of payment in kind, the level of his income is not easily assessed. As late as 1882, for example, a royal commission report cited the case of a shepherd who received potatoes, oatmeal, coal, a house, a cow and 53 sheep, but no money.[32] Moreover, the hours could be long; 'Shepherds or cattlemen might as well ask for a golden sovereign as for a Sunday off', one East Riding labourer informed an investigator.[33]

Sheep were widely distributed, though of relatively greater importance in upland areas where they could survive on meagre pasturage which allowed for little other farming. Agricultural labourers were enumerated by the censuses throughout Britain, but were notably concentrated in the southern and eastern counties of England. Much of the contemporary literature concerned with farmworkers dealt with those predominantly rural areas where few alternative forms of work existed. Where the market for labour was overstocked, wages were low and conditions wretched. Even allowing for the tendency of reformers to score debating points against the agricultural interest, for landlords and their tenant farmers were generally Tories, the weight of evidence confirms the endemic poverty of the labourer. J. S. Mill, for example, in 1846 thought the 'Irish potato digger' would pause before changing places 'with the anxious, care-worn, and not much better fed Dorsetshire labourer'.[34] Sixty years later, wages in Dorset were still among the lowest in any county – an average of 16/1 a week, according to Rowntree and Kendall – but by then observers were profoundly aware of what was termed the rural exodus or the flight from the land. In spite of the fall, which became evident from the 1860s, in absolute terms the numbers employed in agriculture remained large; but the sense of decline probably made it more difficult to organise the labourer. There had been a phase of activity, led by Joseph Arch in the early 1870s, and the upsurge of the 'new' trade unionism some twenty years later gave a renewed impetus in the countryside. This in turn fell away, although the Primitive Methodist George Edwards formed the Eastern Counties Agricultural Labourers' and Small Holders' Union in 1906. In a speech to inaugurate the union, Edwards gave 'the isolated condition of the labourers', the 'great distances to travel' and 'the miserably low wage the labourer receives' as obstacles in the way of organisation, and by 1911 only 3569 members had been recruited.[35] There was also the sense that the land offered poor prospects for the worker. Mothers of farm labourers, asked about where they advised their sons to find work, would reply, 'Not on the land – there's nothing for them',[36] and, although for other reasons as well as respect for maternal wishes, the numbers employed in agriculture fell. Those nearer to towns were most easily able to find better wages and living standards, as well as less arduous social pressures than those sometimes imposed by squire and parson. 'The sturdy sons of the village have fled', one observer of rural Essex declared with an element of condescension, 'they have left behind the old men, the lame, the mentally deficient, the vicious, the born tired.'[37]

Rural industry

In spite of the urbanisation of nineteenth-century Britain, which by 1914 made the typical worker a town dweller, the survival, though in a depleted state, of rural industry should not be overlooked. In the countryside, as would be expected, there were links between farming and several small-scale trades. Often, as with lacemaking and straw plaiting, the work was mostly done by the wives and daughters of labourers. Makers of furniture and baskets were more usually men, though the materials used depended on local supplies and the willingness of landowners to maintain them. A theme of observers of the countryside was the loss of rural crafts, and the story is indeed one of decline. There were a number of reasons for this. By mid-century, mechanised production had begun to supersede some types of small-scale production, a trend that was to continue until 1914. Mass-produced household furniture undercut the woodland-based carpenter, although the flexibility of the individual worker meant that some were able to switch to garden furniture, hurdles and fences. The use of other roofing materials lessened the demand for thatchers, while rural depopulation and, by the 1880s, falling rents meant the erection of fewer cottages and farm buildings.

Moreover, the line between traditional crafts, which embodied generations of skill, and exploitative, poorly paid labour, akin to the sweated homework of the city, was a fine one. Compulsory education helped to reduce child labour, while the small improvement in living standards meant that the families of some labourers could give up cottage production. Even goods made with simple tools and the use of skills in which the worker might take pride had to be marketed, and in this respect too larger producers had the advantage. Efforts were made by sympathetic, usually paternalistic, groups to preserve countryside crafts. For example, the first lace association was started in 1874 and others, 'generally founded by ladies of leisure and energy', followed.[38] However, although such initiatives had little impact on the market for the products as a whole, even by 1914 rural industries, while diminished, had by no means disappeared.

Shipbuilding

For Britain, as an imperialist nation with heavy investments in its export economy, shipping was a vital industry. Of the world's merchant shipping, about a third was British-owned between 1860 and 1914, a period when the size of the fleet increased almost threefold. It was, moreover, the practice of Britain's owners to invest in larger and more modern vessels, selling off less efficient ships to other countries. Together with a rapid economic transformation, as steel and steam replaced wood and sail, these circumstances meant a large growth of employment in the shipbuilding industry. Although it was subject to cyclical fluctuations, with consequent periods of unemployment, workers in the various trades involved – including carpenters, plumbers, brassworkers, boilermakers and blacksmiths as well as shipwrights and engineers – were among the better paid. The nature of shipbuilding gave rise to demarcation disputes among the various craft unions, as each strived to advance its members' interests. However, those shipyard workers outside the ranks of the skilled were expected, as in other industries, to accept long hours and sometimes dangerous conditions. In shipbuilding towns, partly-built vessels were a visible reminder to the local community of its source of employment in the way that the pithead was to miners and the factory chimney to millworkers. The growth of shipbuilding provided work in the north-east of England, in Belfast, Barrow and, especially, on Clydeside, where in the years after 1870 about half the total British tonnage was launched.[39]

Workers in metal, and related trades

The census of 1901 counted, for the first time, more persons employed in metal manufacture and related trades than in agriculture. The category, however, is a wide one, and includes only some elements, such as shipbuilding, that had a distinctly regional character. Nor were the towns most associated with iron and steel single-industry communities to the extent of coal-mining settlements. Even Middlesbrough, so involved with the iron trade that one of its football league clubs played as Middlesbrough Ironopolis, also had many engineering workers. Nevertheless, virtually a creation of the nineteenth century, in which it grew from a small farming village, with a population of 154 in 1831, to a town of over one hundred thousand inhabitants in 1911, Middlesbrough was dominated by its ironworks, in the vicinity of which 'every sense is violently assailed all day long by some manifestation of the making of iron'.[40]

Similarly, the character of several other towns was in part determined by one or other of the metal trades. Sheffield, by 1830, had long been celebrated for the production of cutlery and other edged tools; by 1914 the city still had a reputation for such goods, but by then the eastward expansion of the steel industry into Brightside and Attercliffe had shifted the balance from the small-scale workshop of the 'little master' to the massively capitalised steel mill. This dual nature of the metalworking trades had a consequence for many years on the organisation of the local labour movement. From 1908 to 1920 there were two trades councils. The long-established Sheffield Federated Trades Council comprised the small local unions of the cutlery and silver trades, led by men who were mostly Liberal–Radical in politics. Their views were regarded as insufficiently advanced by some of the socialists who were representatives of the nationally organised heavy iron and steel industry. Intent on promoting independent labour politics, the latter broke away to form the Sheffield Trades and Labour Council in 1908. Ironically, in 1910 the Parliamentary Committee of the Trades Union Congress, most member unions of which were affiliated to the Labour Party, accepted the invitation of the Federated Trades Council to hold its annual congress in Sheffield, and further dismayed the socialists by attending a reception hosted by the Lord Mayor, Earl Fitzwilliam, a colliery owner who had recently been involved in a bitter dispute with miners.[41]

Other varieties of labour

By their nature, some occupations were common to every modestly sized centre of population. Painters, woodworkers, domestic servants, carters and so on were widespread. Even small towns had their own breweries and flour-mills, although the former were affected by the growth of railways which favoured the development of such centres as Burton, which became known for the production of Bass, and the increased importance of imported wheat led to the establishment of large mills, such as those of the Rank company, at coastal sites. On the other hand, numerous towns continued to be celebrated, and sometimes pitied, for specific industries. Dundee was a byword for jute (as its sobriquet 'Juteopolis' indicated), Leicester grew as a centre of boot and shoe manufacture, the 'five towns' of the Potteries depended on china and Widnes became so known for the production of noxious chemicals that the planner Patrick Abercrombie suggested 'no-one ought to live there!' There were also those occupations that many Victorian commentators and moralisers wished to see an end to. Hawkers, thieves and beggars, such as those portrayed by Henry Mayhew in his investigations of the 1850s, were regarded as a drag on social progress. So too was 'the ne'er do weel and the habitual out-o'-work' of London's East End, who in the 1880s Beatrice Webb contrasted with the steady millhands of Bacup, where the 'Co-op' and chapel reflected the people's values.[42] Casual workers on the docks or in the so-called sweated trades were also regarded as both a parasitic feature of the labour force and, once political parties accepted the idea of a mass electorate, poor material for citizenship. Those who tried to make a living as members of what were variously termed the 'residuum', the 'submerged tenth', the 'lumpenproletariat' and the 'dangerous classes' had few defenders. These and other aspects of the Victorian labour market indicate some of the complexities of generalising about the nature of class-consciousness, community and culture.

Summary

Although the criteria adopted in the nine censuses between 1831 and 1911 were not uniform, and some occupations, especially those of women, were missed, the returns indicate the vast range of employment that existed in the period. It is clear that with industrialisation and the growth of urban populations, the structure of the labour market changed. Agriculture became relatively less important; there was an increase in the number and size of factories (although smaller-scale, workshop methods of production remained significant); the demand for coal rose inexorably; and still throughout the period the majority of workers were not employed on the land or in the factory or coal mine.

Moreover, it has to be emphasised that these generalisations apply to the whole of Britain. In a book such as this, which aims to provide a short survey of a period that is both relatively long and complex, simplification is inevitable. Nevertheless, the persistence of regional variations should not be forgotten; indeed, with specialisation and the emergence of locational advantage (sometimes termed 'external economies'), some industries became more concentrated in certain parts of the country. This chapter has also sought to re-evaluate the concept of skill, and to suggest that it should not be narrowly conceived. The growing tendency of workers to form trade unions can in part be explained by the special abilities possessed by sections of the labour force.

Finally, the difficulties faced by both contemporaries and present-day historians have to be acknowledged. It is an impossible task to enter into the lives of the millions of workers of a century and more ago. Even for a small sample, the evidence is both incomplete and (if one thinks, for example, just of the scale of the local press) overwhelming. Then there is the problem of how to deal with perceptions. For instance, visitors to working-class areas were generally inclined to deplore the miles of grimy, mean streets, unrelieved by colour or beauty. The lives of the workers were also assumed to be equally dreary and monotonous. For many, each day was defined by harsh and ill-rewarded work, though, as a later chapter will show, observers from outside often missed or misunderstood recreational and associational aspects of workers' lives. Similarly, there was a failure to see family life from other than an outsider's perspective. In part an exception to this, Lady Bell allowed that the spectator who suddenly came across the 'gaunt assembly of abodes' near Middlesbrough's ironworks would form 'a gloomy picture of what life must be like in them'; yet there were 'people living in these hard-looking, shabby, ugly streets who have been there for many years, and more than one who has left' had 'pined to be back again'.[43] Such aspects of working-class life will be considered more fully in a later chapter, but first more tangible issues will be examined.

2

WAGES AND WORKING CONDITIONS

The Market for Labour

In the nineteenth century, as in other periods, it seemed self-evident to all but a few that work was at the centre of the life of the worker. Men, women and all but young children were expected to be gainfully employed. Idleness not only offended against the divine order, for the Bible taught that man earned his bread by the sweat of his brow, but it was also an intolerable distortion of the market economy. In spite of its inadequacies, the New Poor Law of 1834 tried systematically to ensure the worker would seek paid employment rather than endure the punitive regime of the workhouse. Everything was done by educationists and political economists to emphasise how sharp was the fall from the status of worker to that of a pauper. At about the same time, there was a reorganisation of policing, so that those tempted away from honest toil faced incarceration in prisons that bore comparison with the workhouses, while operating even more harshly.

Promoters of the work ethic could point to the huge range of employment available. Each census, for example, identified hundreds of occupations. The state sought to dismantle restrictions on entry into the labour market, in keeping with Adam Smith's dictum that every man should be 'free to pursue his own interest his own way, and to bring both his industry and capital into competition with any other man, or order of men'.[1] The ethos of unfettered competition, articulated in a humane way by Smith, was vulgarised to such an extent that even John Stuart Mill, who stood in the same tradition of political economy, was repelled by those who thought that 'the normal state of human beings is that of struggling to get on'. He also rejected the view that 'the tramping, crushing, elbowing and treading on each other's heels' were inevitably the 'disagreeable symptoms of one of the phases of industrial progress'.[2] But others revelled in the idea of the 'British Beehive', with its combination of hierarchy and industriousness.

By the mid-nineteenth century, the labour market was as unrestricted as it had ever been. The Combination Laws, for instance, which had limited the rights of workers to form trade unions, were repealed in 1825. Acts governing apprenticeship, dating back to the Elizabethan period, were also rescinded, and, although this old legislation had become virtually a dead letter, its formal abolition was in keeping with the new orthodoxies of the time. However, the government policy that most characterised attitudes to labour was the Poor Law Amendment Act of 1834. At its centre was the belief that the worker should be responsible for finding employment and living on the wages it paid. Those who could not reach such a level were to be tested by the principle of 'less eligibility': they were offered help that was conditional on their entry into a workhouse, where their situation was to be less eligible than that of the independent labourer of the lowest class. It was believed that no pauper would henceforth choose the regime of the workhouse rather than seek employment in the free labour market. In practice, the new poor law had to cater for much larger numbers than were anticipated. A spate of poor harvests between 1836 and 1842 pushed up food prices and contributed, as did the financial crisis of 1839, to depressed trade. These were difficult conditions in which to enforce a new law that was already disliked; in many areas workers were swept into opposition that often involved rioting and did much to fuel the incipient Chartist movement. Nevertheless, the operation of the poor law was insufficiently rigid for some ideologues, who also complained that the legislation of 1834 failed to end the law of settlement, seen by advocates of an unfettered labour market as an interference with the mobility of labour.[3] The Poor Law Amendment Act, while influenced by the theory of laissez-faire, probably did more through its bureaucratic structures to frustrate than to facilitate the political economists' desire for a competitive market.

For much of the nineteenth century, there were two corollaries to this assumption that workers should be free agents when selling their labour. The first was that each adult male was sufficiently knowledgeable about the work he was accepting, and rational enough in making decisions, to agree on a wage that compensated for any peculiar dangers that existed. Thus, in making his wages bargain, the seaman would allow for the risk of shipwreck, the Sheffield cutler would be mindful of the ravages of grinders' asthma and the coal-hewer would be aware of the frequency of mining disasters. More prosaically, workers were expected to act as economic men to the extent that they made provision from their wages for bouts of unemployment and old age. Secondly, for much of the period, the theory of the wages fund – or the iron law of wages – was one of the orthodoxies of political economy. This doctrine, devised largely by Malthus and developed by James Mill, maintained that a fixed amount of capital was available to pay the labouring population. Workers' combinations, according to the population theorist, Revd Thomas R. Malthus, were 'not only illegal, but irrational and ineffective'.[4] The theory was invested with greater authority when Mill's son, John Stuart Mill, incorporated it into his influential *Principles* (1848), where it remained until he and other political economists abandoned the position in the later 1860s.

A number of applications followed from these apparent principles of political economy. Employers of labour, it was maintained, should be free to hire and dismiss workers according to their needs, akin to utilising any other factor of production. In reality, capitalists were not always so ruthless, though this did not save them from those critics who denounced, in Thomas Carlyle's striking phrase, the way cash payment had become 'the universal sole nexus of man to man'.[5] The state, it was widely held, had few grounds on which to interfere with a self-regulating market system (in which other elements, such as profits and rents, were determined by similar economic laws). The interests of women and children, where it could not be assumed that adult males would take responsibility for them, might be legislated for, though, by the later nineteenth century, some of the arguments for state intervention were applied to all workers. Trade unions, if freely entered into by workers, had by the logic of non-intervention to be tolerated, but orthodox political economy denied that such combinations were capable of permanently improving the wages of their members. In the short term, collective action might lead to better rates of pay, but, according to economic law, these improvements would be at the expense of other groups of workers. Before long, market forces would reassert themselves and wages would again find their natural level. Trade unions were regarded as legitimate organisations when they functioned as friendly societies; by encouraging their members to develop thrift and foresight, they helped to ensure provision for unemployment, sickness, industrial injury and old age. Only in the decade or so before the First World War did it begin to become accepted, and then in the teeth of much opposition, that the state should take a role in these areas.

Standards of Living

Beguiled by their theoretical constructions, mid-nineteenth-century political economists were seldom disposed to make statistical inquiries into the wages of the working population. Had there been more information about the rewards of labour, it is possible that the 'standard of living debate' would not have been so prominent a feature of modern historiography. However, that often acrimonious controversy in many respects replicated the arguments of the nineteenth century. While some, such as Carlyle, believed that the economic changes associated with the Industrial Revolution had meant a worsening of the lot of the poorer classes, others welcomed the new methods of production. By 1816, in his novel *Headlong Hall*, Thomas Love Peacock satirised the views of 'the perfectionist' and 'the deteriorationist'. One associated the manufacturing system with

> seas covered with vessels, ports resounding with life, profound researches, scientific inventions, complicated mechanism, canals carried over deep valleys and through the bosoms of hills: employment and existence thus given to innumerable families, and the multiplied comforts and conveniences of life diffused over the whole community.

To which the other responded:

> Wherever this boasted machinery is established, the children of the poor are death-doomed from their cradles. . . . Nor is the lot of their parents more enviable. Sedentary victims of unhealthy toil. . . . They are mere automata, component parts of the enormous machines which administer to the pampered appetites of the few, who consider themselves the most valuable portion of a state, because they consume in indolence the fruits of the earth, and contribute nothing to the benefit of the community.[6]

With regard to the working class, as well as other sections of society, elements of this debate continued in such forms as the 'condition of England question' in the 1840s and the arguments between 'individualists' and 'collectivists' at the end of the century.

Sound statistical evidence, such as might resolve some of these controversies, does not, however, exist. Even on the matter of wages, perhaps the prime influence on living standards, information is deficient, particularly for the earlier period. Moreover, were there more and better information about the wages paid to workers, great caution would still be needed when reaching any conclusions relating to standards of living. This is because there is incomplete evidence about other aspects of the issue. These include the regularity of wages, in a period often characterised by underemployment, as well as regional and occupational variations, the household or family income (not only that of the main breadwinner); and the extent of non-money income. Furthermore, other factors impacted on living standards, such as the conditions of employment and variations in the price and availability of basic food-stuffs. In recent years, historians have developed methods of studying evidence of the physique of workers; yet this attempt to determine varia-tions in living standards has proved as debatable as other approaches to the issue.[7] In spite of these complications, it is nevertheless useful to examine these various factors in more detail. By doing so, it is not only possible to reach some tentative conclusions, but the exercise will also complement other aspects of the experience of labour in our period. In particular, it will provide some indication of the extent to which collective effort affected the wages bargain as well as workers' struggles to attain some autonomy in the workplace.

At a very simple level, it cannot be disputed that the average real wage was higher in 1914 than in 1830. One authoritative source accepts the calculations that suggest, over this period of eighty-odd years, the increase was in the order of some eighty-odd per cent.[8] But the growth in wages was far from even. Between 1830 and 1850 the average real wage probably did not rise; it might even have fallen slightly. Not until the early twentieth century was the term 'the hungry forties' coined to describe the 1840s, though some historians have found it appropriate for a decade of Irish hunger and Chartist agitation. After 1850, it is more generally accepted, average wages did little better than rise in line with prices, until the mid-1860s, when real improvements became discern-ible. A leading authority has recently concluded a survey of the standard of living in the period after about 1770 in these words:

> For the majority of the working class the historical reality was that they had to endure almost a century of hard toil with little or no advance from a low base before they really began to share in any of the benefits of the economic transformation they had helped to create.[9]

A fall in prices from the early 1880s, particularly in the price of food, the major element in working-class budgets, underpinned the further improvement in the average wage. Between 1900 and 1914, however, as the cost of living began to rise, real wages struggled to keep apace of higher prices, and probably fell back by two or three per cent. It has, however, to be kept in mind that behind these broad trends were the myriad experiences of individual workers. Circumstances could vary immensely. An irregularly employed worker without dependents, for example, might be economically better off than a skilled one with a large family to support. However, as knowledge of contraception spread from the 1880s – the establishment of the Malthusian League in 1877 was symbolic of this development[10] – family size fell, at first among more skilled workers. Fewer children to support, especially at a time when compulsory education was reducing opportunities for child labour, was equivalent to an improvement in wages.[11]

The Working Week

Moreover, during the same period in which average wages rose, there was a fall in the length of the average working week. As with other aspects of the period, the statistical evidence is too incomplete to allow more than an indication of the main trends.[12] In 1830 the more fortunate among factory textile operatives worked 'six to six', although there was pressure for the norm to become a working day that ran from 6 a.m. to 6 p.m., with Saturday work ending in mid-afternoon. In some factories workers were expected to be at their machines at 6 a.m. and, apart from half an hour for meals, to continue until 8 or 9 p.m. Reformers campaigned for a ten-hour working day, and gained a little ground in 1833 when legislation restricted the employment of children and young persons. This tended to make it less practical to keep adults working for long hours, but not until 1847 did the 'Ten Hours Act' have the effect of establishing a normal working week of 58 hours (on Saturdays work finished at 2 p.m.). However, some employers adopted the relay system, to stagger the work of young persons and thus extend the day of adult men. In 1850 another act prohibited relays, but increased weekly hours to 60: 'Free Trade in everything, especially in flesh and blood, is henceforth to be the order of the day', commented the radical Joseph Rayner Stephens.[13]

Yet although the factory, which symbolised the Industrial Revolution, and the conditions of child labour in cotton and woollen mills that were widely deplored by social reformers have resulted in a considerable body of historical scholarship,[14] the industrial wage earner represented a minority of the labour force. Away from the factories, hours of labour, while numerous, were often more irregular. When harvesting, farm labourers usually worked from dawn to dusk, though in other seasons they found less to do. In workshop trades in particular, the practice of observing 'St Monday' (the tradition of extending weekend leisure time beyond Sunday) survived, despite the efforts of employers, into the twentieth century.[15] Workers on piece-rates often worked long hours later in the week to make up for the time taken off on Monday, while coal miners tended to have a preference for leisure which led them to sacrifice their earnings for one or two shifts, usually towards the beginning or the end of the working week. The 'result of keeping St. Monday, St. Tuesday and even St. Wednesday' was high coal prices, according to the *Derbyshire Times* in 1882. 'Let us therefore have no limitation on output, but cheap coal and plenty of it', added the paper hopefully.[16]

Hours of labour, like wages, varied widely over the whole period. By the early 1870s, in larger and better organised industries, such as textiles, engineering and building, a working week of between 54 and 56 hours was fairly widespread. This was made up of nine to ten hours during the week, with an early-afternoon finish on Saturdays. (One consequence of the Saturday half-day was the growth of professional football; of the twelve clubs that formed the Football League in 1888, six were in Lancashire and six in the Midlands.) By the end of the 1880s, the demand for the eight-hour day was common among trade union leaders. Though the movement for eight hours had an ethical basis – that of the day's 24 hours equal periods should be devoted to sleep, labour and leisure – it was mainly driven by the wish to reduce unemployment. By limiting the length of the working week, it was argued, the supply of labour would more equally balance the demand. However, some of the more traditionally minded trade union leaders were unwilling to commit the Trades Union Congress, where many of these debates were staged, to campaigning for the legal eight-hour day. They accepted the capitalists' predictions that British industry would become uncompetitive if hours were reduced, while also arguing that government legislation would interfere with negotiations between employers and men. Advocates of legislation held that previous reductions in the length of the working week had not produced the consequences that had been forecast, and pointed out that the occupations most in need of legal protection were usually the worst organised. Although some groups of workers were able to negotiate the eight-hour day before 1914, only in the exceptional case of coal miners was legislation enacted, in the form of the Coal Mines Regulation Act of 1908.

Behind these rough generalisations concerning wages and hours of labour lies an almost infinite range of differing circumstances. Indeed, the working-class autobiographies that survive from the period, together with various other records that allow for the piecing together of individual lives, show that each person's experiences, then as now, had a unique character. However, to make some sense of the past, a level of simplification is necessary. The loss of employment, for example, affects each person differently, and yet in the nineteenth century the lack of work had to be faced by the majority of workers at some point in their lives. It is possible, therefore, to make some general assessment of the extent and impact of unemployment and to offer some conclusions about its significance.

Unemployment and Underemployment

To the classical economist imprisoned by theory, long-term unemployment should not exist. In any market, supply and demand would move into equilibrium, at which point a natural price would emerge. In theory, a worker in need of employment would offer his labour and accept a wage that represented the market rate. Only gradually were the complexities of unemployment realised. As late as the 1870s the respected economist Stanley Jevons sought to explain fluctuations in trade, and hence in employment, by harvest variations caused by climate changes arising from spots on the sun. Given the view that periods of unemployment were inevitable, it followed that each worker should show foresight and make provision. The state ensured there was a last resort, the poor law, but otherwise remained inactive until the 1880s. Then, in the winter of 1885–6, unemployment reached a high level. On 8 February a meeting of the unemployed in Trafalgar Square ended with smashed windows in the gentlemen's clubs of Pall Mall and looted shops in Piccadilly. Subscriptions to the Mansion House Fund for poor relief increased markedly. Soon after, the President of the Local Government Board, Joseph Chamberlain, who was regarded still as a radical Liberal, issued a circular calling on local authorities to provide municipal employment as an alternative to the workhouse. This palliative did help to prepare opinion for the Edwardian legislation, the Unemployed Workmen Act of 1905 and the national insurance scheme of 1911, but older attitudes were slow to shift. For example, the belief that unemployment was inevitable and even beneficial was shared by the social reformer Charles Booth, who wrote in 1903:

> Those who live from day to day, or even from week to week, and even those who live from year to year, may be pinched when trade contracts – some of them must be. There are some victims, but those who are able and willing to provide in times of prosperity for the lean years which seem inevitably to follow, do not suffer at all; and, if the alternations of good and bad times be not too sudden or too great, the community gains not only by the strengthening of character under stress, but also by a direct effect on enterprise.[17]

The small minority of workers who belonged to trade unions usually qualified for small but regular sums when out of work. These benefits, which provided help in spells of unemployment, including payments to assist travel in search of work, were an important feature of craftsmen's unions. However, the skilled worker was in a position to pay relatively high subscriptions to his trade union. Most workers were not and had to depend on less formal methods of surviving the loss of employment. These might include help from family members – such as loans or the temporary adoption of children – though often whole communities might be affected, and impoverished, by spells of unemployment. House rents would be left unpaid, in the hope that the debts incurred would be paid off before landlords issued notices to evict. As far as possible, local shopkeepers were persuaded to give credit; almost invariably, wives negotiated such concessions, their success depending partly on how conscientiously they had paid off arrears on previous occasions. In Edwardian Salford, a 'tick book', showing the sum owed and that a woman was trusted to pay it off, was 'an emblem of integrity and a bulwark against hard times'.[18] Pawnbrokers' shops, widely relied upon as sources of short-term credit, were occasionally overwhelmed by unredeemed pledges, as customers had not the means to recover the clothes and household goods they had pawned. In Sunderland, for example, during 1884 the local press noted that even 'decent women and thrifty housewives' were being forced to rely on the pawnbroker.[19] For small sums, it was as cheap to borrow from a moneylender, without the need to part with the sort of articles a pawnbroker would take. However, if debts mounted up, the interest rates exacted by moneylenders were oppressively high, and women in particular were liable to be harassed by debt collectors. Charities helped unemployed workers, although usually

only those deemed to be of a respectable character, especially where religious observation was expected. Less respectably, and in consequence
less widely recorded, begging, theft and prostitution could ensure survival in the absence of paid employment.

Some of these means of support were also necessary where workers
faced chronic underemployment. This aspect of the Victorian economy
is even more patchily recorded than are levels of unemployment. In the
so-called casual trades in particular, the demand for labour fluctuated
widely. In the great ports, dock workers were expected to present themselves early each morning at the dock gates, where a proportion would
be taken on, perhaps only for half a day, depending on the number of
vessels that needed unloading. As the trade union organiser James Sexton
wrote of Liverpool in the early 1880s:

> Two men offered themselves for every job, and wages came tumbling
> down, shrinking from thirty shillings for a full week – quite good pay
> in those days – until the average cannot have been a ha'penny above
> fifteen shillings, and few men could hope to get full employment for
> any week.[20]

In spite of attempts to organise dock workers, the position was much the
same on the eve of the Great War. According to one survey, during the
summer of 1913 the earnings of a docker during a period of eleven
weeks were 26/3, 18/8, 7/8, 23/2, 47/4, nothing, 41/4, 20/10, 19/2, 18/2
and 14/4 (an average of about 21/6 per week).[21] Among farmworkers,
too, for most of the nineteenth century an over-supply of labour pushed
down wages and consigned many to underemployment. Often this was
seasonal, as farmers, once the autumn harvest had been gathered in,
required fewer workers. Employment by the day, or the task, became
more common, at least until late in the century, when what contemporaries called the 'rural exodus' or the 'flight from the land' made labour
less plentiful and caused modest improvements in wages.

Non-Wage Income

Moreover, it is necessary to consider the nature of non-wage income in
our period. Many workers were able to improve, marginally, their living
standards by means other than the money wages they received. The
most common form of additional income were various perquisites, the

extent and availability of which varied greatly. Those in one of the largest of occupational groups, domestic servants, received very small sums in money wages. A London servant girl in 1851 would be paid less than £10 a year;[22] but she would also get board and lodgings and probably some clothes. Servants who came into contact with better-off families would receive gratuities and enjoy, probably unofficially, some of the food and drink intended for their employers. However, dismissal could render a servant homeless. Where accommodation was provided, as also was the case with some farmworkers, railwaymen and miners who paid low rents for cottages owned by their employers, workers who agitated for change, or who did not comply with their employers' notions of accept-able behaviour, were more vulnerable.

In agriculture, despite underemployment and chronically low wages, the labourer's struggle to survive was aided by various 'perks'. However, from the late eighteenth century, some commentators noted a lessening of the number and value of perquisites available to the farm labourer and his family. In corn-growing areas, for example, the decline of glean-ing was observed. After the main crop had been harvested, it was the traditional right of workers, or more usually their wives and children, to go into the fields and gather, or glean, those ears of wheat missed by the harvesters. Similarly, fields of barley were also searched, in a way that was equally back-breaking, though the grain collected was often used to feed the labourers' hens. More important was the wheat, which, when ground into flour, would go to make bread in the winter months. One calculation, based on a survey of nine parishes in the early 1830s, shows that gleaning represented between 6 and 9.5 per cent of families' annual income.[23] However, though the practice survived, in parts of Essex, for example, until after the Second World War (when the grain collected was used as animal feed),[24] newer farming techniques, including the mechanical reaper, made the main harvest more efficient and left less for the gleaner. Some farmers, moreover, were suspicious that labour-ers, mindful of the gleaning stage that would follow, were tempted to harvest wastefully, and tried to restrict the practice.

Farmers were similarly uneasy about the allotment system. The enclos-ure of wastes, a process which continued in some counties well into the nineteenth century, meant a loss of villagers' customary rights, such as gathering wood and grazing animals. In compensation, some paternal-istic observers advocated the renting of allotments or the enlargement of gardens attached to labourers' cottages, to enable the cultivation of vege-tables and perhaps the support of a few livestock. Had he not kept a pig, many a labourer and his family would have had a near-meatless diet. Where allotments were available, farm labourers could, by working in the evening or on days when farmers did not require their services, supplement their incomes. However, some farmers resisted making available land to rent as allotments, arguing that labourers might get ideas above their station or neglect their other duties in favour of cultivating their own patches of land. It was also suggested that allotment holders would be tempted to steal crops from the farmers' fields and pass them off as their own produce. On the question of pilfering, the amount of evidence that survives probably represents only a small proportion of the cases that occurred, but where game was concerned the severity of the punishment inflicted on poachers indicates the vigour with which the propertied classes were determined to defend their interests.

Probably more than any other source of labour, agriculture offered a greater variety of opportunities – only briefly indicated here – for non-wage income. But workers in other occupations too had customary rights and perquisites. Increasingly, the available evidence suggests, these were enjoyed in the face of employer opposition. Historians have taken the view that the newer ideology that regarded the worker as an economic man, paid money wages in an open market for labour, led to efforts by employers to eradicate practices deemed little different to theft. Some historians have explained the growth of factory and workshop production as partly motivated by the employers' attempts to supervise their workers more closely. Yet older customs persevered. In 1869 James Greenwood described a 'species of dishonesty' known 'by the cant name of "perks", which is a convenient abbreviation of the word "perquisite", and in the hands of the users of it, it shows itself a word of amazing flexibility'. After citing numerous examples, he concluded with an attack on tailors who, when taking material for their own use, 'playfully' designated it 'cabbage'. He deplored the failure to acknowledge that such actions were theft:

> As with the tailor, so it is with the upholsterer, and the dressmaker, and the paperhanger, and the plumber, and all the rest of them. I don't say that every time they take a shred of this, or a pound of that, that they have before their eyes the enormity of the offence they are about to commit. What they do they see no great harm in.[25]

Pilfering was notoriously endemic in all large ports. A Thames waterman in the 1880s, Harry Gosling (Companion of Honour, Justice of the

Peace and Labour Party Member of Parliament when he published his autobiography in 1927), regarded pilfering as 'helping yourself to the things you need, and this has always been a rule of the river ever since the first ship came up the Thames with merchandise'. Gosling allowed that 'a lighterman might take a few pounds of coal', but this was insignificant in comparison to owners who fuelled their vessels with coal stolen from their customers.[26] Dockers sold 'a lot of cheap tea and sugar' in the shop run by Aunt Liza, a relative of Arthur Harding, an East End criminal; ironically, when his uncle sold stolen whisky he ended up in prison, for not having a licence.[27] Where prosecutions were made, court reports show the great range of goods taken and the attitude of some defendants that their offences were not the equivalent of common theft.[28]

In almost all occupations perks were looked for as a matter of course. One engineer recalled how early-twentieth-century workers would appropriate materials to do 'jobs for the king' – the making of tools and other goods for use at home or to sell – and would routinely use a makeshift Bunsen burner to tap into the firm's gas supply to boil water for tea.[29] Some employers established factory canteens, taking the view that the perquisite of subsidised meals was preferable, as it restored some authority in the workplace, to workers breaking off for meals. Undoubtedly, as well as a wish to augment their incomes, workers who sought out perquisites were also motivated by the desire to exercise a degree of control over the conditions of their employment. 'Thou shalt not muzzle the ox when he treadeth out the corn', replied Sidney Webb when asked about miners' allowances of coal during the Sankey Commission (1919), and there was some acceptance of this view by employers. Not all employers were themselves entirely honest in their conduct, as Gosling pointed out when justifying workers' misdemeanours. In his autobiography, John Paton detailed petty fraud in the Glasgow milk trade in the 1900s. As a milkman his wages were 24s a week, for seven days' work that began at five in the morning and ended in the middle of the afternoon. But the dairy's measure was designed to show the issue of two gallons of milk more than was the case, which meant that each milkman had to give short measure, or pay some 2s a day to the employer. However, by 'flicking the wrist' when supplying customers, it was possible not only to cover the shortfall but also to add another 6s a week to the milkman's wage.[30] As Henry Mayhew in his survey of the London poor in the 1850s commented, 'there is no business or trade, however insignificant or contemptible, without its own peculiar and appropriate tricks'.[31]

However, the efforts by workers to get their perks represented in many industries an attempt to counter the employers' exactions. Survivals of the truck system, whereby workers were paid in kind or by coins or tokens that were not legal tender, continued throughout the nineteenth century, despite a series of parliamentary acts designed to remedy such practices. The Royal Commission on Truck, which reported in 1871, took evidence about the general stores owned by mining and colliery companies which put pressure on employees to buy from them, at relatively high prices. Moreover, where legislation made it difficult for unscrupulous employers to underpay wages, they not infrequently responded by developing a scale of fines for minor misdemeanours, deductions for damaged or imperfect goods, and charges for materials or other facilities that were in reality essential for the carrying out of the workers' employment.[32] Non-wage income, therefore, was not necessarily to the benefit of workers. Rentals at below the market price, for houses owned by employers, could have the effect of making workers more subservient, and be a benefit taken into account when wages were offered.

Akin to pilfering from the workplace, though less socially sanctioned, were various types of petty crime. Mayhew's survey of London labour provided examples of, among other acts of dishonesty, shoplifting, thefts from drunken persons, card-sharping, the taking of washing from clothes lines, and so forth. Other large towns would have provided similar opportunities. Until policing became more systematic, 'hush-shops', where beer was sold without a licence, were common, as was the distillation of spirits. Stills were often operated by the Irish, experienced in the production of poteen. Peter Gaskell estimated that in the early 1830s there were over a hundred illicit stills in Manchester alone. By 1870, however, the Commissioners of the Inland Revenue took the view that illegal distillation had been virtually eliminated in England, although this form of activity, as with illicit gambling, is impossible to quantify.[33]

The foregoing discussion, while only brief and impressionistic, does indicate some of the problems that affect any attempt to survey the wages paid in different occupations between 1830 and 1914. On the one hand, there could have been relatively few workers who were not subject to periods of unemployment, through such causes as sickness, fluctuations in trade and industrial disputes. On the other, most workers seem to have found modest ways of supplementing their wages. Nevertheless, it is possible to make some generalisations about the incomes received by different sections of the working class. Wage levels are not only a primary indicator of standards of living, but they also provide a key to the way different groups of workers regarded each other.

Skilled and Unskilled Wages

However, in spite of the reservations that should be made about the character of 'unskilled' labour, it remains the case that workers who could define themselves as 'skilled' generally enjoyed better pay and conditions. This type of worker usually served a seven-year apprenticeship, not so much because the trade involved took so many years to master, more because this was a means of restricting entry. As skilled workers tended to belong to trade unions, employers were obliged to co-operate with them over such matters as entry into the trade. In those occupations able to establish a 'closed shop', which meant that all those employed were trade union members, the rank and file held considerable power. A London hatter recalled that at the end of the nineteenth century 'an apprentice was taken on only by permission of the union' and had to train for seven years. Payment was by piece-rate, according to the prices displayed in the workshop ('the Magna Carta of hatters, who had fought and suffered to establish it'). This meant that wages varied; a man who was 'very quick and efficient' would manage £5 a week, while 'an elderly bachelor who could afford to take things easily, was satisfied with 35s'. Moreover, each hatter was free to decide when to start and finish work, to talk, sing and smoke while he worked, and to have 'his meals in the shop at what time he liked'. However, the trade was seasonal, and as the season waned the shop closed on Mondays and then on Tuesdays and Wednesdays. Complete unemployment could come at a moment's notice.[34]

Among other craftsmen who enjoyed a similar status, if often different working conditions, were stonemasons, carpenters, compositors and engineers. Where piece-rates were impracticable, skilled workers would try to ensure that all were paid the recognised rate for the job. Moreover, there was a preference that employers should agree to pay by the day, rather than the hour. Hourly payments – for example, in the building trade in the 1860s – were seen as a means of quickly laying off men during bad weather or avoiding payment of higher overtime rates. In addition, payment by the hour made it more difficult for carpenters to obtain 'grinding money', the allowance of up to one-quarter of a day each week for sharpening tools. 'If we have no recognised number of hours a day,' asked Edwin Coulson of the London Bricklayers' Society, 'how can we withstand their [the employers'] capricious arrangements?' Yet, by the 1880s, the shift from day to hourly payments had been largely made. In contrast, in newspaper printing, employers moved towards time-work. Linotype and other new methods of printing, introduced in the 1880s and 1890s, led to protracted and complex negotiations between employers and the trade unions. When some pieceworkers' earnings rose to £4–£5 per week, employers switched to what was known in the industry as 'stab', or time-work.[35] In engineering, the great majority of turners, fitters, patternmakers and smiths were on time-work, although there was a tendency by employers to introduce methods that lent themselves to piece-work payments. To discourage workers from slacking, attempts were made, usually opposed by the trade unions, to levy fines. The attempt in 1879, for example, by the Barrow Shipbuilding and Iron Company to limit workers to one visit each day to the lavatory, for a maximum of seven minutes, regulated by a fine of one shilling, was successfully resisted by a strike;[36] yet the incidence of various fines, which were a feature of many occupations, remains problematical.

Although, in various ways, there was friction between skilled workers and their employers, in general as well as greater security of employment the so-called labour aristocrat enjoyed much better pay than those workers conventionally regarded as unskilled. The ever-shifting character of the labour market makes generalisations hazardous. With mechanisation and other technological changes, for example, the income of some occupations declined, while others were able to maintain their position. Nevertheless, the income of skilled workers was often twice that of the labourers who worked with them. Indeed, in occupations where craftsmen and unskilled workers were employed together, the former generally sought to maintain marked wage differentials. In early twentieth-century London, for example, where the wages of those in regular employment tended to be a little higher than in the provinces, Charles Booth noted a skilled man would average 40s a week. A man in regular unskilled work, of a type 'which demands but little experience or muscular strength', would get between 18s and 20s a week, while more would be paid 'when the work demands any special powers'.[37] Thirty shillings might be the weekly wage for work requiring physical strength, though typically after middle age the worker would have to accept a less arduous job. The relatively unskilled but regularly employed worker and his family were examined in detail by a group of Fabian Society women a few years after Booth's survey of the 1890s. Such people were 'respectable persons whose work is permanent. . . . Painters' labourers, plumbers' labourers, builders' handymen, dustmen's mates, printers' labourers, potters' labourers, trouncers for carmen, are common amongst them.' They were distinct from the poorest people, 'the river-side casual, the work-house in and out, the bar-room loafer'. The title of this study encapsulated the size of these workers' wages.[38]

The Fabian women emphasised the need for greater state assistance to improve the welfare of wives and offspring. They called for baby clinics and the provision of milk for children. Further, they endorsed the demand for a minimum wage, taking up the arguments of Philip Snowden, the Labour MP who had shortly before published *The Living Wage*. Snowden cited the calculations of the statistician A. L. Bowley to produce the following table showing the weekly income of about eight million regularly employed men:

Under 15s	320,000	4%
15s to 20s	640,000	8%
20s to 25s	1,600,000	20%
25s to 30s	1,680,000	21%
30s to 35s	1,680,000	21%
35s to 40s	1,040,000	13%
40s to 45s	560,000	7%
Over 45s	480,000	6%[39]

Snowden suggested that 30s a week would be a fair minimum wage, although he coupled this with the proposal that labour disputes should be settled by compulsory arbitration rather than strikes. This idea was resisted by many trade union leaders while the spirit of state intervention, though evident at the time, was too weak for there to be widespread support for such a far-reaching scheme.

Working Conditions

Winston Churchill, the future Prime Minister, in the summer of 1908, addressed a miners' gala at Porth in south Wales. He told those assembled:

Proper and regular hours of healthy labour are the only foundation on which a highly complicated modern system of industry can stand. If you can show the people in the next few years that they did not suffer by the institution of an eight hour day for the miners, but on the other hand that they gained, you will strike a great blow, not only for yourselves but for humanity in general.[40]

Such willingness to involve the state in matters previously left to the vagaries of market forces was increasingly typical of the Edwardian period. The reasons for this need not be detailed here (as they are discussed in Chapter 6), but politicians like Churchill were aware of the need to manage a predominantly working-class electorate at a time when the young Labour Party was gaining the affiliation of the trade unions. Moreover, the efforts needed to win the Boer War had led to a questioning of Britain's efficiency as an imperial nation, as had the growing challenge of Germany, as both a trading and naval power. In the German system of national insurance, some observers found an example that Britain should follow; in 1911 a scheme to provide insurance against sickness for some sections of workers, and against unemployment for those in trades regarded as most subject to cyclical unemployment, was introduced.

Also in the decade or so prior to the Great War, some workers, in the so-called sweated trades, received a degree of protection with the formation of trades boards that could fix minimum wages. Civilians in government employment, such as those in ordnance factories and shipyards, were granted conditions that were meant to provide an example to private employers, and, though inconsistently applied, contracts placed by government departments were meant to include a fair wages clause. Workmen's compensation was legislated for, thus overturning the principle that the worker, by accepting the employer's wage, had also contracted to take whatever risks to health and life the work entailed. Labour exchanges were established by the state to facilitate the worker's search for employment. And a modest old-age pension was introduced to give a little more security to retired workers.

In spite of the improvements in wages, hours worked, and the other conditions of labour that took place between 1830 and 1914, life remained harsh and dangerous for many workers. The hot and noisy textile factories that so attracted the attention of early reformers were better regulated, but technical innovations led operatives to complain about the faster tempo of work and the practice of 'steaming', which allowed the use of inferior cotton.[41] Although the fatal accident rate among coal miners showed a downward trend, several hundred deaths occurred each year. Those killed numbered 1276 in 1912 and 1753 in 1913.[42] The worst disaster in British mining took place on 14 October

1913 when an explosion in the Senghenydd pit ended 439 lives. South Wales had the highest average death rate of all British coalfields, due in part to the dry and fiery character of Welsh coal. As well as a high level of non-fatal injuries, miners were also subject to such occupational illnesses as nystagmus and pneumoconiosis.

In many other industries too workers were at risk from various diseases. In woollen mills, deaths were caused by anthrax – 'woolsorters' disease' – contracted from imported fleeces, and the subject of a parliamentary campaign waged by Fred Jowett.[43] 'Phossy jaw' (atrophy of the facial bones caused by handling phosphorus) afflicted matchmakers and workers in the pottery trade were liable to suffer from lead poisoning. In chemicals and rubber production, both expanding areas of employment in the decades before 1914, workers were at risk from occupational diseases. The continued mechanisation of industry, often involving the introduction of rapid-action machinery, added to the dangers of, if not death, then serious accident. Work on the railways was dangerous, particularly in shunting yards and when repairing the track. In 1906 of every 10 000 railwaymen employed eight were killed in the course of their work (the comparable figures for merchant seamen were fifty-five and for coal miners, thirteen).[44]

At the start of our period, medical men had debated the effects of different types of labour on health. For example, the Leeds surgeon Thomas Turner Thackrah linked factory work and ill health in 1831. But some doctors denied the connection, arguing, as did Daniel Noble of Manchester, that urbanisation, not the growth of manufacturing, was the cause of disease. Yet by 1861 the distinguished doctor John Simon was urging on the Privy Council the need for legislation, for 'the canker of industrial diseases gnaws at the very root of our national strength'. The sufferers, he reckoned, were 'the bread-winners for at least a third part of our population'.[45] Gradually officialdom recognised the existence of 'dangerous trades' and the need for a degree of safety legislation, although this mitigated rather than eliminated the risks that workers faced. Legislation termed the Workmen's Compensation Act (1897) made employers liable for accidents in the workplace, but this did not prevent, or protect against, illness developed over lengthy periods.

Age also affected the living standards of members of the working class. Seebohm Rowntree described the cycle of poverty that was characteristic of many workers' lives. This depended on parents' occupations and the number of children in each family, but in old age, when work could no longer be undertaken, the worker will 'sink back again into poverty'.[46] Older, as opposed to elderly, workers were also likely to find work more difficult to obtain. By the early 1900s the trade unions of skilled men had recognised this. Benefits were available to members, if they had made a certain level of subscriptions and subject to inquiry by branch officials, at 55, in the case, for example, of the Amalgamated Society of Engineers and the United Society of Boilermakers and at 50 in the Amalgamated Society of Carpenters and Joiners. W. J. Davis, the leader of the brass-workers' union, pointed out to the delegates at the conference of the Labour Representation Committee in 1902, that a mechanic or a labourer 'if on the wrong side of 45 years of age, when applying for work, is often told that he is too old'.[47] Less well-paid workers were more likely to end up as, in the terminology of the period, aged paupers. Analysis of the former occupations of those in workhouses showed among men a large proportion of general labourers and of farmworkers who had 'followed the plough to the workhouse door', while women had often been domestic servants and charwomen.

Finally, though the statistical evidence is characteristically less complete than might be hoped, it appears that the improved living standards of those workers on which this book focuses were on a relatively lower scale than the improvements enjoyed by other social classes. Those employed in middle-class occupations appear to have improved their economic status significantly between 1830 and 1914. The advanced Liberal Leo Chiozza Money, for example, writing in the early 1900s, drew attention to the great disparity between the mass of the population and the well-to-do. Drawing on the calculations made in the 1860s by Dudley Baxter, he attempted to show that, although the annual income of the manual worker had increased from an average of £30 per head in 1867 to £45 in 1905, the proportion of national wealth going to the working class had fallen slightly, to below forty per cent. Middle-class radicals such as Chiozza Money emphasised the conspicuous consumption of the upper classes which appeared to be such a feature of the Edwardian period.[48] To many commentators the motor car, affordable only by the wealthy, symbolised ostentation. Sweeping along country roads, the car not only coated the labourer and his cottage garden with dust, it could also be dangerous (motor vehicles were involved in 373 fatal accidents in 1909 and 1328 by 1914). Since the Industrial Revolution, observers had regularly drawn attention to the contrast between what Disraeli in the 1840s characterised as the 'two nations' of rich and poor. With the growth of organised labour after 1900, such criticisms became more frequent. For example, the Labour MP Philip Snowden, speaking in the House of Commons in 1911, roundly stated:

> The working people are getting poorer. The rich are getting richer.... They are getting enormously rich. They are getting shamefully rich. They are getting dangerously rich.[49]

Much as defenders of the established order might deplore views of this sort, and point to improvements in status of the working class, the impression remained of disproportionate wealth in the hands of a privileged and selfish elite. Moreover, this narrow social class faced growing criticism. There was a long tradition of radical MPs taking up causes to benefit the working class – in various ways, for example, William Cobbett, Feargus O'Connor, John Stuart Mill, Joseph Chamberlain and Sir Charles Dilke – sometimes with the support of middle-class writers and publicists such as Richard Oastler, Robert Owen, Charles Kingsley, Frederic Harrison and William Morris. Some of these figures had supported the widening of the franchise and reformist legislation affecting factory labour, the truck system, public health, the adulteration of food and so on. After the general election of 1906 pressure grew for measures to redistribute wealth. The introduction of death duties in 1894 had been a step in this direction (although their immediate purpose was to allow higher naval expenditure). In 1910, the Liberal government did increase income tax, and Lloyd George's land tax proposals caused bitter opposition, but, by the outbreak of war in 1914, little had been done to remedy what reformers regarded as the gross maldistribution of wealth.

Summary

On first approach, it might seem self-evident that the wages bargain is central to working-class living standards. Conventional political economy favoured the unfettered operation of a labour market in which supply and demand would determine price – that is, wages. And to some extent, then as now, take-home pay was the single most important indicator of economic status. However, the character of the nineteenth-century labour market was somewhat different from the economist's model, based as that was on simplifying assumptions. Few workers earned wages that were full and regular over their working lives. Most individuals were liable to accidents and illnesses, when at best they would receive small sums from trade unions or friendly societies. A large proportion of occupations carried a high risk of industrial disease. With old age, work was often more difficult to come by. Moreover, involuntary unemployment could result from broader changes, such as depressed trade, over which the individual had no control. In some trades, older customs and practices, which included perquisites, had to be conceded as the organisation of production changed, while mechanisation frequently required more intensive effort from the workforce. Compared with the employing and professional classes, improvements in workers' living standards probably lagged behind.

On the other hand, it is possible to see ways in which workers did seek to establish their autonomy, to become more than 'hands' or abstract factors of production. Faced with the unprecedented demands of industrial capitalism, they developed not only strategies for survival but also means of confronting the holders of economic and political power. Increasingly through collective action, they sought to control their conditions of labour. For most occupations, wages were slowly improved and the working week reduced by a few hours. Legislation afforded remedies to some dangers and abuses, both in the workplace and the home. Moreover, workers' organisations, which will be treated more fully in a later chapter, were established and strengthened in this period.

3

LABOUR MIGRATION

The Meaning of Labour Migration

The processes of population growth, industrialisation and urbanisation ushered in an age of great population movement, both internal migration and external emigration.[1] Between 1815 and the Slump of the 1930s some 50 million Europeans crossed the Atlantic for new lives in the United States. Around 10 million of these originated in Britain and 5 million in Ireland.[2] Australasia, Canada and other parts of the British Empire also proved to be attractive destinations for migrants. Millions of people also moved within Europe, especially in the north, where the lure of work encouraged a drift towards the North Sea.[3] With population growth and redistribution, a new social fabric unfolded in both Europe and America. The declining importance of the countryside was paralleled by the rise of great urban centres, such as Liverpool and New York, which, along with thousands of smaller towns, symbolised the industrial age. In Britain, during the nineteenth century, working-class life came to be typified, not by the yeoman's ivy-clad cottage or agricultural labour, but by the proletarian's terraced house and the regimented toils of human and machine. In this process of transformation and development, labour migration was to play a vital part.

The scholarly appraisal of migration – its causes, patterns and consequences – began with E. G. Ravenstein's important papers of the 1880s.[4] In more recent times, Brinley Thomas advanced the understanding of migratory patterns by identifying a link between the building cycle and both internal migration and emigration from Britain. He noted peaks and troughs in migratory patterns of approximately 20 years' duration which aligned broadly with high and low points in investment and construction.

Thomas suggested that the export of capital from Britain to America led to falling internal migration within the former and an increase in emigration to the latter. Two key points emerge from this path-breaking research: first, that labour migration should be viewed as a sensitive and important economic indicator; and, secondly, it must be recognised that there was an interconnection between emigration and migration within the 'Atlantic economy'.[5]

Historians once tended to view migration as a first-time once-and-for-all shift from rural to urban areas, with overseas emigration similarly presumed to have occurred between the rural regions of one country and the urban centres of another (say, from Wiltshire to America's east coast). It is now agreed, however, that the majority of emigration actually occurred from urban areas, having been preceded, in the case of rural workers, by short-distance 'step' migrations within the country of birth. This was as true for Norwegian peasants (*husmenn*) as for Scots crofters or Devonshire farmhands.[6] As Redford has shown, the process of migration from the land to the town occurred in a 'complex wave-like motion', which began in earnest in the mid-eighteenth century but did not peak until after the 1840s when comprehensive transport links were put in place. Some of this motion occurred from early industrial towns, for example in east Lancashire and west Yorkshire, to newer centres, in the same counties, but most came from rural areas. Although rural depopulation is difficult to measure, due to the insensitivity of the census, it is clear that surplus population in the countryside fed into the towns and cities.[7] Many of the great urban-to-urban transatlantic migrations – from Liverpool or Glasgow to New York or Boston – involved people who had moved from countryside to town in their own country before embarking, at some later stage, for overseas destinations.[8]

Although it has long been common to stress the increasing integration and homogenisation of economy and culture in the nineteenth century, more recent research has offered a number of alternative perspectives, in particular regionally distinct patterns of development. In relation to the question of migration, for example, it has been suggested that increased population mobility encouraged an outgrowth, a diffusion from a core, of local customs and practices. This type of regionalisation helped to enforce local identities, and some types of customary behaviour, rather than destroying them.[9] The nature of migration certainly suggests that such a regional perspective is plausible. Most initial population movements occurred over short distances. Among rural tradesmen – carpenters, coopers, blacksmiths and the like – the drive to leave the home village or small town was generated as much by the prospect of holding on to their trade as of changing it. Return migration also was quite common, with migrants drifting back and forth from their place of birth. This was certainly the case with many Welsh migrants and with peripatetic Irish seasonal labourers. The Welsh, for example, often clung on to a distinct rural culture long after arriving in new urban settings, and then maintained close contact with the home country.[10] Certainly, rural migrants helped to promote the image of towns as loosely connected 'ethnic villages', where different regional or national groups perpetuated pre-industrial culture and customs.[11] Therefore, while migration can be seen as a process of 'uprooting' – an undertaking by sometimes desperate and reluctant villagers – it also has been viewed as a rational response to new opportunities for self-improvement which increasing numbers of both rural and urban workers embraced as the century wore on.[12]

Urbanisation and Mobility

In any study of migration, urbanisation must be ascribed particular importance. The population of Britain in 1914 was very different from that in 1830. It was both larger and more concentrated. Established urban areas became much increased in size, and new urban centres continued to spring up long after the initial phase of growth which had seen places such as Manchester and Liverpool dominate the popular imagination. Cromar suggests that 'the growth of towns in nineteenth-century England and Wales is seen as an index to the development of the "industrial state" and the social relationships which accompanied the new industrial order'.[13] This claim is not surprising, for, if anything typified both the new living arrangements and the new working experiences of the British working class, then it was the urban environment. Although growth rates were uneven, varying by region, several key centres experienced rapid growth in the early industrial period. Big town or cities such as Birmingham, Liverpool and Manchester doubled in size in the third quarter of the eighteenth century, though none contained many more than 50 000 people – a figure that by 1901 would be matched even by such places as Luton and Wallasey. By the 1830s, Liverpool, Manchester and Glasgow had each passed the 200 000 mark. While towns became larger and more numerous, those of between roughly 10 000 and 200 000 constituted a much more typical social experience for the emerging working class. Textile centres such as Bury, Bolton and Bradford grew tenfold in the years 1780–1830; the wool capital, Leeds, grew sevenfold to more than 120 000; and industrial centres such as Sheffield and Wolverhampton experienced fivefold increases.[14] Similar patterns of development were observed in the medium-sized towns of south Wales, the Black Country, Tyneside and central Scotland.

In the critical early phases of growth (certainly before the 1860s) towns and cities experienced huge two-way flows of population, with natural increase alone seemingly unable to meet the labour demands of local industries. The ratio between natural increase and migration-fed growth is, however, difficult to ascertain and many estimates are misleading. It is a received wisdom to suggest that early urban growth (that is, pre-1850) was sustained by rapid in-migration, while growth thereafter tends to be explained by the fertility levels of a largely young urban population. Recent research by Baines, however, suggests that the role of migrants in the later period is often underestimated when most growth is attributed to natural increase. Migrants, too, were mostly young, and Baines calculated that they accounted for around two-fifths of urban population increase in this period.[15] What is more, in certain areas, for example the Highlands of Scotland, kinship and clan ties were such that migrants usually travelled in small family groups that included members of the right age to reproduce, once favourable economic circumstances had been achieved in the towns and cities of the Scottish central belt.[16]

Victorian statisticians recognised that the urban experience began not with great cities but with more modest towns. This was reflected in migration patterns as well as in the distribution of population in the industrial regions. Census enumerators were told to regard settlements of over 2000 as towns, even though many of these were far from obviously urbanised. By 1851 just over 50 per cent of the people of England and Wales lived in urban centres of this size or greater (see Table 3.1).[17]

However, the simple division between urban and rural hides some important aspects of nineteenth-century spatial geography and culture. In the coalfield regions of south Wales and County Durham, both rural and urban characteristics – such as open spaces yet cramped housing – existed in parallel long after the classic period of the Industrial Revolution. In 1821, the majority of Durham and Northumberland colliers lived in settlements of less than 2000 people.[18] In these regions, even much later, towns tended to be small and dispersed, and were un-nucleated, having no recognisable central business districts. The scattered nature

Table 3.1 Urban and rural populations of England and Wales, 1851–1911 (millions)

	Total	Urban	Urban (%)	Rural	Rural (%)
1851	17.93	8.99	50.2	8.94	49.8
1861	20.07	10.99	54.6	9.11	45.4
1871	22.71	14.04	61.8	8.67	38.2
1881	25.79	17.64	67.9	8.34	32.1
1891	29.00	20.86	72.0	8.11	28.0
1901	32.53	25.05	77.0	7.47	23.0
1911	36.07	28.16	78.1	7.91	21.9

Source: *Census of England and Wales, 1911*, vol. I, p. xv.

of mining meant that factories, centres of commerce and administrative buildings were absent from these towns, most of which were simply linked villages. Such urban areas were thus amorphous; they were towns only inasmuch as someone chose to label them census enumeration districts or urban sanitary districts. There was a world of difference between tightly defined towns such as York and Carlisle, with their medieval walls, and the scattered settlements of the Rhondda, yet both were defined in later century censuses as 'urban'.

One effect of the urban–rural mix of the mining districts was that migration tended to be even more localised than was the case in the larger towns. Although the modest market town and mining centre of Chester-le-Street had a small but regular flow of migrants from Norfolk, the majority of inhabitants between 1851 and 1891 came from no further afield than north Yorkshire, the majority being Durham-born. Durham and south Northumberland colliers were known for their intensely inward-looking 'localised' mentality and a resistance to out-migration. They fought hard to control entry into their trade, principally by excluding alien labour. These attitudes support Langton's argument that workers often associated long-distance labour migration with black-legging and employers' attempts to break strikes. This view was prevalent on the northern coalfield, especially during the miners' strike of 1844 when striking colliers on Lord Londonderry's lands, threatened by the introduction of Irish labour from the owner's Irish estates, attacked the 'knobsticks'. A similar explosion of violence occurred between native and Irish miners at Seaton Delaval and Holywell, Northumberland, during the same bitter dispute. The Lancashire coalfield was also marked by a considerable degree of localised migration; although colliers regularly passed between Wigan, Prescot and St Helens, few were drawn in from other areas.[19] While the long-established colliery villages of Durham were remarkably homogenous throughout this period, there was in-migration from other areas to newer pit developments on the fringes of the 'Great Northern Coalfield', for example Tow Law, and also to developing iron-making centres, such as Consett, both of which attracted significant numbers of Scots and Irish workers in the 1850s and 1860s.[20] Yet even the most dynamic urban centres still counted high proportions of short-distance arrivals. For example, although in 1871 40.7 per cent of the population of Barrow, a classic nineteenth-century boom town, had been born in Staffordshire, Ireland, Cumberland, Yorkshire, Worcester and Scotland, more than half (52 per cent) were Lancashire-born.[21]

London had a unique history of urban development. From the fifteenth century it was the largest city in Europe, with travellers from across the continent finding their way there. It was (and remains) a richly cosmopolitan place. Jews and Irish, Scots and Welsh, had formed ethnic clusters prior to the eighteenth century.[22] Distinct crafts and religions led to the settlement of German tailors and French Huguenots. As restrictions on labour movement fell away at the end of the Middle Ages, increasing numbers of people were drawn, mainly from the southern counties, to the capital. This influx more than compensated for London's high death rate; by the twentieth century some 20 per cent of all English-born people were resident there. Its population was far from static, with a steady but uncounted flow of people passing in and out of its boundaries. Between 1861 and 1911, London burgeoned from 2.8 million to 4.5 million inhabitants. While much of this was due to net in-migration, natural increase accounted for 85 per cent of all growth by the end of the century. Yet London was not a centre of industry or of large factories. Few of its businesses employed large quantities of labour; workshops and small concerns prevailed, and 86 per cent of employers in 1851 had fewer than ten employees. Women outnumbered men, because, according to Waller, 'domestic service and the prospect of marriage were the prevailing forces'; this coincided with a huge reduction in labour opportunities for rural women (down from 229 000 in 1851 to 67 000 in 1901), especially in the shires of the south. Like their counterparts elsewhere, migrants to the metropolis were young, mainly in their twenties. Rural migrants tended also to avoid London's inner city, where three-quarters of residents were London-born, and many others were Irish and (especially later in the century) Jewish and Italian. Although it peaked in 1851 at 108 548, the Irish population remained an important presence until well into the twentieth century. Mobility was high among all classes of workers, but for casual labourers, whose job security was lowest, rates of movement were highest. Once there, however, migrants did not necessarily stay put, and Booth discovered that 40 per cent of families in Bethnal Green had moved within one year. In general, migrants from other counties were attracted to London in direct proportion to their distance from the south-east of England. Among these migrants, turnover was high, with a large part of the working-class populace occupying the same housing for only a few months.[23]

London was unique in size but not in the patterns or effects of labour migration. Historians have understandably shown much greater interest in the growing cities of the industrial north, especially in Liverpool, Manchester and Glasgow, where large industrial and commercial enterprises were far more common than in London. In Manchester, mills and factories encapsulated the newer industrial way of life (even if they were located mostly away from the city centre). This differed from Liverpool, where the dominance of the docks meant that work was casual and that factories were uncommon, although food-processing concerns, for example Tate and Lyle's sugar refinery, became more apparent as the period progressed. Glasgow's economy rested on a number of enterprises. As a commercial port, Glasgow, like Liverpool, had risen quickly in the eighteenth century. Textiles, engineering and shipbuilding all became increasingly important in the second half of that century. Glasgow was the hub for a cluster of growing Clydeside towns, places where shipbuilding and engineering would earn an international reputation for scale and quality. Additionally, the Clyde's thriving dock frontage afforded thousands of jobs that were similar to those on Merseyside – casual, hard and organised into small and localised territorial units. These three cities represent important peaks in the vista of labour mobility and in-migration. Their patterns of growth were remarkably similar in pace and extent, even if founded on very different economic bases. In 1801, Liverpool's population stood at 82 000; within fifty years this had grown to 376 000. The corresponding figures were for Manchester 75 000 and 303 000 and for Glasgow 77 000 and 357 000 (see Table 3.2).

All three cities experienced remarkable periods of growth between 1811 and 1851. In only one recorded instance during that time (in Manchester in 1841) did the decennial growth rate fall below 30 per cent. Moreover, in Manchester (in 1831 and 1841), in Glasgow (in 1821) and in Liverpool (in 1831), growth rates reached 45 per cent or more.

Table 3.2 Population growth in the major northern cities ('000s)

	Liverpool	% inc.	Manchester	% inc.	Glasgow	% inc.
1801	82	–	75	–	77	–
1811	104	26.8	89	18.6	101	31.6
1821	138	32.7	126	44.9	147	45.5
1831	202	46.4	182	44.4	202	37.4
1841	286	39.6	235	29.1	275	36.1
1851*	376	31.5	303	28.9	357	29.8
1861	444	18.1	339	11.0	420	17.6
1871	493	11.0	351	3.5	522	24.3
1881	553	12.2	462	31.6	587	12.5
1891*	630	13.9	505	9.3	658	12.1
1901	685	8.7	645	27.7	762	15.8
1911	753	9.9	714	10.7	1000	31.2

*Highest figure recorded in years when boundaries were changed.

Sources: *Reports of the Census of England and Wales*; *Census of Scotland, 1851–1921.*

These major cities obeyed the laws of migration by deriving the majority of incoming labour from surrounding hinterlands. Lancashire and Cheshire were dominant in the cases of Liverpool and Manchester, though the high proportion of young people among migrants demonstrates that many of these Lancashire-born residents were actually the sons and daughters of recent arrivals. In each of these cities, the Irish presence was enormous. Liverpool had nearly 50 000 Irish-born in 1841 and almost 84 000 in 1861; Manchester's Irish-born population ranged between 33 490 and 52 076 in the same years; and Glasgow's peaked at 68 330 in 1871. What is more, what the demographers call age-cohort heaping (in this case, clustering in the 15–35 age group), and the predominance of young males in the migratory flow, suggest that Irish labour probably registered up to one-third of the male workforce in these great centres.

Scotland provides us with one of Europe's most striking examples of the delicate balance between urbanisation and migration. By the mid-Victorian period, Scotland's central belt was probably the most highly urbanised region in the world. Rural migrants flooded into the towns of the Clyde and to the two great cities of Edinburgh and Glasgow. Work opportunities were, in the main, plentiful, even if markets were highly susceptible to the cycle of boom and bust. Yet Scotland also was one of Europe's main sources for emigrants to the New World. Throughout the period from 1815 to 1914 it vied with Norway for an unenviable second spot behind Ireland. But Norway and Ireland were rural economies whose subsistence crises were far more pervasive than that which racked Scotland's western Highlands. Scotland's poor rural population was a diminishing part of an increasingly and overwhelmingly urban and industrial population. So what accounts for Scotland becoming the urban–industrial economy with the highest incidence of out-migration in Europe? One of the first points to note is that the Scottish Highlands emitted a constant flow of migrants to both Scotland's central belt and to Canada, America and Australasia. It is important to recognise that the Scottish economy was particularly reliant on the export sector, and thus to economic fluctuations. Moreover, Scotland lacked the tertiary service sector which buffered England's industrial economy against further recessions. In addition, by the 1860s a majority of emigrations from Britain to America were part of a Europe-wide urban-to-urban shift, driven by the fact that skilled workers' wages were so high in the New World and because transport costs were falling. It is also important to remember that huge, but uncounted, proportions of Scots workers moved in continuous, and largely unreciprocated, labour migrations to the big towns and cities of England, where, throughout the nineteenth century, wages were higher than in Scotland.[24] If European emigration by, say, the 1870s was a complex mixture of old and new factors – rural hardship and urban opportunity – then Scotland was uniquely placed to send forth masses of people on both counts. Even then, its urban and industrial growth might be seen as a positive factor which prevented an Irish-type problem permeating areas other than the Highlands and Islands.[25]

Britain's other cities were small in comparison to London. They were, nevertheless, important regional centres. By the 1850s, Birmingham, with a population of more than 230 000, had become a major urban centre and the focal point of the increasingly densely populated and industrialised West Midlands region, drawing in labour migrants from Warwickshire, Worcestershire, the West Country and Wales, as well as from further afield. Newcastle, which in 1831 had a population of only 54 000, expanded massively over the following decades to reach 267 000 on the eve of the First World War. Newcastle was at the heart of the North-East's shipbuilding, mining and heavy engineering region – a district which included many other major towns along the Tyne and Wear rivers (North and South Shields, Wallsend and Howdon, Gateshead, Hebburn, Jarrow and Sunderland) as well as the smaller industrial towns and mining villages, fanning out between Ashington, Barnard Castle and Easington. Further to the north, by the 1850s, Edinburgh had become a major commercial city as well as a long-standing national centre of government and law. Its hinterland, which combined rural pursuits, such as farming, and semi-industrial developments, for example mining, lacked the dramatic growth rates and sheer size of Clydeside's urban areas, but, with Leith fast becoming a major port, the area of Midlothian was of both regional and national importance. The same could be said of Leeds, the dynamic and fast-growing centre of the worsted industry, which proved to be a major recipient of local and distant labour alike. To the south, Bristol, despite passing its heyday in the eighteenth century, continued to be a magnet for rural in-migrants from some of the poorest parts of England.

Most of Britain's cities were at the centre of thriving regional economies, which included agricultural lands and smaller, often quite specialised, towns. There were several other regions of urban population, however, which lacked the focal point of a large city. The Potteries centred on Stoke-on-Trent and had no town to compare to Birmingham; Sheffield, in the 1850s, was unlike Manchester or Liverpool in being an isolated and semi-rural string of urban villages rather than a great city (though its near-neighbour, Rotherham, nurtured exceptional growth in the 1860s). Sheffield's isolated and semi-rural character was reflected in the profile of its labour migrants, most of whom came from the city's rural hinterlands. In 1861, three-quarters of the city's 185 172 population had been born in Yorkshire, with Derbyshire (5 per cent) and Nottinghamshire and Lincolnshire (5.9 per cent) providing the next significant categories. Although the arrival of the railways meant that steelworkers and miners from Lancashire, the North-East or Wales could find their way to the growing 'steel city', migrants from distant points of departure such as Ireland and Scotland constituted less than 5 per cent altogether.[26]

Perhaps the most impressive developments in the early Victorian period occurred in Lancashire, where commercial, industrial and factory development was most notable. This county, the seat of cotton manufacture, and the leading sector of the Industrial Revolution, saw unparalleled urban growth and labour migration. The earliest and most striking developments occurred in mill towns such as Bolton which grew from around 18 000 in 1801 to 181 000 in 1911; Oldham (12 000 to 147 000) and Preston (12 000 to 117 000) were also to the fore. At the same time, the county's coal and engineering industries also stimulated considerable population redistribution and there was significant growth. Wigan, for example, expanded from 11 000 to 89 000 between 1801 and 1911. Other major industries, such as glass and chemicals (along with coal), also gave rise to urban growth in Lancashire. This was certainly the amalgam of stimuli that prompted St Helens to burgeon from 15 000 in 1851 to 97 000 in 1911.[27]

The nature of towns, and of the industries within them, clearly influenced patterns of migration. While women in search of domestic work had a good chance of finding it quite close to home, men were often compelled by the demand for their skills to travel much further. Male mobility was determined by the economic specialisation of many regions: thus, whereas women's domestic work was universally available, employment opportunities in many skilled trades were not. Skilled Welsh migrants to England, for example, were attracted to industrial centres which offered mainly male work – for example, Tyneside, Sunderland, Middlesbrough, Portsmouth and Plymouth. At the same time, cities of regional importance, such as Liverpool, Birmingham and Bristol, also drew Welsh migrants, mainly from the Welsh counties nearest to them. Similar patterns can be observed among the Irish, although the Welsh in Liverpool in 1871 were distributed more evenly across the labour market than the Irish; the Welsh were under-represented in unskilled work and over-represented in the ranks of the skilled and semi-skilled.[28]

Rural Depopulation and Migration

Much of the literature of migration in Britain during the Industrial Revolution highlights linkage between rural depopulation and urban growth, particularly in the 30 years after 1820. During the French Wars (1789–1815), the effects of rural population growth were cushioned by the prospect of steady work and of increasing wages. With a slump in postwar demand, and increasing commercialisation and the move to larger farm units (via enclosures and the like), the pull of the town and the push from the land exerted a complementary force on the increasing pool of unskilled farm labour. By 1831, there were five landless labourers in England and Wales to every owner-occupier, a ratio that had doubled since the 1690s.[29] As agriculture became more efficient, with more food being produced by fewer workers, rural labour demands became more seasonal. Consequently, underemployment was added to the problems of this landless class. While farmworkers in Lancashire or Warwickshire could make their way to Manchester or Birmingham, the effects of the agricultural revolution were felt most acutely in those regions where alternative work, whether rural or urban, was not available, for example in Dorset or the Scottish Highlands. The patterns of population change in rural areas between 1851 and 1911 suggest a broad band of decline from Cornwall, Devon and Dorset through to the Fens of East Anglia; across middle and northern Wales to the Vale of York; from the north Pennines to the Borders region of north Northumberland.[30] In all areas, migration followed a wavelike motion. Rural incomers to the towns came first and foremost from the immediate countryside, usually in the same county, before the motion carried in those from more distant points. This has been demonstrated with particular clarity by Redford, and in Withers's study of Highland migration to Dundee, Perth and Stirling.[31] Overall, rural population depletion was consistent and general through the Victorian period, only falling after 1901 with a post-depression upturn.[32]

Migration from rural areas was both more frequent and shorter in distance than movements between urban areas.[33] There had long been a degree of short-distance mobility among rural workers, notwithstanding the rigours of the Elizabethan Poor Law and the various acts of settlement which were aimed to restrict population movement. Indeed, scholars now recognise that there was significant pre-industrial labour migration, with young people from far and wide finding apprenticeships and work in domestic service, especially in London.[34] The highest levels of rural out-migration occurred in short hops, especially from the immediate hinterland of large cities such as Liverpool, Manchester and Leeds and around closely situated new towns, as in Durham, west Cumberland, the west Midlands and Clydeside.[35] The rural hinterlands of major urban centres usually had higher wages than was the case in other rural areas; but the major towns also offered the highest industrial wages. Thus, although nearby industrial activity is thought to have forced up agricultural wages, differentials remained relatively balanced in a regional context so that rural dwellers still migrated. For this reason, even farmers in prosperous regions were concerned about their inability to hold on to hired labour. Transient, well-paid workers, such as navvies, carried the message and example of occupational as well as physical mobility to the envious farmhand.[36] The disturbing effects of progress were felt long and hard in the shires. Commentators were blinded by the light of urban and industrial growth when they commented that there was nothing left in the rural backwaters. C. F. G. Masterman captures the essential characteristics of this point of view:

Outside this exuberant life of the cities, standing aloof from it, and with but little share in its prosperity, stands the countryside. Rural England, beyond the radius of certain favoured neighbourhoods, and apart from the specialised population which serves the necessities of the country house, is everywhere hastening to decay. No one stays there who can possibly find employment elsewhere. All the boys and girls with energy and enterprise forsake at the commencement of maturity the life of the fields for the life of the town.[37]

Between 1851 and 1911, the rural population declined in both absolute and relative terms. However, while the absolute number of rural dwellers fell only by around 11.5 per cent, the large rise in the overall population meant that the proportion of rural dwellers had declined by more than half. In the former year 9 936 800 people (49.8 per cent) lived in rural areas; in 1911 the figure was 7 907 556 (22.9 per cent). Particularly significant outflows occurred in the 1850s, which although stemmed in the 1860s were greatly increased in the 1870s and 1880s, with the end of Britain's so-called agricultural 'Golden Age', and the beginning of a period of agricultural depression. Although there was considerable return migration, the overall trend was one of permanent contraction and decline. Between 1851 and 1871, the total number of agricultural workers fell by more than 250 000. However, most of the loss from rural areas – which, between the 1850s and 1890s, occurred at around 75 000 per annum – was in the form of excess, not absolute, population decline.[38]

The decision to migrate from the rural areas was not taken lightly. The first link forged in the chain of migration or emigration was often made by farmworkers whose ancestors had worked the land for centuries. Once the process had been initiated, however, future movements became more likely. Further stimulus was provided by the success stories of previous generations of migrants. As early as 1833, the Petworth Emigration Society had produced a one-shilling booklet of letters from previous emigrants to Canada. The letters were reissued within a year. Poor Law officials and private charities also encouraged, and sometimes assisted, migration or emigration.[39] Departures from the poor rural south were slow. Earlier in the period, laws of settlement still bound men and women to their parishes. If they fell on hard times while tramping to other places, they risked removal to their place of origins (as occurred in Liverpool in the late 1840s when many Irish migrants were forcibly returned to Ireland, despite the likelihood that death would befall them). The financial outlay of labour migration was also significant and rural workers tended to lack the complex networks and institutionalised support systems – other than those provided by family and friends – that facilitated the often peripatetic lifestyles of skilled migrants. A break was also applied by what might be termed the 'rural mentality'. Rural folk, especially in the most isolated communities, were particularly suspicious of strangers and hostile to change. To them, London might have been on the other side of the world, while a journey of just 20 miles meant pulling up roots that were long and deep. These people may have seen trains but probably had not travelled on them; they knew of towns and cities but may not have visited them; and they listened to their religious leaders who sometimes preached of the immorality and vice that lay waiting for the unsuspecting country folk. Then again, more enlightened church views could see local clerics emerging as facilitators. When Canon Girdlestone organised the migration of labouring families from Halberton, Devon, to Kent and the northern counties in the late 1860s and early 1870s, he had to do everything for those who departed, as a later writer recalled:

> their luggage [had to be] addressed, their railway tickets taken, and full and plain directions given to the simple travellers. The plan adopted when the labourers were leaving for their new homes, was to give them, as Canon Girdlestone did, plain directions written on a piece of paper in a large and legible hand. These were shown to the officials on the several lines of railway, who soon getting to hear of Canon Girdlestone's system of migration, rendered him all the assistance in their power by readily helping the labourers out of their travelling difficulties . . . .

The image conveyed is one of a pathetic group of individuals almost incapable of helping themselves. Indeed, some were so ignorant of geography that they even asked if they were travelling across the sea. Yet these same rustics were keen enough to take their families from a backward region where wages were no higher than 8s per week to northern towns where they earned not less than 13s.[40]

A particular growth in rural out-migration occurred in the 1880s, which precipitated an upturn in the economic conditions of those who stayed put. However, workers in the towns became increasingly restive at the sight of so many agricultural labourers moving in to search for work, citing the depressing effect upon wages and worsening overcrowding in what became a new assault on the problem of rural depopulation.

Observers in the shires also noted the depletion of population, lamenting its economic origins and its social effects. Smallholdings Acts were passed in 1892 and 1907 in an attempt to encourage the rural population to hold its place. This legislation offered landless labourers a stake in the land they worked, but, as Mingay and Chambers pointed out, 'more than Acts of Parliament were needed to turn a centuries-old rural proletariat into a race of peasant cultivators'.[41] Consequently, 'the drift from the land continued to disturb observers of the rural scene. From census material of 1901 it can be inferred that fewer than half the farmworkers aged 15–24 a decade earlier remained in the industry.'[42] Over the duration of our period, the share of the population engaged in agriculture, horticulture and forestry had declined from around 50 per cent to about a much diminished, though still significant, one-third.[43]

The distinction between urban and rural areas became increasingly hazy as the century progressed. Indeed, an element in the depletion of the most rural regions can be accounted for by the transformation of rural districts into semi-rural or partially urban ones.[44] West Cumberland, around Whitehaven, south Northumberland, just north of Newcastle and North Shields, and large areas of the West Midlands, provide useful examples of this change; mining districts in general became much less rural as 1914 approached. Indeed, it has been argued that very few genuinely rural districts existed in the early twentieth century away from the south-west of England, central Wales, the northern Pennines area, the Lake District and northern Scotland.

Labour Migration Within Rural Areas

Labour migration was not simply an urban phenomenon, even if by the 1860s the majority of labour migrants moved between towns. Indeed, rural areas were not as static as the emphasis upon urban growth might suggest. In 1871, for example, almost one-fifth of inhabitants in the isolated rural parish of Furness and Cartmel, in the Lake District, had been born in other counties.[45] There were also backward flows, from established urban centres to developing ones. The earliest examples of work-related mobility came in the rural sectors, as mechanisation, enclosures and improved efficiency increased the seasonal aspect of farm work and thus enlarged farmers' and landowners' needs for casual labour. From the early 1800s, in Ireland, the Highlands of Scotland and in the south of England, farmworkers increasingly came to the market place looking for casual employment. These workers – men and women – tramped between regions and crop-types, competing sometimes violently for available work.

Rural poverty and displacement created a valuable supply of needy workers, but it also led to increasing pauper migration, with the Scots and Irish prominent. One of the most important transient non-industrial migrations was that of Irish seasonal harvesters or spalpeens. Seasonal passage became a key part of both Irish and British life in the mid- to late-eighteenth century, and continued long after. This migration is often viewed as a precursor of permanent settlement, although it was actually a parallel movement which did not peak until long after the Famine. While harvest migration of this sort was in some respects a precursor for making a permanent move into the town or city, in the most backward areas, most notably western Ireland, the cash generated from seasonal work was meant to secure a link to the land, not break it.[46] Cheap fares made temporary migration more popular in the 1820s, and by this time few regions – from the Highlands of Scotland to Norfolk and Kent – were without regular supplies of Irish labour. These workers travelled from most Irish ports, including smaller ones such as Dundalk, Drogheda and Londonderry. By 1841 one in thirty-seven of Mayo's residents were seeking work on farms throughout England and Scotland.[47]

Population growth and commercialisation in agriculture also affected small farmers in northern Scotland. In the early part of the nineteenth century there were effectively two Scotlands: the Highland region and the industrialising central belt. Both were undergoing significant changes, and in the more traditional north population increases were significant in the period 1750–1830. The Highland Clearances of the early 1800s marked the final destruction of the clan system, which undermined an economic as well as a cultural system. With enclosures underpinning the shift towards larger farm units and with more landowners bringing in sheep, thousands of peasant cottars and their black cattle were driven closer to the sea and nearer to a susbsistence crisis. New farming practices in the Highlands led to increased demand for seasonal agricultural labour, and this also undermined the traditional peasant proprietor. As in Ireland, the famine of 1846–50 exacerbated these problems, especially in the far north-west where dependence upon the potato was most significant.[48] The concept of labour migration took a savage twist at this point as many landlords used the famine as an opportunity to rid their estates of surplus tenants. Few, however, were as brutal as Gordon of Cluny, who hunted reluctant migrants with dogs before having them bound, gagged and despatched. In all, more than 2700 of his tenants were sent to Canada between 1848 and 1851.[49]

Despite the opportunities afforded by the more normal patterns of free migration – both overseas and to Glasgow and Edinburgh – many displaced Scots cottars remained in their native counties, with the hope of securing paid farm employment. It was here that they came into conflict with Irish harvesters who crossed over each year looking for work. The new rural order in Scotland had created a class of Highlanders similar to the Irish spalpeen who wandered the country searching for seasonal labour. While the same basic economic grievances occupied Highlanders and the Irish, competition for meagre work opportunities sometimes led to violence between them. Despite competition and undercutting, however, seasonal farm employers in the Lowlands of Scotland continued to hire Highlanders until the second half of the century.[50]

The story of these itinerant farm workers reminds us that the relationship between technology and labour supply is vital, even if the link between the two is not always clear. While it has been argued that machines drove labourers from the land it is perhaps even more likely that the lure of towns, and the problem of rural depletion, led farmers to look for new technologies to replace an unreliable and diminishing labour pool in regions where surplus labour tended to join the stream of out-migration.[51] An increasing preponderance of large farms and an emphasis by larger farmers on the need for seasonal workers, rather than on continous application to smallholding, undoubtedly encouraged both rural labour migration and technological innovation.

The Migration of Industrial Workers

Labour migration, as we have seen, was not simply a rural-to-urban phenomenon, Nor was it an undifferentiated movement of agricultural workers to urban work, though this aspect was important. Many movements were contrived, providing the starkest possible evidence of Brinley Thomas's argument that labour flowed after capital and investment. In March 1843, for instance, between '750 to 900 persons living in different parts of Liverpool were suddenly uprooted from familiar surroundings and placed together in the semi-rural district of Crewe'[52] because it suited their railway employers' new investment plans. In general, the building of railways led to a large increase in the volume of itinerant industrial labour. In the 1870s, noteworthy examples of labour migration were taking place between south Wales and Middlesbrough, with iron-masters and their workers taking part in a regular movement from one iron region to another. An even more striking case of directed labour migration occurred in the 1880s when the firm of Cammells decide to dismantle its Derbyshire steelworks and to move it to west Cumberland where iron deposits were rich and plentiful. As a result, between 1881 and 1891 some 1800 ironworkers uprooted from Dronfield and moved to Workington.[53]

During the 1840s, the so-called period of the 'railway mania' saw around 200 000 roving navvies working on lines up and down the British Isles. This was one of the most notable migrations in Victorian history. The navvies' work was extremely severe, but well paid; their living conditions were primitive, but their leisure culture intense and ribald. They were responsible for some of the most impressive feats of civil engineering in the Victorian period: the Tring and Edge Hill cuttings, the Forth rail bridge and the Ribblehead viaduct are just some examples. More importantly, they added fluidity to the construction-industry labour market: many years after the zenith of the 'railway age' these men were still building roads, digging new canals, excavating huge docks – providing muscle and no little skill wherever they were needed.[54]

Labour migration was common among skilled, often unionised, workers. Indeed, as Hobsbawm has shown, it was an important cultural practice among artisans; tramping provided an outlet for excess labour. It was a sign of solidarity, efficiency and of the effectiveness of the union which funded and supported such migrations. Tramping represented a broadening of horizons and a deepening of skills. It also was extremely intricately organised. Workers were sent forth with documents from the union attesting their good character and detailing their paid-up union subscriptions. Many received route maps, names and locations to head for. On arrival in a new town they headed for a 'house of call', an 'unofficial labour exchange', often a pub, where they received food, sometimes beer, accommodation, and the chance of a job, if one was available. If not, they received more money and directions to the next town. This went on until they found work or were forced to return home, which could mean a round trip of 2800 miles for compositors in the 1850s![55] Recent studies have suggested that localised economic conditions were the main cause for this form of labour migration, and that the development of a more integrated national economy reduced the possibility of avoiding unemployment in particular trades simply by moving to other regions. The national slump of the 1840s exposed the inadequacy of the tramp and led unions to replace or supplement it with a system of unemployment pay.[56]

Migration, however, remained a part of the skilled worker's response to dearth. Declining regions, and older, waning industries often experienced a steady outflow of skilled labour. Thus, many ironworkers in Cumberland in the 1840s and 1850s had migrated from old iron centres such as Staffordshire. Mining communities in south Wales and Lanarkshire benefited from the outflow of Cornish copper and tin miners. In the 1850s, many miners in the flowering haematite iron industry of north Lancashire were also the displaced victims of industrial decline in Cornwall. These men brought many valuable skills into the region and, with their families, formed distinctive social enclaves. The descendants of these same workers must have been among the steady of flow of iron miners leaving the Cumbrian coalfields for the South African gold and diamond mines in the 1880s. Cornishmen were also prevalent among the hardrock miners of North America, just as Irish miners from Cork were very heavily concentrated in the copper mines of Butte, Montana, in the later nineteenth and early twentieth centuries.[57]

Skilled female labour also comprised an important part of the migrant streams between certain areas and industries. Women textile workers from Ulster were more important in the Dundee flax and jute industry than were men. Highland women also found work in similar circumstances, and, like their Irish counterparts, came to outnumber male migrants in towns such as Perth. For unskilled or less-skilled women, migration was also an option. Domestic work traditionally attracted young girls from outlying rural districts to the nearest town, although there was something of a reversal of this trend in the later nineteenth century when holidaymaking and hotel building in rural settings resulted in many young girls moving from towns to the countryside for 'live-in' work as household servants, chambermaids, cooks and so on.

The trade cycle, temporary downswings in production and available work, affected export-orientated trades such as shipbuilding much more acutely than other industries. This clearly helped to forge a culture of migration among shipyard workers, though the situation was complicated by regional divisions of labour and increasing degrees of specialism in particular yards (ocean-going liners in Belfast and submarines – as early as the 1870s and 1880s – in Barrow). Shipbuilding workers thus flowed fairly frequently between the major industrial centres: the Clyde, Tyneside, Wearside, Merseyside, Barrow and Belfast. In the early nineteenth century skilled workers such as shipwrights had sought to protect members of their union from competition by eliminating geographical mobility. A similar motivation was thought to be behind the Sheffield outrages of the 1860s, when violence and murder were sparked by competition from undercutting, less-skilled labour, some of which was thought to have come from outside the city.[58]

By the turn of the century, however, high levels of mobility led to a more integrated approach to labour issues by both masters and workers. In shipbuilding, for example, union men in Barrow and Belfast attempted to follow the wages patterns and conditions of employment experienced by their counterparts on the Clyde. Most of the skilled men had been trained in Scotland and this provided a vital flow of information about procedures and practices. Even in the larger centres of Tyneside and Wearside the Scots influence was significant, because the men had 'very largely come as young shipwrights from Dundee, Montrose, Aberdeen'.[59] Economic fluctuations meant that many workers spent months, even years, without work, or else in a state of underemployment. Yet, despite regular migratory rhythms among the men, shipbuilding afforded no opportunity for skilled workers to transfer from one trade to another – not even temporarily and certainly not at a comparable rate of pay. Thus migration occurred between yards, or from shipping to engineering (but within the same trade), and this was the main coping strategy for skilled workers pressed by economic recession or industrial conflicts. Even in the good times, the turnover of labour was high. The shipbuilding town of Barrow grew from 47 292 to nearly 64 000 between 1881 to 1911, but in the same years there was a total permanent loss from the district of 11 800.[60] High levels of mobility, which, by the later nineteenth century men favoured as a control mechanism for their trades, and which consequently lowered (but did not eliminate) regional wage differentials in the industry, also resulted in a high turnover in unskilled labour, most of which was Irish Catholic and hailed from Ulster.[61]

Irish Labour Migrants

Irish migration provides examples of all these different sorts of migration. Irish workers, because of the nature of the Irish economy, were overwhelmingly rural-to-urban migrants, passing as they did from one of Europe's most pastoral nations to certainly its most industrial. The Irish were a marginal migrating people, shunned by native workers who feared for their jobs, reviled because of their Catholicism (even though many were Protestants), but embraced by employers looking for cheap and flexible manual labour. The Irish maintained unusually high levels of mobility; many viewed Britain as a stop-gap measure – as a part of some grander plan to move on to North America or Australasia.[62] While many achieved this goal, most lived the rest of their lives in Britain, sometimes at the margins of subsistence, always drifting to where work was available. Irish migration provided British capitalists with one of their most important, resourceful and flexible labour forces. Attracted by opportunity and driven from their homeland by pressure upon unevenly distributed resources, low wages, underemployment and a failure to industrialise, thousands of Irish labourers entered, and sometimes unbalanced, the British labour market at particularly important moments, for example during the Famine crisis of the later 1840s and early 1850s.

Irish settlement in Britain came to be viewed as a particular problem in the years after 1815 when a collapse in Irish agriculture led to a significant increase in pauper migrants. By the 1820s, local authorities, especially in the coastal districts, were beginning to complain bitterly about the costs of maintaining the peripatetic poor of Ireland. The clamour undoubtedly influenced poor law reformers and led to calls for the introduction of an English-style poor law for Ireland. The Poor Law (Ireland) Act (1838), however, had no discernible effect on the rate of migration from Ireland, where population pressure continued to mount. By the early 1830s the Irish were fully spread across the established industrial regions of Britain. Apart from in London, the Irish were most prevalent in Lancashire, west and central Scotland, the North-East, Yorkshire and the west Midlands. As Table 3.2 indicates, the Irish-born community in Britain was already sizeable in 1841 but grew most rapidly in the 1840s and 1850s, as a direct consequence of the Great Famine (1845–51), when due to the 'Potato Blight' (a fungal infection of the crop) and attendant hunger and disease, emigration reached flood proportions. Liverpool alone received more than 500 000 arrivals in 1846 and 1847, and all centres of settlement noticed considerable increases in the numbers of destitute Irish incomers.[63]

The pattern of Irish settlement changed as the century wore on. Throughout the period, Irish harvesters remained important to British farmers and found work as far afield as Sutherlandshire and Kent. Permanent settlement was noticed first in London; then in the Scottish textile towns of Ayrshire, Wigtownshire and Dumfriesshire, and in early industrial Lancashire. By the 1840s other places were experiencing

Table 3.3   The Irish-born population of Britain, 1841–1911

	England & Wales	%	Scotland	%
1841	289404	1.8	126321	4.8
1851	519959	2.9	207367	7.2
1861	601634	3.0	204083	6.7
1871	566540	2.5	207770	6.2
1881	562374	2.2	218745	5.9
1891	458315	1.6	194807	4.8
1901	426565	1.3	205064	4.6
1911	375325	1.0	174715	3.7

Sources: *Census of England and Wales, 1851, 1871*; *Census of Scotland, 1851, 1871*.

large-scale influxes of Irish labour migrants. While the migrants accounted for anything up to thirty per cent of the male workforce in the big cities – such as Liverpool and Glasgow – they were if anything more prominent in smaller Scottish towns such as Girvan or Dundee. By the 1870s Tyneside and west Cumberland were as important, in proportionate terms at least, as these other more familiar Irish centres. Irish workers also showed an unusually high degree of mobility within Britain, and they were probably more mobile between types of work as well. The Irish were under-represented in the skilled trades and were over-represented in the worst kinds of hard manual labour (chemical works, dock labour, and so on) though perhaps not as much as was once believed. Although the highest levels of Irish settlement occurred between the early 1830s and the mid-1850s, there was still a regular flow of Irish labour into Britain on the eve of the Great War and beyond.

In terms of labour effect, the impact of Irish settlement is difficult to assess and historians disagree as to the wider economic implications of what contemporaries regarded as a flood of Irish settlers. The nineteenth-century view was quite clear: whether for good or ill, Irish workers were thought to have played a decisive role in the Industrial Revolution. Irish labour was commonly held to have checked the upward pressure on wages; native workers considered the Irish to be a threat to their liveli-hoods because of an alleged willingness to work harder, longer and for less pay. Yet Irish labourers were not alone in being accused of undercutting wages or strike-breaking. In fact, all forms of rural–urban migration posed some sort of threat to established workers. John McEwen, a Perth millowner, said in 1834 that the children in his employ were Highlanders who worked for lower wages and kept out their Perth-born counterparts.

In Disraeli's 'Condition of England' novel, *Sybil* (1845), it was Suffolk 'hagricultural labourers . . . sold out of slavery, and sent down by Pickford's van into the labour market to bring down our wages', who drew the venom of Mowbray's hard-pressed workers. In Gaskell's *Mary Barton* (1848), striking Manchester millworkers were moved to violence by the threat from workers who were 'weary of starvation'; 'foot-sore, way-worn, half-starved' imports from the outlying textile towns. Yet, as if to emphasise the ambiguities of this issue, another of Gaskell's famous novels, *North and South* (1854–5), revolves around a strike in which local workers riot because of the introduction of Irish 'knobsticks'.[64]

Historians are divided on the issue of Irish labour and its impact on wages and conditions. E. H. Hunt considered that Irish workers played a decisive role in the economy, going as far as to argue that the volume of migration was so great that it slowed out-migration from the poor agricultural districts of England, thus increasing hardship in these areas. A more recent econometric interpretation by J. G. Williamson, however, contends that Irish numbers were not large enough to influence wage rates, although this argument founders because it underplays the regional features of the early Victorian economy and of Irish settlement. Irish labour may have been well spread across the west of Britain, and eastwards into London, Yorkshire and Durham, but it was also very densely compressed in key areas, such as south Lancashire, where its effects were likely to have been considerable.[65] As with other questions relating to wages and standards of living, the absence of comprehensive data suggests that a complete picture will never be known to us.

Summary

By 1914, although rural areas remained important, England, Scotland, and, to a lesser extent, Wales, were highly urbanised countries, noted for their large cities and numerous towns. Most of their populations lived in urban areas, while the majority of workers were engaged in industrial or commercial pursuits. Migration is crucial to our understanding of the way towns were formed and of the nature of urban and rural life. It also tells us something about the precarious nature of employment opportunities. From the large-scale influx from Ireland and the trail of landless labour moving from village to town, to the 'tramping artisan', few groups of workers remained static for long periods. Most labour migration was characterised as short-distance and regular, although the railways and improved road transport broadened this spatial dimension considerably in the post-1850 period.

Most early migrations emerged from rural beginnings, frequently with short-hop movements to the nearest sizeable urban centre, after which movement became common. Migrants thus went first to Shrewsbury or Kilmarnock rather than directly to Birmingham or Glasgow, although, in each case, a move to the city was also likely. Many rural out-migrants travelled in family groups, some with children; but the largest demographic group was young and male (though women were by no means absent). As migration became fixed in the lifestyles of urban–industrial workers, family movements became more common. The majority of migrants – whether Devonshire farm labourers or Clydeside shipbuilders – following paths that had been trodden by previous generations; many expected to find at least a few friendly faces at the journey's end. Yet there remained a sense of the unexpected about migration; and also a notion of danger.

While increasing knowledge of the intricacies of labour migration has led historians to conclude that the process was less hectic and fearsome than was once assumed, there are problems with such a view. Many migrants felt compelled to leave in order to improve their life-chances; others were forced, by hardship and want, into making a decision·for which they were sometimes ill-equipped. Migrants who left the country-side for the town also placed themselves and their children at greater risk. The young were far more likely to die of such endemic diseases as scarlet fever, whooping cough and dysentery in the town. However, despite the fact that mortality rates were much higher in the towns, workers still took the risk that this entailed, and transplanted themselves and their families, because throughout this period a general labourer could earn more than twice as much as a farmhand.

4

COMMUNITY

Problems of Definition

The concept of community, despite its imprecisions, can be used to examine a number of characteristics of working-class life. It encompasses the immediate living environment of individuals and groups in all its facets, from personal or family ties, often set in the home, to the shared space of the street or neighbourhood. Community describes the relationship between people, especially among those who lived in close proximity, experiencing similar environmental, occupational and social circumstances. Communities are 'imagined' as much as they are real.[1]

Working-class communities were noted for the solidaristic networks which united members of the same class, in part by dividing them from their social superiors or inferiors. An individual's or a group's sense of community was shaped by work as much as by family. The day-to-day observation of street life and participation in popular leisure pursuits also helped to cement the individual to the community. Interaction with familiar individuals was, therefore, central to the experience of living in a community, as was a sense of being different from strangers. What is more, communities had a particular resonance in the nineteenth century, when the home, street and workplace represented the totality of most people's daily physical space and experience.

Although communities are changing and evolving entities, historians' understanding of them was slow to develop. As Raymond Williams stated many years ago, 'community, unlike all other terms of social organisation, never seems to be used unfavourably'.[2] For so long, the very notion of communities had a connotation of traditional identity, permanence and continuity. More recent studies have recognised, however, that the term is more than simply a label attached to an event or process. Historians now employ community as a deeply evocative concept which is likened to class, gender, ethnicity or race in terms of its power to describe relationships.[3] A recent study has suggested that community 'performs many different functions in the description and analysis of society'.[4] We might also note that academic interest in nineteenth-century working-class communities has grown because these same communities are now threatened with extinction following the decline of the heavy industries upon which they relied.[5] This has applied particularly to former mining, heavy engineering and shipbuilding centres such as south Wales, the North-East and Clydeside.

Historians and social theorists broadly agree that the nature of communities changed during the nineteenth century, not least because of migration and urban growth. The sentiments of community-mindedness may have remained, but the social fluidity and spatial geography of communities undoubtedly presaged changes. Historians tend to employ Ferdinand Tonnies's *gemeinschaft* (community) and *gesellschaft* (society) dichotomy to distinguish between the idyllic (often rustic, romantic and pre-industrial) notion of community and the individualistic traits of modern civic society.[6] In Tonnies's formulation, community is based upon traditional and customary relationships which were natural rather than created. By contrast, society is manufactured and (in a sense) artificial, governed by laws and an overt notion of reciprocity between members.

Still greater conceptual rigour is required as the term 'community' is at once useful and problematic. Communities tend to be seen as things of solidarity and social stability, creations of mutuality and compromise; yet this is far from always the case. Communities were not simply the passive creations of subconsciously aligned individuals but were also sources of conflict and division. Nor were they only about 'warm face-to-face social relations'.[7] In the rapidly urbanising world of Victorian Britain, community was shaped partly by outside perception: the notion of middle-class 'supervision' and 'influence' and attendant pressures to create ordered civic hierarchies and for individuals to be socialised to dominant notions of identity. These were taken to be key aspects of a healthy and functioning community. Such a hierarchical, structural perception of community is descriptive rather than explanatory. To focus upon communities as defined by local government officials, bureaucrats and the enfranchised middle class is to ignore the independent or 'bottom-up' aspect of working-class communities and the fluid, unstructured, cultural aspects which permeate them. The web of connections implied by mechanistic notions of community crumbles when we consider the 'real' social geography of the new urban centres such as Manchester. It was precisely because the existing social structures were breaking up that the middle classes tried artificially to re-create what once had been deemed natural: communities. Thus, the Manchester described by the social reformer, J. P. Kay Shuttleworth, was far from homogenous:

> The township of Manchester chiefly consists of dense masses of houses, inhabited by the population engaged in the great manufactories of the cotton trade. Some of the central divisions are occupied by warehouses and shops, and a few streets by the dwellings of some of the more wealthy inhabitants; but the opulent merchants chiefly reside in the country, and even the superior servants of their establishments, inhabit the suburban townships. Manchester, properly so called, is chiefly inhabited by shopkeepers and the labouring classes. These districts where the poor dwell are of very recent origin.[8]

This sense of division and separation was, however, a key feature of Victorian urban life, or rather of the way in which commentators viewed that life. Not just in the sense that there was a physical separation of the classes – in truth there had always been an element of that, even though many exceptions might be noted – but because labour relations, expressions of class, and discontentment with the world in which people lived, were often given substance by the apparent iniquities of the new urban world. Viewed from within, communities were positive and reinforcing. They captured the way people lived, from their physical surroundings and housing to the things they enjoyed and consumed. This chapter seeks to pull together some of these interconnected ideas of community. By focusing on the everyday lives of ordinary labouring people, and by leaving out any integrated discussion of work and the workplace, the chapter attempts to present a social history of community on its numerous levels: living conditions, family and kinship, the neighbourhood, diet, leisure culture, and so on.

Living Space

The house, home and neighbourhood – the physical space in which people conducted their daily lives – were important features of working-class

communities. Labour historians traditionally have paid particular attention to the experiences of urban workers because the growth of towns
and cities was such a noticeable feature of the age, although studies of
rural workers are now much more common. Towns generated most
social comment and provided the most damning statistics of the modern
age: low life expectancy, disease, overcrowding and insanitary environs.
By contrast, the rural world has long been characterised as idyllic: a
place in which seasonal work patterns laid greater emphasis upon free
time and merrymaking. The assumption that the shires were inhabited
by happy, ruddy-faced peasants was undoubtedly strengthened by the
fact that death rates were much lower than in the towns. Clean and
unpolluted air, and plenty of fresh food, were commonly cited as comparative advantages enjoyed by farmworkers.[9] Yet the rural world was
far from an idyllic place. As was true of the urban world, socio-economic
status was the main determinant of a person's life expectancy and ease of
life. The middle class lived longer than workers, whether farm labourers
bent at the ploughshare or immiserated millhands. Yet, although the
millhand had an even shorter life expectancy because of the condition of
the towns, the farm labourer had a much lower income and was reliant
upon the allowances of bread and beer, and a cheap, if often squalid,
cottage which constituted a vital part of his meagre wages.

Although an increasing proportion of working-class communities
were to be found in urban areas, the countryside nevertheless hosted a
significant proportion of ordinary people's lives (nearly fifty per cent in
1851, though declining more markedly thereafter). Few people in the
mid-nineteenth century, as Burnett has observed, 'came to terms with
the idea of permanent residence in the city'.[10] At the heart of the idea of
rural life was the idealised and partly mythical country cottage, a vital
component in the English idea of social perfection. The cottage was seen
as a dwelling place attuned to the local landscape in a way that tenements
and terraced houses never could be. Yet the rural world encompassed
more than simply sparsely populated hamlets; and the rustic dream-
scape could also hide a nightmare. Thus, when Robert Rawlinson visited
Wordsworth country – the Lake District – in the late 1840s he was appalled
by what he found in industrial and market towns alike. While the burghers
of Whitehaven, Carlisle and Kendal were chastised, as might be expected,
the opprobrium which rained down on the authorities in market towns
such as Penrith and Keswick is perhaps more surprising. Rawlinson
refused to be beguiled by the slate-built charm of many of Keswick's
dwellings when he claimed that 'The whole place is encompassed by foul

middens, open cesspools and stagnant ditches, or by still fouler drains.'
The small proto-industrial town of Ulverston was similarly lambasted
for its 'nuisances injurious to health ... which are removable'. He complained that 'there are neither proper sewers nor drains' and 'cesspools
are crowded amongst the cottages', while 'fever prevails in the houses of
the poor'.[11] Such opinion concerning semi-rural and rural spheres is
important, for it was not only the great industrial towns that were seen to
be at fault. Many of the rudest dwellings of agricultural labourers, for
instance, were found in the hill-farming regions of the Pennines, the
Lake Counties, mid-Wales and northern Scotland; many of these were
worse than their urban equivalents, though the danger from disease was
much less apparent. The primitive rural homes of north Northumberland shocked James Caird, who in 1850 complained of finding places
where pigs and cows lived under the labourer's roof.[12]

Rural dwellings were more varied in quality than their urban counterparts, with the size, construction and state of repair dependent upon age
and region. Bricks were used more often to build rural housing as the
century progressed, and the best of the older housing was constructed of
stone. Throughout the country many houses, especially those dating to
before the eighteenth century, were made of wood, with rubble or stone
footings held together by wattle and daub or laths and plaster.[13] Yet
mud was common in the Midlands, and cob and thatch in the west of
England, where accommodation was worst of all. While most rural
dwellings were distinct and separate entities, in some regions – for example
in Northumberland, where the labourers were scarce and farms were
large – workers were provided with what William Cobbett called 'a sort
of barracks; that is to say, long sheds with stone walls, and covered with
what are called pantiles'. He viewed with concern these rudimentary
and austere dwellings:

> They have neither gardens nor privies nor back doors, and seem alto-
> gether to be kept in the same way as if they were under military discip-
> line. There are no villages; no scattered cottages; no-upstairs; one little
> window, and one door-way to each dwelling in the shed or barrack.[14]

Much rural accommodation, however, originated in the distant past,
with the effect that large families often found themselves residing in cottages which had been built for a less populous age. Other dwellings, such
as the often temporary hovels of squatters, were built without inherit-
ance in mind. However, the commonest complaint did not concern

building materials (which in any case improved with the availability of commercially produced bricks) but overcrowding. It is important to recognise that the majority of rural workers were tenants whose wages were adjusted downwards to take account of the low-rent accommodation which came with the job. Thus, cheap or free housing was of little monetary benefit; what is more, the right of residence only lasted for as long as the individual concerned was employed by the farmer who owned the cottage. This certainly had a dampening effect on agitation for improved wages and conditions. Similar examples of supposedly benevolent capitalism were common in mining communities, where houses were often built and owned by the coal employer, which serves to support Daunton's opinion that one of the many social or ideological functions of housing (that 'universal need') was 'the management of the workforce'.[15]

The housing conditions of the urban working class is an emotive subject. Contemporary commentators have left us with the impression that one of the most awful effects of industrialism was the degeneration of housing, caused by a huge increase in the size of the urban population. Writers such as James Kay Shuttleworth, the Manchester doctor, educationalist and social reformer, enforced the view, still held by many social historians, that living conditions at mid-century counter the claims of 'optimist' economic historians that early industrialisation led to improvements in the standards of living of ordinary working men and their families. Kay Shuttleworth portrayed the social environment of the Manchester labouring class as a product of poor housing and living conditions; although he suggested these factors were exacerbated by the allegedly immoral and unrestrained attitudes of the Irish, who, 'Debased alike by ignorance and pauperism, they have discovered, with the savages, what is the minimum of the means of life, upon which existence may be prolonged.'[16]

The living conditions and housing of the urban working class were so varied that only the briefest sketch can be given here. In the early nineteenth century, many urban dwellers were probably crammed into old, airless, damp and sometimes dilapidated accommodation. This was certainly the case in Liverpool, where the Victorian problem of overcrowding, poor sanitation and disease was at least predicated upon the fact that so much of the housing had been built for an eighteenth-century population.[17] By 1841 Liverpool and Manchester were the mostly densely populated urban spaces in the world. Population density for England and Wales averaged 275 persons per square mile, whereas the figure for Liverpool was 138 224 and for Manchester 100 000. Dr Duncan of Liverpool – the country's first Medical Officer of Health – calculated that certain streets and alleys in the city had a density equivalent to 657 963 people per square mile.[18] Perhaps unsurprisingly, mortality rates were also fearfully high. In 1840 Liverpool's death rate was 34.4 per 1000; the figure for Manchester was 33.3 (compared to 27 in London). The average age of death, moreover, was 17 years in Liverpool and 20 in Manchester (compared to 26.5 in London). The conditions of the labouring classes were hardly much better in Glasgow, Newcastle, Leeds, Birmingham and many other towns and cities; nor was this just a problem in such large centres. Old walled towns, for example, were particularly inapt for dealing with expanding populations; examples included the old parts of Edinburgh, Hull, London and York.[19] This is why Norwich was so badly affected by the smallpox epidemic of 1870–2 which killed 45 000 people in England and Wales.[20] Eighteenth-century towns were also ill-equipped to deal with the mobile and expanding populations of the industrial age.

Throughout this period, the average number of persons per house was 5.45 nationally, although this figure does not account for the desperate overcrowding experienced by many working-class people. The physical shape of these communities was, however, contested ideological ground. For those who lived two or three families to a house, over-crowding was simply a question of poverty and the lack of personal space; but for philanthropists and reformers overcrowding comprom-ised hygiene and morality by encouraging unnecessary familiarity between people of both sexes. Yet few families could afford homes which met with the approval of moral guardians who demanded that 'where there are children of both sexes, *mere decency* requires *four rooms*, – three for sleeping and one for daily use'.[21]

Many of the housing problems of these new urban communities were caused by pressure on space and time. Lodging houses provided many young migrant workers with rudimentary places to rest, and contem-porary writers regaled their audiences with sordid tales of beds occupied day and night by rotating shift-workers, with entire families crammed into single rooms, and criminals and prostitution lurking on every stair-well. Not all lodging houses were corrupted, and some aspired to be more than glorified brothels. However, Mayhew deplored the propor-tion of London's lodging houses that were of the lowest sort, by which he meant places in which criminals and prostitutes resided.[22] The White-haven surgeon, T. F. l'Anson, told Robert Rawlinson in 1849 that the town's high incidence of fever was due to overcrowding in local lodging houses: 'nearly all the cases in Ribton Lane were from two lodging houses which are always crowded with Irish', he claimed.[23] Even the more reputable ones were choked with young single males, and were overcrowded to a dangerous degree. Other large town houses could take on the appearance of small lodging houses when they fell into a cycle of room-letting. Multiple occupancy was not something that workers and their families chose (indeed they avoided it where they could), but it was a necessary condition of existence for the poorer or transient groups. Respectable families, too, could be found in overcrowded tenement houses, which, although difficult to distinguish from lodging houses, offered families the chance to rent a room for as little as 1s 6d or 2s 6d a week.

The worst of all urban accommodation was the cellar. Although some were ventilated by windows that also afforded natural light, the majority were dark, damp, miserable and overcrowded. Their sole advantage was a low rent, though their relative disadvantage was compounded by the fact that, while the poorest members of the working class lived in them, they were often let by the more prosperous working-class families occupying the houses that sat above such subterranean accommodation. The factor of cost undoubtedly encouraged the Irish to congregate in them, sometimes more than one family to a room. Commentators such as Peter Gaskell on Manchester wrote of the 'loathsomeness' of these Irish cellars, made worse by the residents' 'domestic companion, the pig'. Kay Shuttleworth also regarded the pig with horror, while Angus Bethune Reach, writing for the *Morning Chronicle* in 1849, reckoned he had seen the worst cellar in Manchester. Besides the usual dampness, darkness and overcrowding, and scenes of drunkenness and dissolution, Reach was shocked to find 'a well-grown calf' sleeping next to a fully-clothed man.[24] While as many as one-fifth or more of the working populations of Liverpool and Manchester lived in these lamentable dwellings, cellar living-space tended to be a feature of older residential areas; it did not occur universally, and was absent from new towns.

One housing type to prosper amid the urban blight was the back-to-back, described as the 'speculative builder's answer to ... mass demand'.[25] Either two-up-two-down or one-up-one-down, these houses were relatively cheap and efficient in terms of materials and space. Despite their poor reputation, the better ones were a significant improvement on the majority of urban and rural housing, for they were generally built from solid materials, usually brick, and were likely to have staircases and cooking-ranges. Although the rooms were smaller than was normal with other houses, each dwelling was meant to be self-contained and private. Some had attic rooms and cellars, but the main focus of the house would have been a kitchen, another downstairs room and two bedrooms. The worst examples of back-to-back building, however, compounded many of the worst effects of rookeries, courts and other overcrowded urban properties. Social reformers such as Edwin Chadwick complained that many back-to-backs which had sprung up by the 1840s were jerry-built, with too little brickwork, inadequate ventilation and little or no drainage. Chadwick suggested that the lack of space between the rows meant they actually re-created the old environmental problems associated with tightly pressed court-dwellings. He also criticised the fact that 20 dwellings or more might share one wash-pump and a single privy.[26] The back-to-back house was most common in Birmingham and in many towns across Lancashire and Yorkshire, with the West Riding having a particularly dense concentration; London had very few.

The classic 'Coronation Street' terraced house was beyond the means of most working-class families in the 1830s and 1840s, although these artisans' dwellings were being constructed in large numbers from mid-century. By the 1870s the two-up-two-down 'through terrace' – with its access at both front and rear, sometimes with a small garden or backyard, and of solid construction and adequately ventilated – was becoming the standard dwelling of urban Britain (this is notwithstanding the fact that many of the poor and casually employed still lived in tenements, back-to-backs, rookeries and courts. They would continue to do so until the Second World War). The traditional terraced house was a far cry from the worst of the back-to-backs, never mind the lodging house or the cellar. Many were built in the 1850s and 1860s at a time when covered sewage systems and adequately piped clean water were also being provided by municipalities. These houses, with their separate rooms, enabled greater definition of the spheres of domestic activity, from chatting or reading to eating or sleeping. By-laws introduced by some local authorities to reduce overcrowding meant that builders and landlords faced a less than maximum economic return because they used space less efficiently than either tenements or back-to-backs.[27] Nevertheless, they were more efficient than the suburban semi-detached homes which became the vogue in the inter-war period; and, in any case, resourceful builders were able to improve on their efficiency by turning out flats modelled on the terraced principle. This was particularly evident in the North-East where 'Tyneside flats' – which effectively divided two-up-two-down terraced homes into two separate dwellings – became the region's most distinctive housing type. By the 1890s, up to 60 per cent of the populations of Gateshead and South Shields occupied such flats. These flats doubled the number of families that could be housed in a street, which had an effect on community life in the vicinity of such accommodation by pressing more people into the available space.

Different authorities and localities dealt with the problems of urban communities in contrasting ways. From the 1830s, there were numerous national inquiries into the physical and atmospheric environment of the towns, and various efforts were made to improve the lot of the labouring classes; this reformist zeal was stimulated by a combination of fears: about disease, moral decay and political agitation. The authorities in Liverpool – renowned as Britain's unhealthiest urban centre – tried to close all cellar dwellings in a clean-up campaign of the early 1840s, but the initiative collapsed during the winter of 1846–7 under the weight of more than 500 000 Irish famine victims who flooded into the city. In 1851–2, legislation was passed to enforce minimum standards in Britain's lodging houses, though many dwellings went unchecked by the authorities. Liverpool was also the first place to embark on a comprehensive programme of municipal house-building. Elsewhere, bans on back-to-back building were gradually introduced and by 1875 (at the time of the Artisans' Dwellings Act) few were being constructed. In Lancaster, house-building was left in the hands of small-scale private speculators, with larger firms playing no role in building, owning and renting working-class housing.[28] Glasgow and Dundee builders chose to answer the need for accommodation by raising the skyline towards the heavens, constructing large tenement buildings. Despite their foreboding, prison-like appearance, these constructions represented an efficient use of land. Many of the individual flats within these constructions were designed to be too small for multiple occupancy, and though dreary and austere, the better models were significant improvements on the jerry-built back-to-backs or the ramshackle rookeries of old towns of previous eras.

The physical state of working-class communities inevitably defined those who inhabited them. Behind the blackened walls, and amid the foul middens, were people whose shared experience of deprivation and squalor undoubtedly bonded them. These communities were physically and psychologically inward-looking, defined as much by negative perceptions as by the shape of the streets. The neighbourhoods in which people lived were physical expressions of their class and status, not least in a period which witnessed the sustained suburbanisation of richer elements in society. Within these physical boundaries communities were forged and reforged, as people migrated in and out. Communities were not fixed – at least not in the sense that they comprised the same individuals and families from one year to the next. Yet there were continuities to the traditions and customs which captured the idea of community. Some of these were rehabilitated or imported from earlier lives in different places; some were new inventions based upon the needs of the urban world. In the end, though, people were at the heart of things.

People

Labour historians today lay far greater stress on the continuities in people's lives during the period of industrialisation. While it is accepted that industrial culture had a heavy impact upon the nature of social relations – not least by uprooting and redeploying large numbers of people who once were part of traditional communities – it is now common to question how far fundamental organisms, such as the family, were altered by the process of economic development. It seems likely that many features of rural life were maintained in the new urban communities. The influence of Marxism lies at the heart of the once common perception among historians that the Industrial Revolution proletarianised the family by transforming it from a unit of production and consumption to one of consumption alone.[29] In this explanation, as far as social relations were concerned, the kinship-orientated family was replaced by an 'affective individualism' inspired by capitalism. Traditional perspectives also emphasised that pre-modern family relations were marked by a greater morality than was the case in the nineteenth century, with increasing numbers of children being born out of wedlock under the changed circumstances of the later period. These notions have been found wanting by more recent research.[30] What seems apparent, however, is that the family was, as Peter Burke has argued, a 'moral community';[31] thus, changing perceptions of the family were as much to do with evolving notions of morality as with changes to the essential structure of families themselves.

Economic pressures also had an important influence on changing family patterns. However, the nature and extent of these pressures is less than clear-cut. It has been argued that the Industrial Revolution – by breaking the linkage between agriculture and domestic production (the dual economy) and by promoting a system of wage labour – weakened the position of women and children (which had been strong in the context of the domestic economy). Under capitalist systems of labour organisation, male work and moneyed wages were emphasised at the expense of domestic work and non-monetary contributions to the family budget. A similar line of argument, deriving most impetus from Marx's and particularly Engels's writings, has maintained that migration to towns broke traditional family bonds by demoting the roles of extended family members (grandparents, uncles, aunts, and so on) and placing much greater emphasis upon the nuclear family members (parents and children). Studies of the pre-industrial family have, however, shown that families tended to be nuclear long before the nineteenth century.[32] While village life almost certainly involved the existence of close kinship networks – grandparents, uncles and aunts living in close proximity – an extended family rarely lived under the same roof. What is more, research on family structure in urban settings has shown the importance of extended household members, including blood relations as well as lodgers.[33] Indeed, evidence suggests that despite the large-scale migrations discussed in the previous section, urban communities were not entirely different from their rural counterparts. Communities in both towns and villages were strengthened by the family unit; in both places, people were united by the themes common to the wider group's social class. Sociologists have likened urban communities to urban villages because of the extent to which they operated on a small and localised scale in everything from the location of work to the choosing of a marriage partner.

None of this means that women's participation in the economy withered away in these years. In fact, the belief that work patterns and experiences shifted in a linear fashion in our period must be refuted. But we do have problems assessing those aspects of women's work that lie in the half-light, if not in total darkness.[34] Census returns tell us about the surplus of women in the 15–49 age category (due to higher mortality among males); and overall (that is, nationwide) patterns of employment in domestic and laundry work, mills and factories, and so on, are easy enough to ascertain. But if we move beyond aggregate figures to ask about the social impact of work, the image becomes hazier. Women worked shifts, just as their menfolk did. A sweatshop seamstress would work through the night if the opportunity arose because she knew that the following month might be slack time. Part-time employment also occupied far more women than we are aware of, but little can be done to quantify such experiences. Yet we must deduce, even though measurement is impossible, that work – whatever its type – influenced the cultural lives and social roles of women.

The role of women in these communities was important, although in a world which placed increasing emphasis upon waged labour, men were destined to hold the real status and power in an increasingly less ambiguous fashion. As Robert Roberts has written, 'the matriarchs stood guardians, but not creators, of the group conscience and as such possessed a sense of social propriety as developed and unerring as any clique of Edwardian dowagers'.[35] Women's social and economic roles were regarded as subordinate to those of men; yet they were also at the fore-front when it came to providing their families and communities with survival and coping strategies in the face of the everyday travails of working-class life. As Ellen Ross notes, they were 'instrumental in organising ties between households, thereby facilitating the creation of shared working-class values and identities'. Just as men were linked by their experience of paid employment outside the home, so, too, were women brought together with their kin and neighbours, exchanging goods, experiences and skills and sharing the day-to-day lives that 'wove together individual conjugally-based households' into communities.[36] Women had a special place in the home or at street level; it was their responsibility to raise children and to feed and clothe their families. Mothers trained the next generation of young girls to become obedient wives and good mothers themselves. Women were the moral guardians of the communities and streets in which their families lived. Their gossip, which was more than idle chat, served a social function that enabled information to pass between these arbiters of community morality. Through such networks, women imposed their values on the community at large; here they condemned errant neighbours with a 'matronly snub' or by 'smashing of the guilty party's windows'.[37] Shame, opprobrium or exclusion were channelled by women as they saw fit; in some respects this must have appeared to be a sanitised version of the earlier *charivari* or 'rough music' – the ribald forms of collective justice doled out by the sort of traditional communities brought to life by the novelist, Thomas Hardy, in *The Mayor of Casterbridge* (1884).[38]

Women's roles were competitive as well as co-operative. Fights between children, or acts of bullying, could easily escalate into a full-blown brawl between mothers. Scrubbing the front step or maintaining a window box might be a measure of the tensions between neighbours, as was the woman's feeling of pride if her husband had the cleanest white collar for church on Sunday. Religious leaders were well aware of the importance of women. They tried harder to maintain the women's religious devotion than the men's because women shaped the children's attitudes. Catholic authorities, for instance, were particularly concerned about mixed marriages, and considerable pressure was exerted to convert the man and to make sure the children were brought up in the mother's faith. As Fielding has suggested: 'It was the woman's duty to maintain the family's integrity.'[39] The Virgin Mary may have been the role model assigned to Catholic women, but those of other faiths, as well as those with no faith at all, were expected by outside agencies – social reformers, philanthropists and newspaper journalists – to adopt the important function which the Church ascribed to Catholic women. Although, many Protestants would have baulked at the notion of ascribing Catholic role models to their co-religionists, from the 1840s the state showed a gradually increasing approval for the Catholic Church's civilising and educative mission among the Irish poor.[40]

However, we must not exaggerate the saintly disposition of maternal forms of control. Like men, women were fallible. Some mothers were just as likely to be found drunk on the streets as their husbands; in which event, the censure of middle-class moralists was usually many times amplified. The domestic life of women was never smooth-running: the exigencies of work, family budgets, childbirth and illness in the family made sure of that. But the housewife's control of the family budget was based entirely on the supposition that she could extract money from the wage packets of her husband and sons. Failure to do so weakened her position both within the family and beyond. Incidents of wife-beating, neglect and abandonment testify to the fragility of women's roles; and the sight of barefoot and dirty children playing in the streets certainly compromised the idealised image of the all-powerful matriarch. The woman's need or desire to contribute materially to the family's income could excite the social commentator who felt that paid employment for women – in factories and sweatshops – undermined the bond between mother and child. Yet women were undoubtedly more powerful when engaged in full-time work. Women in mill towns, such as Preston, where in 1901 and 1911 approximately one-third of married women were at work, had much more say in the affairs of the community than in engineering or shipbuilding towns, where female employment was scarce. On the other hand, full-time women workers paid less attention to domestic duties; they were, for example, among the first to buy bread, fish and chips and pies, a habit which drew criticism from women who made

everything themselves.[41] Women's roles, thus, were marked by contra-
dictions.

In addition, in the public sphere of the home men possessed the
instruments of power; for working-class communities were, in this respect,
overwhelmingly patriarchal. The devolution of day-to-day domestic
authority to women should not obscure the dominant position which
most men enjoyed, or could enjoy. The family revolved around them:
food was prepared to their tastes and at their convenience; and women's
work – washing, ironing and cooking – followed the rhythm of the men's
work routines. Special places, such as the front parlour with its high-
backed armchair, were reserved especially for men, while the scullery or
kitchen was a place for a man to eat or wash but not to work. Children
were not often allowed into the front room, where their father and his
friends smoked their pipes and chewed the fat, while their mother might
enter only to clean the room. Children's play was also prescribed by the
sleep requirements of a father or older brother who worked nights. But
this suggests that the patriarchy of Victorian society, though grim, was
essentially benign; but this is not the case. Violence against women and
children was, in an essentially and pervasively violent society, a commonplace occurrence. Morover, far less protection existed then than
now. Victorians tolerated public executions until the 1860s, military and
prison floggings until later, and were treated to a weekly parade of violence in the magistrates' courts of every borough. But we know very little
about what went on behind closed doors, though Saville suggests that
neighbours ignored abuses until the violence became extreme.[42]

Men's work routines also delineated the life patterns of women. Miners'
wives in County Durham slept in snatches when they had shiftworking
husbands and sons, for these men would come in and out of the house,
requiring food and hot water, at regular intervals throughout the night
and day. A miner's wife who presented testimony to the Sankey Commission in 1919 succinctly summarised her role: 'my husband and three
sons are all on different shifts, and one or other of them is leaving or
entering the house and requiring a meal every three hours in the 24'.[43]
The mother of Jack Lawson, the former miner and one-time Labour MP,
would rise at three in the morning to get his father off to work at Boldon
colliery and again at five to do the same for the boys. Lawson's mother
did this in part because, such were the dangers of mining, 'it might be the
last time she would see us'. For the miner's wife, it was 'unthinkable that
we should go to work while she was in bed'.[44] It is impossible to know
how typical Lawson's mother was; after all, it was only the untypical

worker who went on to become a Labour MP or to write an autobiography. The example does, however, tells us something of how women
were perceived.

The man's sphere was more obviously public than the woman's; or,
rather, men enjoyed a full life outside the home, free of the limiting
effects of children and domestic duties. Manly pursuits were not usually
conducted in the home. Burnett captures this domestic demarcation
well: 'Husbands who worked all day and dutifully brought home their
wage-packets . . . were not expected to share in the routine housework:
they might mend shoes, repair household articles, dig their allotments,
and, perhaps, play with their children, but they expected their meal to
be on the table.'[45] Or, as Catherine Cookson remembered, 'in those
days, a man went out to work and that, to his mind, was enough . . . . [I]t
lowered a man's prestige if he as much as lifted a cup.'[46] Whereas their
wives lifted and carried more than cups. Working-class women marry-
ing in the 1890s, when in their late teens or early twenties, would have to
contend with an average of ten pregnancies throughout their childbear-
ing years;[47] and, with this, came physical and emotional stress, not least as
a result of stillbirths, infant mortality, and the general rigours of carrying
children full-term and then raising them till they were independent
young adults.

The surviving children mixed elements of both male and female roles.
From an early age, girls and boys were groomed for their future roles.
Most parents tried to strike a balance between, on the one hand, education and nurturing and, on the other, work and exploitation. Thus, while
both sexes went to school and were taught rudimentary reading and
writing skills, boys tended to stay in school longer and girls at home to
help their mothers. Census records offer the sketchiest evidence of family
structures in the nineteenth century, and on issues such as female work
these impressions are sketchier still. It was common for one daughter
gradually to be drawn away from the other siblings, sometimes condemned to a life of drudgery and spinsterhood because of the needs of
an ailing mother or a widowed father. Younger girls also worked, both
inside and outside the domestic sphere, though this usually stopped at
the point of marriage. At the beginning of this period, young boys might
begin work before the age of ten, though this became less common after
1833 when the first act in a series of factory laws was passed. Many jobs,
such as running errands, were done on a part-time basis, alongside the
normal childhood routine of schoolwork and domestic chores. Even at
the end of this period, boys were entering apprenticed trades in their

early teens, spending five or seven years learning a craft under skilled supervision. Family and kinship networks were a vital part of the recruiting network for mills and mines and for skilled apprenticed trades in, for example, the shipyards. By the later Victorian period, school occupied the majority of a child's day, and the youngster would remain at school until a progressively later age, rising eventually to 14 years of age in 1918.

Working-class communities were also distinguished by their common diet. Food consumption is a vital element of any individual's standard of living and is a measure of both class and status. It is impossible to know precisely what people ate in this period, how much they ate, and how their diet changed óver time. Impressionistic evidence is plentiful, whereas comprehensive runs of quantitative data are non-existent. We do know that consumption of certain items increased or changed over our period. Tea and coffee sales increased significantly in the second half of the nineteenth century, at the same time as steamships, refrigerated transport, and canning introduced Argentinian meat, corned beef, and North American grains into the diet of the British working class. The majority of workers, however, were tied by economic necessity to a simple diet, the staples of which were bread and potatoes. Cheaper cuts of meat, particularly bacon, offal and sausage, provided the main animal protein consumed, and were a regular, if not daily, part of their meals.

The diet of agricultural labourers, though often supplemented by the workers' own-grown food, usually reflected their low wages, in some areas as little as 7s or 8s per week in the 1860s. 'Tea-kettle broth', made by pouring boiling water on bread, onion and seasoning, was the simple fare with which many north Devon labourers began their 10- or 11-hour-day's work. Bread and hard cheese were common midday foodstuffs, with supper usually comprising bacon, potatoes and cabbage. Meat, other than a few scraps of bacon, was a rarity; some had to make do with greasing their vegetables down with a little fat. These same workers were allowed to buy 'grist corn' at a fixed price and were granted a daily ration of three or four pints of 'unsaleable and almost undrinkable cider'. At the same time, butcher's meat 'found its way sometimes on Sundays – but only on very rare occasions – to the peasant's table'. The more varied diet of rural workers was undoubtedly an advantage over their urban counterparts. But many of them were 'crippled up by rheumatism' at the age of 45 or 50, because of their constant exposure to damp, as well as 'feeble from the lack of a proper amount of food'.[48]

Although food consumption correlated quite clearly with income and social class, the family of a well-paid but heavy-drinking mechanic would have eaten less well than the family of an abstemious general labourer, even though the latter's wages might have been half the former's. At the same time, both families would have suffered heavily if the breadwinner was unemployed or incapacitated by an accident. Much of what we know about food comes from social commentators who existed outside the communities. Details of family budgets are sparse, and qualitative evidence (including working-class autobiography) tends to be impressionistic. All classes commented, for example, on the monotony of the poor Irish labourer's diet. A large pot of Murphies (potatoes) and cabbage, sometimes with a little bacon, was a common and much denigrated staple in the diet of these migrants. 'Stirrabout', a thin stew bulked with oats and potatoes, was another cheap dish. Herrings were also part of the Irish diet, consumed irregularly but in higher quantities than most other forms of protein. While the native working class was thought to crave better quality food, not least animal produce, commentators alleged that Irish migrants were only content to eat potatoes because the money they saved could then be spent on drink. Observers failed to appreciate that the potato is one of the most nutritional staple foodstuffs and had been cited 60 years earlier by Arthur Young, the writer and leading exponent of agricultural improvements, to explain the beauty, complexion and physical prowess of the Irish peasant.[49]

The clothes of the poor also excited a prurient middle class, with sensationalised images of barefoot street urchins and semi-clad female workers arousing particular passions. Joseph Adshead's study of the poor in Manchester in the early 1840s carried the observation of a gentleman who claimed he had seen 'some children stitched up in calico, I suppose to keep them warm, and save the trouble of dressing and undressing'. Mr Buckland, a missionary to the poor, told the same author how he came across '[s]everal families [that] were almost in a state of absolute nudity'.[50] Even in better-off families, young children wore their older siblings' cast-offs and repaired clothes. There were, however, clothes for special occasions, what were termed 'Sunday best'. Even these suits and frocks were not always of the most recent vintage, though pride was taken in them being smart and presentable. Men wore very particular sorts of clothing for work that were chosen for toughness and durability rather than for show. Equally, the emergence of the railway companies meant more men going to work in uniforms which immediately demonstrated the wearer's occupational status: a stationmaster could never be mistaken for a fireman or driver. In trades such as mining, men were levelled by the grime and dust that covered them head to foot. Religious leaders often remarked on the failure of working men and women to attend church through embarrassment at their lack of presentable clothes. Some blamed the state of affairs on drink, as was common, but others, like the Revd Dr Goss, opined from the pulpit that as 'Christ had no fine dress' he would prefer to see among the congregation a 'sprinkling of those who had no coats'.[51]

Culture and Leisure

In 1830, there were few restrictions on the length of the working week, and little time was left for the pursuit of pleasure. During the early industrial period, when Lancashire factories were taken to be the embodiment of work's harsh regimen, considerable pressure was exerted for the working class to be given more leisure time. W. Cooke Taylor, writing in 1842 to Dr Richard Whatley, Archbishop of Dublin, demanded more free time for Lancashire's labouring class – but there was a moralising sting in the tail:

> No one feels more strongly than I do the great but neglected truth that moral education, in spite of all the labours of direct instructors, is really acquired in hours of recreation. Sport and amusements are, and must be, means by which the mind is insensibly trained; the lectures of the school-room will be utterly ineffective when they are counteracted by the practical lessons of the playground.[52]

By 1914, the working week had been universally shortened by a series of campaigns for more humane hours. However, even at this later point, fully employed males and females still worked long and hard. Saturday mornings were still part of the normal working week for most people. Without overtime, the average worker could still expect to put in more than fifty hours per week. Despite the looming presence of work, and even partly because of it, leisure activities were a robust and important aspect of life in working-class communities. Some of these pastimes – for example, reading or church societies – were deemed by moral reformers to be character-building and indeed 'rational'. Others, including heavy drinking and prizefighting, were considered to be barbarous and degrading. As a result of this dichotomy between the 'rational' and the indulgent, Victorian commentators, and subsequently historians, viewed leisure as contested ground. Historians have disagreed over the extent to which leisure culture was created by, or was imposed upon, the working class. In a classic Gramscian analysis, popular culture is explained in terms of hegemony – the imposition of ruling-class values on the working class, something which is suggested in the words of Cooke Taylor, quoted above. More recent research has, however, offered a more fluid interpretation, with emphasis upon the dichotomy of 'rough' and 'respectable', irrespective of class or social status.[53] Whatever the precise political and cultural utility of leisure, however, it is clear that the way men, women and children spent their free waking hours was a vital adhesive in the broader idea of community. It is also clear that the impulse to leisure-time enjoyment remained constant throughout our period, even if the mode or sphere of that enjoyment may have changed. As Golby and Purdue remind us: '[i]f the nineteenth century saw a taming of its cruder and more violent manifestations, ... many leisure pursuits remained in essence the same and were simply modified to suit a society that had become more prosperous, more humanitarian and less disorderly'.[54]

The way in which the working class passed their spare time was a source of great concern for middle-class observers. The apparent problems of leisure were linked to the way people felt about their changing world. Politicians and journalists alike were fearful of the social effects of urbanisation – the growth of whole areas of working-class population, beyond the control of priests and social missionaries, where a 'mob' might quickly form. Meanwhile, events in Europe offered regular reminders of the dangers of political upheaval. The same impulse that inspired the early Victorian evangelical revival also saw the middle classes promoting self-improvement for their inferiors while also demanding the constitution of an effective police force. That so many social theorists and commentators alighted on the issue of popular culture, was part of a wider desire to transform society without revolution.

Leisure was, however, also a part of working-class survival strategies; controlling free time was a crucial aspect of any battle to resist the further regimentation of work. In defending leisure time and particular sorts of pastimes, the working class was stressing its independence. Thus, Liverpool dock labourers preferred to work harder for more hours per day in a three- or four-day week than to work more days. Indeed, as their historian writes, 'the casual system gave them an independence denied to other workers. Perversely, the drawbacks of the system were transformed into virtues', and the men 'were proud that they worked when they wanted to'.[55] In a hard and brutal working environment, such as the docks, men needed leisure time to rest and to spend their wages; working lives were much shorter than in many other forms of work and this imbued men with a fatalism that was reflected in robust leisure pursuits. A similar mentality affected the railway navvies, with their once-a-month 'beanos' of drinking and violence. More generally, the concept of St Monday (or even of St Tuesday or St Wednesday), which had been a feature of pre-industrial work rhythms, remained stubbornly imprinted on the work and leisure culture of many groups of workers in the mid-Victorian years, particularly those in small-scale workshops or who worked at home, although the tradition was strong among the colliers of the North-East.[56] If leisure was about control, then it concerned working-class self-control as well as improving tendencies of moral reformers.

    The extent to which the processes of industrialisation and urbanisation transformed people's lives is debated. Continuities and changes in popular leisure culture constitute an important part of any consideration. Pre-industrial popular culture is usually characterised as vigorous yet benign; boisterous, but not, ultimately, a threat to the social fabric. Rural leisure tended also to be closely associated with local customs, and it was usually shaped by the religious calendar (though this declined as time went by) and by the seasons.[57] Many aspects of traditional culture declined due to the pressures upon common space exerted by enclosures and the commercialisation of agriculture, although great social occasions, such as the Michaelmas hiring fair, continued to bring together town and country in a ritual of drunken revelry and community-wide indulgence. Mass football games and various forms of fighting – boxing, wrestling and cudgelling – were common events; a rich variety of blood sports, including cockfighting, also drew attention from gamblers, including local squires, who sometimes had considerable sums riding on the events organised by labourers.[58] These forms of rural leisure were often actively promoted and funded by local elites, in a marked contrast to the rather dismissive air exhibited by better-off townspeople in Victorian times. The rich and varied popular culture of 'Merrie England', with its emphasis upon participation and acquiescence by all tiers of the rural community, was in terminal decline in the eighteenth century when the division between 'polite' and 'popular' culture became more apparent. Many of the pre-industrial pastimes that disappeared in this period were reinvented in the Victorian years; but examples such as the maypole were 'shorn of any sexual or subversive connotations'.[59] Certain aspects of rural culture maintained their importance in the town. Workers in Manchester kept pigs for the same reason as their rural counterparts: because pigs had economic value. For the Irish, the pig was 'the gintleman who pays the rint'. And in mining villages, where rural met urban, the pig was usually a welcome house guest. Jim Bullock remembered how killing the pig was a notable occasion in his childhood village of Bower's Row, near Castleford. His father selected the pig and the children ran about the village taking orders for various joints of pork. The ritual was completed when 'a team of six burly miners' arrived with a large table, accompanied by the butcher in his blue and white smock. The pig was hoisted on to the table, whereafter the scene was 'very similar to a bull-fight: everybody prepared for the kill . . . the village butcher stood back like a matador, waiting to administer the final coup de grace, swiftly and efficiently'. Once the deed was done, there was no waste; every bit was used in some way – even the bladder, which the boys blew up for a football.[60] Similarly, while hunting rituals changed over time, and between town and country, long-lining and rabbiting were much the same in a village or on the out- skirts of a town. The urban worker's company terraced house sometimes came with a small allotment of land, which, just like the rural garden, might provide the green-fingered gardener with a variety of items for the family table or for sale.

Despite the more recent intellectual vogue stressing the independence of working-class culture, it is nevertheless difficult entirely to erase a train of thought which suggests leisure culture was a source of conflict between classes. In fact, culture welled up from the bottom in addition to being promoted or imposed from above, and the two levels of analysis are not distinct from each other. Leisure helped to delineate the community's physical space as well as defining differing moral positions: pubs were symbols of communities but also sources of conflict between indulgers and abstainers. In the towns, enclosures were also an issue, albeit less so than in the countryside, having the similar effect of proscribed certain leisure activities in the village. There were riots when urban spaces were enclosed, as occurred at Plumstead Common in London in 1876, while Newcastle's Town Moor was still being used for horse racing in the early 1880s. Many forms of opposition to working-class leisure culture were also apparent. A key problem was time: week-long fairs and endless days of merrymaking were at odds with the regimented work rhythms of industrial life.[61] Critics also suggested the sprawling games and public indulgence of rural culture were impossible and undesirable in the con- fines of the town. As part of the general pressure exerted against ruinous indulgence, the extent of gambling was many times curtailed by law, which meant much of it went underground. Common gambling houses were outlawed in the mid-1850s, but working-class communities continued to gamble by throwing a veil around such activity in an attempt to outwit the police.[62] Equally, although laws were passed in 1822 and 1835 to prevent cruelty to animals, and though the Society for the Prevention of Cruelty to Animals (SPCA, later prefixed 'Royal') was founded in 1824, working men continued to organise clandestine activities, including dogfights and badger baiting. Similarly, cockfighting was outlawed in 1839 but continued in a clandestine fashion. Much of the impetus for a higher or 'rational' form of recreation came from the churches, many of which provided by the 1850s a whole range of organised pastimes to counteract the remnants of eighteenth-century leisure attitudes and the siren's call of the public house.

The churches occupied a somewhat ambiguous position in working-class communities.[63] The religious census of 1851 (a one-off and crude attempt to measure faith through church attendances on a given Sunday) seemed to suggest that religion had never been less popular in British society. What is more, the established Anglican Church suffered the most serious decline, while the few growth denominations included Catholicism, Methodism and Judaism (especially following the Jewish immigration from the Russian Empire in the later nineteenth century).[64] The religiosity of society was declining steadily and this caused great concern for moral reformers. Most Britons, however, remained generally religious, even if church attendances were waning. Religious houses continued to be key features of the physical and mental landscape of the new communities. Churches provided spiritual comfort and sociability to those entering the growing towns; this was never more apparent than in the case of the Irish Catholics, whose arrival in the urban centres coincided with the greatest social upheavals in the process of industrialisation. Sometimes, the needs of a desperate Irish flock encouraged the Catholic Church to offer an important social function.[65] Protestants of all nationalities, too, shared this social sense, and all churches concentrated on a comprehensive mixture of religious and social functions, including leisure and sporting activities. An example of this occurred in 1887 when a Catholic priest founded Glasgow Celtic football club. The circular announcing the formation of Celtic claimed that 'the main object of the club is to supply the east-end conferences of the St Vincent de Paul society [a Catholic charitable organisation] with funds for the maintenance of the "dinner tables" of our needy children'. Many other towns saw football teams of 'Hibernians', 'Harps' and 'Shamrocks' springing up at around the same time; and churches in most other towns provided a similar mix of the spiritual and the social in forming sporting societies and the like.[66] Much of the energy for reform derived from the fear and loathing of drink. As we shall see in the next chapter, drink was, even more than gambling, viewed as a dividing point between 'rough' and 'respectable' culture.

Many leisure pursuits were fundamentally different in the towns. Generally, urban pastimes were marked by far greater organisation and had the capacity to be larger and more concentrated than in the shires. There also emerged a much more distinct division between participant and observer, especially in team sport, where spectators were becoming increasingly numerous. Sporting activities became increasing highly organised, competitive and commercialised – changes which derived part of their impetus from permeation of the public schools' new emphasis on the value of character-building and manly qualities of team sports.[67] Certain types of leisure facilities needed urban populations to finance and sustain them, for example libraries, reading rooms and bathhouses. The same could be said for music halls, where the entertainment has been seen as epitomising the culture of urban workers. According to Stedman Jones, the music hall 'appealed to the London working-class because it was both escapist *and yet* strongly rooted in the realities of working-class life (original emphasis).' However, with the advent of 'moving pictures', many music halls were converted into cinemas, which by 1914 numbered some 4000.[68]

The towns offered new possibilities for both participant and spectator sports. Football and cricket leagues were facilitated by the clustering of populations and by the spread of transport networks. Horse racing remained consistently popular with the working class, though it had first appeared in the country and continued to thrive both in towns and in villages. However, certain sporting events simply could not have attained their legendary status without the development of urban communities. Up to 100 000 people are said to have watched rowing on the Tyne in the 1840s (though many came in from outlying districts to observe these events); and by 1903 an average of 20 000 paying spectators watched first-round FA Cup matches.[69] The development of transport links helped to expand the frontiers of leisure, not least with the development of day trips and short breaks. The emergence of pleasure towns such as Blackpool, Whitley Bay, Skegness and Southend-on Sea, which offered cheap seaside holidays for the masses, was a feature of the later period. Between 1883 and 1914 the number of visitors to Blackpool increased fourfold to four million. Less fashionable large towns also exploited their commercial leisure potential to interesting effect. The development of Sunderland's seaside suburb of Roker, for example, put day trips to the seaside within easy reach of thousands of miners and shipbuilders, at the same time striking a pleasant contrast to the grime of the town's pits and shipyards.

In urban communities, traditional and modern aspects of popular culture lived in symbiosis. One noticeable feature was, however, the breakdown of community-wide aspects of leisure activity. Gender division became more apparent with the emergence of male-dominated pastimes, from pigeon-fancying to team sports. However, the enduring elements of traditional culture most lamented by local authorities were those which combined drink, violence and gambling. This occurred with all sorts of organised fighting, but was perceived to be particularly pernicious when erupting spontaneously within working-class communities. The people of the Victorian boom town of Barrow in the 1870s witnessed a spate of these brawls. Local newspapers expressed alarm, blaming high wages, drink and the police:

> [prize fights] occur night after night with impunity, at the end of every street; and the police seem powerless in relation to it. Rough brawny men receiving wages higher than they have been accustomed to, squander their surplus funds on strong drink, and become 'pot valiant' or make a quarrel.[70]

Such encounters often led to serious beatings, but in the case of Barrow only once to death. The fatality occurred when a dispute between two workmates – both skilled shipyard workers – was turned into a public fight, with heavy bets placed on the outcome. The fight was attended by a crowd of 150 and lasted for a considerable length of time before one of the pugilists, a pattern-maker called John Hockney, fell dead. Six men were charged with manslaughter: John Ennis, the other fighter, received a sentence of six months with hard labour, while the other five were sentenced to one month, also with hard labour.[71]

As well as being cultural, leisure was also political. The growth of socialism from the 1880s saw the development of a whole range of social organisations designed to attract converts and weld the group identity. Robert Blatchford's *Clarion* newspaper lent its name to an array of social-ist leisure-time pursuits; there were Clarion cycling clubs in Glasgow, and Clarion ramblers in Sheffield. Labour churches and socialist Sunday schools became popular in this period, offering something more than religious instruction for all. John Maclean taught economics to working men in Glasgow, while institutional self-education was available through such organisations as the Plebs League and London's Central Labour College.[72] There is no doubt that the period 1880 to 1914 saw a great awakening in working-class political consciousness; much of it derived from the new-found organisational strength and voice of the unskilled workers, although the skilled remained at the heart of the labour movement's institutional aspects.

The development of youth organisations should also be seen as part of the self-improvement mission associated with many leisure forms, especially in the later nineteenth century. Football clubs, the Boys' Brigade, Baden-Powell's Boy Scout movement, formed in 1908, and, later, the Girl Guides, represented a broad mixture of the disciplined, quasi-military and self-improving way in which the hearts and minds of working-class children were fought over. Sport, exercise and the great outdoors were increasingly thought to be an antidote to the problems of urban life; fitness of body was seen as an aid to fitness of mind; and a mentally alert, physically fit populace would bring its own rewards to the country at large. Indeed, the Edwardians held the view that 'it was their love of sport and the qualities it bred that set them apart from other nations and fitted them uniquely for the task of governing their vast empire'.[73]

Finally, in this period, as now, many took their leisure in an unstructured fashion. Middle-class observers often expected more of workers, after long arduous hours, than mere relaxation. By the time boys left school, one investigator reported, their 'great source of amusement' was the street. There the boy 'spends a large part of his spare time in loafing'; with his pals, he can be found 'playing games, singing, exchanging witticisms, and generally making himself obnoxious to the police and the public'. Almost all boys, moreover, smoked 'Woodbines or "Coffin-nails", as they facetiously term them'. As they became older, their behaviour became more adventurous:

> A large number of them gamble on pigeon-flying, football, etc. – a habit that has the most unfortunate effects in unsteadying the character. Many of them, even at fourteen, parade the streets arm in arm with girls. The Girl, however, is not a serious factor . . . till he reaches 16 or 17; at that age he begins "walking out" . . . [74]

Once such boys became adults, and work dominated their lives, leisure became something to seize and defend. Men who worked hard needed time to recover, and, though it pained the clergy, Sunday was the only full day on which complete indulgence could be enjoyed, as the Rector of Bethnal Green in 1895 acknowledged. His comment is worth quoting at length. He told the audience:

> You must prepare your minds for this, that a vast majority of the men in your district will have spent their Sundays for the last twenty-five years, and their fathers before them, in the following way: they will have lain in bed till about eleven or twelve, having been up early all week; they will then go round when the public-houses open, which they do at one; they will have what they call a 'wet' till three . . . they will then have dinner, the great dinner of the week, which the missus has been preparing all the morning. Then comes a lie down on the bed in shirt sleeves until five, with a pot of beer and *Lloyd's Weekly*; then follows tea, and after tea a bit of a walk round to see a friend or a relation; then fairly early to bed to make up for a very late Saturday night . . . [75]

Such ways of spending leisure could have a strengthening influence on the sense of community. Boys who 'loafed' the streets would develop, almost incidentally, attitudes of 'them and us', which were also elements of a collective existence, as was the proclivity of men to have their 'wet' and visit friends and relatives. As for women, their leisure activities were often imperceptibly intertwined with the routines of daily life about the house. They snatched brief leisure opportunities to gossip, which added to communal networks.

Summary

The problems of adequately summarising the idea of community will be apparent from the range of issues discussed in this chapter. From the community sprung so many other features of working-class life. Indeed, it is arguable that the community *was* working-class life, given that labouring people lived overwhelmingly among other labouring people. Together they were bonded by shared aspirations, experiences and outlooks. Communities were organic insofar as they linked numerous elements of life to the individuals they comprised. Communities were clearly shaped by the nature of the work that sustained them: isolated mining communities were different from shipbuilding communities which were based in large towns, while mill-based communities, with their heavy emphasis on women's work, were different again. At the same time, many features linked urban communities, despite differences in available work. The primary functions of community, such as sociability and friendship, were the same across time, regions and occupational groups. However, communities were spheres of conflict as well as coalescence in this period because those inside and outside struggled to impose their ideas upon the way the working class lived their lives.

Self-improvement was increasingly and persistently promoted long before the notion of state welfare became widely accepted. Yet the philosophy of improvement could be deployed to benefit the community and its members' class as much as to inculcate what was presented as the superior ethos of bourgeois society. Notwithstanding the existence of poor relief and limited social reforms (in working conditions, housing and education), the Victorian world put the role of the individual ahead of the masses; and this was to have a dramatic adhesive effect on the 'idea' of community. Groups were recognised as more powerful and important than individuals precisely because so little help was available outside familiar networks for those who fell on hard times. Consequently, the decision of the individual and groups of individuals to organise for their mutual benefit represents a significant part of any attempt to explain the experiences of labour. Such urges found satisfaction through the associational culture of clubs and societies which dominated working-class organisation in the mid-nineteenth century.

5

SELF-HELP AND ASSOCIATIONALISM

A Victorian Ideology?

An unshakeable faith in the nostrum of self-help lay at the heart of the Victorian idea of progress. The requirement for individuals to help themselves may appear at first to have run counter to the centralising tendencies of the British state in the later nineteenth century, but there are, as we shall see, various ways in which self-help could fall in line with the increasingly impersonal nature of modern society. In the earlier part of the century, social thinkers and legislators came increasingly to view liberal individualism as a near-divine virtue. Moreover, the message seems to have been infectious, for a repeated emphasis upon the self-help credo was pressed hard upon the working class in this period.

Yet the case for self-help was not always perceived as synonymous with individualism. Among sections of the working class, self-help was a group activity, what has come to be termed associationalism. This form of clubbing together was how working people responded to a world in which the state offered little in the way of social provision. There is, however, considerable debate in labour history circles about the nature of working-class associations, such as the co-operative movement, friendly societies, building societies, and so on. Were these signs of collectivism 'the fruit of a hegemonic imposition of "bourgeois" values on a compliant workforce'? Or was it the case that the labour aristocracy was becoming assimilated into capitalist society? Or was it the result of a 'drawing out of strands within working-class experience'?[1] In other words, were

114

organisations such as the co-operative movement or the friendly society dependent upon, or independent of, middle-class control?

Although the middle classes played a significant role in bringing the idea of the club or society to a wide audience in this period, workers themselves had long been forming trade guilds to protect their collective economic interests. Working men and women borrowed many of the symbols and rituals of middle-class associations (Freemasonry, for example, was much mimicked in this respect), but they also pursued their own objectives in forming and maintaining what was a plethora of clubs, societies and associations. From the Oddfellows, the Foresters and the Royal and Ancient Order of Buffaloes (the three largest friendly societies) to trade-union-based mutual association, many working men – most of them were skilled men and very few of them women – boasted paid-up membership of at least one of the many available clubs, which, despite their often ceremonial appearance, were dedicated first and foremost to the economic and social welfare of their members. Regional and occupational variations may have existed, but men of all trades and ethnic groups belonged to such organisations. The range of this sort of activity was quite staggering, with millions enrolling in a conscious attempt to buffer the hard times. Institutions such as the co-operative movement provided a physical presence and often a certain architectural grandeur, as well as a range of social and economic functions in every later-Victorian town, and there were also hundreds of smaller organisations which offered members the chance to share the costs of unemployment, sickness and burial.

Recent historical analyses in the field of labour history have sought to undermine the holistic and deterministic associations of class, with a number of writers preferring to stress radical continuities from the eighteenth century and the primacy of language, over economic context, as the constitutive of working-class experience.[2] However, no discussion of working-class collective self-help, or the related impulse to associationalism, would be complete without reference to the controlling element at play in the emergence of many forms of working-class self-help institutions. In an important analysis of the working men's club movement, Richard Price has argued that the middle classes encouraged the self-education, rational recreation and mutualism of such organisations as the working men's club because of a perceived need to impose a '"safe" and alien ideology and value system upon the working classes'.[3] This viewpoint clearly conflicts with notions of the independence of class culture – the idea that, by forming associations, the working class was looking after its own interests independent of other classes. Yet the two views need not be mutually exclusive, for, although the working class were often quick to adopt the middle-class vision of respectability, they rarely employed it without moulding it to their own tastes. Most clubs and societies were dominated by the better-off skilled workers, the aristocracy of labour, and, although membership of friendly societies was very large in the nineteenth century (more than 8 per cent of the population, even in 1815),[4] poorer members of societies, day labourers and their families, or recent immigrants, were not as well placed to take advantage of systems of provision for sickness or death benefits which might run to several shillings per week. Most workers in this century paid no more than 3s to 5s in rent, and an equivalent cost in assurances was beyond the means of many.

The Self-Help Ethos

The idea of self-help was closely linked to the economic doctrine of laissez-faire.[5] These two creeds were part of a dominant ideology which viewed state intervention as having a deleterious effect on the capacity of individuals to realise their full potential. The state was thought to stifle the entrepreneurial energies of the British character, while social intervention, such as the poor law (regularly refined and rethought since Elizabethan times), was criticised because it supposedly encouraged a culture of dependency. The cornerstone of the laissez-faire and self-help ideal was Adam Smith's *Wealth of Nations* (1776), a devastating critique of the rules and regulations associated with the mercantile system of the eighteenth century. Aspects of Smith's viewpoint were refined by a number of important political economists, such as T. R. Malthus, Jeremy Bentham, David Ricardo, James Mill and Nassau Senior. Popularised in newspapers and periodicals, and in publications such as the *Encyclopaedia Britannica*, laissez-faire had become the dominant economic ideology long before Victoria ascended to the throne. This was shown in one of the last publications of the conservative political theorist Edmund Burke. Writing in the 1790s, Burke denounced the use of the term 'the labouring *poor*', a term employed habitually in the nineteenth century. He considered it offered sham compassion and patronised the poor worker. Instead, he averred in *Thoughts and Details on Scarcity* (written in 1795 but first published in 1800), 'Patience, labour, sobriety, frugality, and religion, should be recommended to them; all the rest is downright *fraud.*' Burke was arguing, as Malthus did in his *Essay on the Principle of Population* (1798), that while work was a normal state, poverty was the natural outcome of the balance of people and resources.[6]

In the aftermath of Napoleon's final defeat in 1815, this type of moral viewpoint was affirmed in the debates about the poor law. Malthus's views on population led commentators and politicians to suggest that softening attitudes towards the relief of poverty had lessened the worker's fear of want, increased dependency upon the state and encouraged population growth. Although the Speenhamland system (effectively a wages supplement, paid from poor rates, developed in 1790s Berkshire) was far less widespread in southern agricultural regions during the French Wars than poor law reformers suggested, there is little doubt that the poor rates were sometimes used to subsidise low farm wages and thus to distort the market. Early critics, such as Sir Frederick Eden, who popularised negative images of Speenhamland and demanded a sterner test for the poor, were eventually rewarded by the Poor Law Amendment Act of 1834.[7] In Britain, as in America, the adherents of laissez-faire tried to suggest that the free-and-easy awarding of outdoor aid led to increasing indigence. The logic of this was simple: the easier the claim, and the greater the comfort, the more the system appealed to people whose only other option would normally be hard work and self-reliance.[8]   .

This was certainly the view of Samuel Smiles, prophet of liberal-individualism, whose book, *Self-Help* (1859), enjoyed enormous sales and was translated into many languages. Smiles sought to articulate the very American idea that men of humble origins could go on to great things if they avoided temptation and worked hard for themselves. *Self-Help* is a compilation of biographies, or hagiographies, of great men who advanced beyond the relatively low circumstances of their birth. The book draws upon all walks of life, deriving advice and instruction from all manner of successful men. Thus, the lives of Joshua Reynolds, Dr Livingstone and Sir Robert Peel are juxtaposed with effusive out-pourings on Dr Johnson, Sir Walter Scott and J. S. Mill. Smiles opened his account with the religious maxim 'Heaven helps those who help themselves.' He considered that 'The spirit of self-help is the root of all genuine growth in the individual'; by this measure, society and the nation would benefit, for self-help also 'constitutes the true source of national vigour and strength'.[9] If Smiles embodied a near-religious vision of the way human society might be improved and protected, there was a less than saintly aspect to his vision, articulated in a later book, *Thrift* (1875). Here, perhaps more than in *Self-Help*, Smiles envisioned the true root of elite fears: if the working man had nothing he might forget the Ten Commandments and begin to covet his neighbour's possessions. If, however, the working class could be encouraged to fend for themselves, without upsetting the natural order of rulers and the ruled, then they might rise above the petty jealousies associated with want: 'When workmen, by their industry and frugality, have secured their own independence, they will cease to regard the sight of others' well-being as a wrong inflicted on themselves.'[10] J. P. Kay Shuttleworth, the Manchester doctor, educationist and reformer, concurred that the prospect for self-improvement made the 'success of the middle classes less a subject of envy than of emulation'.[11] Smiles was articulating an already well-subscribed ethos; he certainly did not create, but he did help to simplify and publicise, what was a pervasive and general commitment in Victorian society to the idea of progress, enlightenment and national well-being via individual fulfilment.

The working class, however, did not universally embrace the philosophy in its pure form. The problem was clear enough to most working people: individuals who began poor seemed rarely to have prospered in the world of towns and machines. Self-help was a fine ideal to expound in the drawing-room, but, as Fraser has correctly pointed out, 'it required only a small logical extension' to develop from the self-help creed a social theory 'in which men found their due place in society in proportion to their talents'. This fear came to fruition, later in the century, in the Social Darwinism of Herbert Spencer, a theorist who stressed Darwin's 'survival of the fittest' in terms of its application to human society.[12] Unsurprisingly, perhaps, amidst the upheaval of industrial and urban growth, millions of ordinary Britons made a conscious decision that it was better to club together than to stand alone. This is not to downplay the importance which some sections of the working class attached to their own individual improvement; but this was usually channelled towards education and the pursuit of knowledge for its own sake. In hard-nosed economic terms, it was clear to ordinary men and women that the world was a safer place, with far greater rewards, when people pooled their skills and resources.

There is, therefore, a dichotomy here: *individual* self-help was the way in which the middle class articulated its vision of a well-ordered society of independent individuals; yet it was *collective* self-help that ordinary workers turned to in order to defend themselves against the privations brought about by misfortune and market conditions. The philosophy extolled the individual, but the practice enforced the collective. What is more, its natural development was political and contentious, as Koditschek makes clear in his study of class formation in Bradford: 'For . . . impoverished and alienated workers who were being stripped of the material foundations of independence and reduced to a common proletarianized state, self-help was not something that could be achieved by individuals; it was something that had to be collectively won for their class.'[13] The self-help creed and the culture of voluntarism simply show the contrasting ways in which the classes adapted to the needs of a rapidly changing, growing population and the orthodoxies of political economy and social attitudes.

The Smilesian ideal was also reflected in government policy. In the century before 1914 very little legislative provision was made for the vagaries of working-class life: unemployment, want, sickness and death. Yet the state was not inactive in either the social or economic spheres; Herbert Spencer, for example, lamented its looming presence as early as the mid-1850s, and a succession of acts of parliament attested to the growing gap between the ideal and the reality of laissez-faire. But self-help dominated the provision of welfare until the 1880s, when Smiles's critics on the left – thinkers such as the Fabians and writers like Henry George and Arnold Toynbee – began to question the utility of the acquisitive society and to ask why poverty and progress marched together. Recruitment for the Boer War (1899–1902) illustrated the unhealthy and undernourished state of the working class, in response to which a clutch of legislation under the reforming Liberal administration that took office at the end of 1905 saw the introduction of school meals, basic old-age pensions, and a limited and uneven system of national insurance. But these early signs of a creeping welfarism were driven by unease about the efficiency of British society in the wake of German and American competition, and a fear of political extremism, rather than by any sea-change in the level of commitment to state intervention. Meanwhile, the long struggle of the Boer War, and its effects in exposing the physical weakness of so many workers, led to a frenzy of self-analysis which ended with the blaming of the working class for shortcomings in the nation's economic and social life.[14]

For the most part, the working class remained responsible for its own economic well-being. In times of hunger, when unemployment bit hard, or when a breadwinner was struck down by an industrial accident, it was not the state which came to the working family's aid. Indeed, Royle has suggested that 'as a proportion of their resources, the poor were their own greatest benefactors'.[15] When working people needed help it very largely came from their families and friends, or from the network of pawnshops which played a vital role in all working-class communities. Yet what working-class communities did for themselves is almost as elusive to the historian as the 'penny capitalism' with which many tried to supplement or indeed replace waged labour.[16] Both Conservatives and Liberals remained committed to a policy of non-intervention underpinned by the ethos of self-help; even if the left saw Smiles as a joke figure by 1900, they did not represent a majority view and were far from influential in the area of social reform.

A desire for change was becoming widespread in the Edwardian period, as social investigators, notably Booth and Rowntree, and writers such as Jack London, began to uncover the true extent of poverty in Britain. But the true potential of state intervention would not be seen for several decades. In spite of the Royal Commission on the Poor Laws and Relief of Distress (1905–9), the 'principles of 1834' were not formally abandoned by the Liberal government. It should not therefore be over-looked that, while much notable social legislation was enacted in the period before 1914 (acts that regulated conditions in mines, factories and workshops, conferred legal status on trade unions, aimed at better public health and housing provision, and so forth), the state's encour-agement of friendly societies, co-operatives and other such associations had a particular impact on the culture and consciousness of the working class.

'Civilising' the Working Class

When considering the issues of self-improvement and self-help, it is important not to mistake the intentions of legislators for outcomes realised by ordinary people. Many of the movements and societies considered here were initially based upon a middle-class ideal of what constituted good and responsible behaviour, but working-class members often carried a very different vision into practice. Golby and Purdue argue that the earlier attempts to 'reform' and 'improve' working-class habits – for example the mechanics' institutes and working men's clubs – were 'overt and often clumsy'.[17] As a result, tensions between middle-class images and working-class realities were often apparent from the start. Nowhere is this more notable than in the history of the Working Men's Club and Institute movement. These clubs developed in the 1850s and 1860s because exist-ing mechanics' institutes failed to recruit enough members, and because of the need to impose a more generalised form of self-improvement and education upon a working class that had so far resisted 'useful knowledge' and scientific education.

The first institute appeared in Brighton in 1848, but disappeared in 1851 because its founder opposed the discussion of politics in favour of poetry and literature. However, F. D. Maurice, the Christian Socialist and radical educationist, noted that 'the subject of Politics has an interest for a large body of English workmen which no other subject has'.[18] Politics, therefore, should not be excluded for fear of alienating the working class but should instead be linked into the wider context of study. The movement achieved a necessary and permanent focus in 1862 when the Working Men's Club and Institute Union (CIU) was founded under the aegis of Reverend Henry Solly, a man committed to improvement through education and rational recreation. By founding the CIU, he hoped to promote new clubs and consolidate those already in existence. 'Thus', Price noted, 'Solly came to a position where the elevation of the working classes could be accomplished by the provision of recreation within a civilised environment' – the working men's club. While Solly sounded a religious and moral note, he did not demand that proselytism be part of the plan; it was his expectation, however, that 'Christianity would result from the effects of the "club spirit"'. Solly went about the business of collecting funds for the CIU with a missionary's zeal. Henry Fawcett, the blind MP, introduced Solly to his wife as the man 'who believes that Heaven consists of working men's clubs'.[19]

Solly's CIU ideal was clear; but how did it appear in practice? What outcome did the men themselves envision? Working-class men who had the wherewithal and time to run clubs and societies could hardly be expected to ignore the great political issues of their day. In expecting that it might be possible to encourage them to reflect soberly on all aspects of life except politics, Solly was being naïve. Once the institutions sprung to life, they developed an identity of their own – an identity which often conflicted with the improving and benign vision of the philanthropists. There is no doubt, however, that many who joined their local institute had in mind some sort of self-fulfilment; and this was encouraged by the wide range of newspapers, magazines and books which these institutes bought, as well as by the classes, discussions and lectures which were available on the premises. Yet education played a minor role next to the club's social function. Temperance may have prevailed in some branches, and certainly dominated Solly's thinking, but it was much more common for a club to supply alcohol. Indeed, when the drink issue was dropped, the movement became more successful. Prior to the national movement achieving financial solidity in the 1880s, the health of the club movement rested mostly on the generosity of local philanthropists, and the national body of the CIU was dominated by aristocratic and middle-class leaders, with the clubs themselves holding only 11 of 46 seats at the outset.[20]

There is little question that the club movement embodied the bourgeois Victorian ideal of acceptable pastime pursuits. Indeed, in the words of the 1875 Friendly Societies Act, working men's clubs were defined as 'institutions for social intercourse, mental and moral improvement and rational recreation'.[21] In its purest form – with temperance, education and non-political pursuits at its heart – the CIU was meant to provide working-class men with an atmosphere conducive to moral and intellectual improvement. By the early twentieth century, however, the working class had seized the CIU system. What was effectively a coup in the 1880s saw the CIU central administration fall into the hands of representatives of the clubs themselves. While the opposition to middle-class control and the resistance to temperance must be noted, so, too, should the sectional divide of the CIU. The attitude of early members earned them disdain from outsiders; a sense that these men were working-class snobs with ideas above their station was not uncommon. The second Working Men's Club and Institute in Barrow-in-Furness, for example, which was opened in the 1870s, made little impression on the drink culture of the town's workers, attracting far fewer members than its chief benefactor, H. W. Schneider, a local industrialist, had intended. The supposed pretensions of its membership earned the club a nickname, 'the House of Lords', which stuck until the 1990s, when it folded. CIU clubs often were divided by neighbourhood and by trade, with shipbuilders, iron-workers, railwaymen, miners and many other occupational groups having their own clubs. There was a strong element of social control in the working men's club movement, with the middle class at first dominating its centres of power. But, as Price suggests, working-class members saw through the motives of their superiors and were able, as time went by, to negotiate a position of greater independence. By the early 1900s, the CIU club had become a centre of Labour politics; club committee men tended also to be shop stewards; Labour Party activists and councillors drank in these clubs and used their committee rooms to discuss their political business. By 1914 the billiard-room revolution was complete, and the influence of the philanthropists, reformers and enlightened employers, who had first funded the clubs, had been eradicated.

One important function of the CIU clubs had been the promotion of education. The furnishing of reading rooms as well as bars, and the promotion of lectures as well as cheap beer, is illustrative of the self-improvement ethos that united the better-off working men of Victorian Britain. Education was a means to end poverty, intemperance and immoral behaviour. The problem was clear to W. Stanley Jevons, professor of political economy and noted logician, who wrote in 1866 that 'the ignorance, improvidence and brutish drunkenness of our lower working class must be dispelled by a general system of education, which may effect for a future generation what is hopeless for the present generation'.[22] During the Victorian years scores of pseudo-anthropological studies of working-class life were undertaken which, among other things, expressed the need for education; although, some, such as Leifchild's examination of Britain's mining communities in 1856, apparently found examples of the working class helping themselves to education. One of the differences between English and Scots colliers, Leifchild felt, was that the latter 'scorn to read the penny and two-penny publications current in other places. They are ready, after their work, to read and enjoy a chapter of [Adam Smith's] the "Wealth of Nations".'[23] The advancement of one group, however, exposed the indiscipline of others. Leifchild continued:

> on the other hand, the English pitmen who are readers and students are quite the exception. Adam Smith's works are a rarity. English miners seldom attack a book that requires steady thinking, or a work on logic, or mathematics (though *some* in the north pursue mathematics zealously). The Scotch often study both, and in such books as Watts' Logic, &c.[24]

While Leifchild shows a barely believable intimacy with the reading habits of the working man, it is his attitude, rather than the veracity of what he wrote, that is illuminating. Leifchild perceived both an absence of reading, and a deplorable level in the quality of such reading as did occur. The link between education and self-improvement was clear to men such as this. The groundswell for reform can be seen in successive legislative interventions in this period: in 1830, working-class children received at most rudimentary education in church and dame schools (the latter being the working class's own schools, characterised by the teacher, often an old 'dame'). Yet, by 1900, a system of compulsory elementary education was being provided by the state. Despite the reforms, working people (especially men) continued to take their own educational needs seriously. Until later in the century, many adults did not benefit from state reforms, while the provision of elementary education – the '3 Rs' – up to the age of ten or eleven merely left others thirsting for a greater knowledge. Part of this need was met through working-class networks in clubs and societies, such as the mechanics' institutes. Men benefited from this system in a way that women could not. Education was, Vincent has argued, a commodity to be purchased like any other;[25] when times were hard, it had to be jettisoned in favour of bread, but it is less than likely that education was ever really set directly against the widening range of consumer goods that were becoming available by the end of the century; the majority of working people had to wait until after the Second World War for their own consumer revolution to take effect.[26] While men were continually exposed to the need for literacy – at work, in the pub or during other social activities – women had much less time and too many domestic distractions to guarantee that levels of literacy, attained in childhood, would be maintained throughout adult life. Thus, while working-class people viewed education as healthy, self-improving and therefore desirable, it was usually better-paid skilled men, not women and labourers, who had the networks to meet this need. The sort of educational opportunities provided by the club or chapel were, on the whole, informal and of limited utility, and tended to 'improve' the recipient morally or spiritually rather than financially.

However, some working men did go on from lowly backgrounds to higher economic status, with education proving to be a crucial rung on the ladder. Others also benefited from the availability of cheap literature in a largely autodidactic fashion. From the ranks of these self-educated men came a class of what Gramsci called 'organic intellectuals', men who were at the forefront of emerging class organisations such as trade unions. More mundane aspects of education were also developing in this period. In the 1870s and 1880s, for example, new civic colleges were rising up in the big cities – Manchester, Newcastle and Sheffield, among many others – and would later be founding institutions of the new provincial universities. These educational initiatives were partly intended to stave off the American and German challenges to Britain's industrial hegemony by improving the quality of technical education. It is unlikely that working men benefited from this tier of education. Although some men could move from the shop floor to the engineer's office, most men were denied such significant degrees of upward mobility. Education remained an important ideal, as did technical skills which people were quick to acknowledge. But the most direct way of improving an individual's economic position was through mutualism and a collectivist ethos.

Economic Mutualism

Voluntary societies and collective self-help organisations had their roots in the eighteenth century. Many of the most famous examples, such as the Whig Green Ribbon Club and the Kit Kat Club, were exclusive in membership and political in disposition. The majority tended to be small and localised (in 1783 Birmingham alone had scores of them),[27] and were often restricted to given trades in a specific location (for example, the silk-weavers of Spitalfields, London). Victorian organisations were larger, more numerous and less localised, although the small, independent societies continued to prosper. By the later nineteenth century, greater population mobility had led to the creation of national networks which enabled workers to transfer their membership from place to place as the motions of labour migration dictated. Of all the various forms which these groups took, the most important was the friendly society.

Friendly societies

Although associational aspects of working-class life, such as friendly societies, have not been fully studied by historians, there are exceptions. While Gosden's now 40-year-old study remains the most comprehensive treatment of the subject on a national level, Crossick's careful study of Kentish London demonstrates quite clearly the multifaceted importance of collective, economic self-help among the artisan communities of Woolwich, Deptford and Greenwich.[28]

The first legislation to protect and promote friendly societies was passed in 1793, an important year in what were politically turbulent times. The words of the act indicated that friendly societies were viewed as a positive influence among working men. The idea of clubbing together to ward off the economic impact of sickness, injury and death, it was suggested, 'is likely to be attended with very beneficial effects, by promoting the happiness of individuals, and at the same time diminishing the public burthens'.[29] Many other acts were passed in the nineteenth century to assist people who wished to form friendly societies, and these were consolidated by a single, annually renewable act, the Friendly Societies Act of 1850, which was made permanent in 1875. This act outlined the basis upon which any number of individuals could form a society; it made rules concerning subscriptions, rules and registrations; most importantly, it also required treasurers to submit a bond to protect the society's funds from embezzlement. Whereas before the 1850 act local authorities had been responsible for registering friendly societies, the creation of a national registry also saw the appearance of a department for administering the act and a full-time paid registrar, Tidd Pratt being the first. With the growth of friendly societies (21 819 were voluntarily registered in 1872), Pratt's workload also expanded. What is more, his work touched on all manner of organisations as they were brought under the friendly society legislation. Thus, as Gosden states, 'Whether a man joined a savings bank, a friendly society or a trade union, shopped at the co-operative store or bought his house through a building society, the Registrar's certificate would follow him.' This was recognised by the Royal Commission on Friendly Societies, in its fourth report of 1874, which went as far as to state that Pratt had emerged as 'the embodiment of the goodwill and protection of the state, in all that goes beyond the police, the poor law, justice and the school'.[30] In legislating in favour of such institutions, smoothing their passage and protecting their members, the state was indulging in the sort of intervention that even Adam Smith or David Ricardo might have concurred with.

The most important friendly societies were the affiliated orders. These were highly organised, successful and of national importance. In the mid-Victorian years over 30 friendly societies had more than 1000 members, and in all over 1.2 million people were registered as being affiliated. The Manchester Unity of the Independent Order of Oddfellows was the most powerful affiliated friendly society with 426 663 members; the Ancient Order of Foresters was in second place with 388 872. The origins of the Oddfellows is cloaked in mystery. One of the order's historians, R. W. Moffrey, claimed that 'there is a filament of truth' to the claim that the Oddfellows movement had been introduced to Britain by Roman soldiers, though a more orthodox explanation dates it to the formation of the Abercrombie lodge, Salford, in 1810.[31] The growth of the Oddfellows after this date was spectacular, reflecting as it did the scale and pace of urban growth. Its earliest successes were in the rapidly growing city of Manchester (with Salford), but by the early 1830s it claimed to have more than 30 000 members in 561 lodges. These had burgeoned to 3500 lodges and 90 000 members by 1842. By 1845 branches of the Oddfellows existed in every county of England. Within three years, membership had soared to almost 250 000, and, though numbers

Table 5.1   The ten counties with the largest number of Oddfellows' lodges in 1845 and 1875

	1845		*1875*
Lancashire	737	Lancashire	507
Yorkshire	600	Yorkshire	444
Staffordshire	160	Middlesex	135
Cheshire	142	Cheshire	123
Warwickshire	141	Staffordshire	123
Derbyshire	134	Derbyshire	122
Lincolnshire	105	Durham	111
Durham	97	Warwickshire	98
Northumberland	93	Norfolk	96
Worcestershire	91	Leicester	82

Source: Derived from P. H. J. H. Gosden, *The Friendly Societies in England, 1815– 1875* (Manchester, 1961), table 4, p. 31.

could fall as well as rise, the half-million mark was passed in 1876. Membership patterns usually (though not always) reflected the development of urban society. Thus, Rutland had only five lodges in 1845 and four in 1875, Huntingdon 10 and 8 and Westmorland 21 and 17, while Lancashire had more than 700 lodges in 1845 and Yorkshire 600 (see Table 5.1).

Although notable growth occurred in the agricultural districts, the affiliated societies were always strongest in the north of England. The declining membership in many of the industrial regions, illustrated in Table 5.1, can be explained by the formation in some towns of breakaway societies during the later 1840s when internecine conflict struck the Manchester Unity.[32] The secession of lodges did not prevent the Oddfellows from continuing to prosper. By this point, friendly societies were part of the fabric of urban society, a reminder again of the mutualist aspiration of the working people. In 1874, there were 489 237 Oddfellows in Britain; by 1908, this had increased to 868 190, although the latter figure includes overseas members. In 1864, the Oddfellows drew in contributions for funerals and sickness totalling £278 971. At this time, the fund for such circumstances had reached almost £1.7 million, of which just over £200 000 was paid out. By 1908, the fund had reached £13 183 171, with some £462 026 being drawn by members or their families. These figures do not include the work of widow, orphan or juvenile societies, which were an important part of all friendly society organisations.[33]

Table 5.2   The ten counties with the largest number of Foresters' courts in 1845 and 1875

	1845		*1875*
Yorkshire	383	Middlesex	466
Lancashire	332	Yorkshire	370
Cheshire	117	Lancashire	357
Lincoln	116	Somerset	221
Middlesex	78	Kent	170
Durham	69	Surrey	151
Staffordshire	35	Cheshire	144
Warwickshire	35	Durham	136
Derbyshire	20	Gloucester	113
Nottinghamshire	19	Norfolk	94

Source: Derived from P. H. J. H. Gosden, *The Friendly Societies in England, 1815–1875* (Manchester, 1961), table 7, p. 42.

In some respects the growth of the Ancient Order of Foresters was even more impressive than that of the Manchester Unity. From its foundation in 1845, when it claimed 65 000 members, the Foresters went on in leaps and bounds: it had topped the 100 000 mark by 1854, the quarter-million in 1863 and in 1876 had close to 500 000 members. Like the Oddfellows, the Foresters were initially strongest in Lancashire and Yorkshire, with the least industrialised counties providing least support at the outset. By 1875, every county of England had a Foresters' court, with Rutland (3), Huntingdon (7), Westmorland (7) and Oxford (8) the only ones in single figures, a pattern which was again similar to that of the Oddfellows. However, a changing geographical profile is apparent in this latter year, as Table 5.2 illustrates, with the inclusions of counties such as Kent, Surrey and Somerset suggesting that agricultural workers were more attracted to the Foresters than to the Oddfellows.

After the Manchester Unity and the Foresters, the other affiliated societies were much less important. The next five could not muster as many members as the latter organisation in 1872, and only the Grand United Order of Oddfellows and the Order of Druids had more than 50 000 members.[34]

The world of the friendly societies was complex and colourful, convivial as well as financial. Behind the impressive but somewhat mundane story of mutual funds, sickness and death payments, there was also a movement of masonic-style rituals, ceremonial garb and public expressions of

solidarity, from the evening lectures to the street parades. The clannish-
ness of these societies is shown in the lecture which new members of the
Manchester Unity received:

> The duties of Oddfellowship will always teach you to stretch out your
> hand to a brother in distress; to offer up your warmest petitions for his
> welfare; to assist him with your best counsel and advice; and to betray
> no confidence he may repose in you.[35]

But for those who were not members, movements such as Oddfellows,
Foresters and Druids were viewed with interest or suspicion. Even the
names, bizarre and exotic, added to the inquisitiveness on the outside.
There is no doubting the emphasis which members placed upon their
court or lodge. Initially, the conviviality of the friendly society was guar-
anteed because of the habit of holding meetings in pubs. As societies
became wealthier, and premises were purchased (most large towns had
an Oddfellows' Hall by the 1870s), the use of the pub declined but conviviality did not. There was some discussion concerning the use of society
funds to buy drink, but the practice of socialising with fellow members
served the same purpose in the end. Certainly, many women felt the
advantages of friendly society customs could be denuded by the indul-
gences of members. As Thomas Wright, 'journeyman engineer', recalled:

> I have frequently heard and read that married ladies in the upper
> ranks of society look with great disfavour on their husbands' clubs; but
> these ladies have, I fancy, much less cause to be opposed to club
> proceedings than the wives of many working men who (the men) are
> members of benefit societies. For the loss to a working man's wife of
> the portion of her husband's scanty and perhaps precarious earnings,
> which is spent in the society's club-room, or through the reckless spirit
> engendered by the drink imbibed there, may and often does mean an
> insufficiency of food and clothing for herself and children.[36]

The friendly society ideology even attracted converts among those
seemingly least likely to be able to afford its costs. Poor Irish Catholic
migrants, for instance, whose numbers increased dramatically at this
time, found themselves pressured by the financial as well as the religious
teachings of their Church. Fearful of the secrecy and anti-religious message of many early trade unions, the Catholic Church in Britain allied its
vigorous anti-combination message for Catholic workers to a range of

its own friendly-type services. Trade unionists were threatened with excommunication, and, at the same time, Catholic friendly societies were formed to promote a church-centred mode of self-improvement. By the late 1830s, almost all major urban centres in northern England had at least one Catholic friendly society. The Ribbon Society in addition offered a network of secular support systems for Irish Catholic migrants. Although Ribbonism was primarily noted as a political organisation dedicated to breaking up the union with Britain, its networks offered conviviality and mutualism which bound the migrants together.[37] On the other side of the sectarian divide, the Orange Order also mixed conviviality, politics and religion with a desire to meet some of the material needs of its members. The Orange Order's association with the often violent pageantry of the 'Glorious Twelfth' of July should not obscure the fact that it also exerted considerable energies on the provision of sickness and burial funds, with money sometimes being provided for tramping.

These were not the only societies providing benefits of this nature. Some trade unions developed a friendly society dimension, and enlightened employers also were known to help their workers to organise mutual societies. For instance, the Furness Railway Company's Employees' Sickness and Benefit Society was founded as early as 1855 and was still thriving in the early 1900s. Indeed, a broad spectrum of institutions offered protection from sickness and death funds; working-class men and women protected themselves from life's uncertainties by paying their weekly dues. There is no doubting the importance of these forms of organisation; the self-help ethos found its practical expression in such tightly knit, well-organised, and ultimately rich societies. Not every individual had the wherewithal to invest in this way; but by the mid-Victorian period millions of workers and their families were taking some comfort at least in the financial clout of their affiliated friendly society.

Credit and debt

Most working people spent more than three-quarters of their wages on the necessities of life: food, shelter and clothing. The vast majority of Britain's labouring population had little to spare; others gave what little they did have to the local publican. As the century wore on, an increasing proportion were able to put something aside for the future. A cycle of poverty and debt shaped many people's lives. The extent to which these savings were preserved until old age, rather than simply being eaten away in times of unemployment, is unknown. However, the demands made on philanthropic bodies and the Poor Law provide an indication. In 1870, in England and Wales, over a million paupers were relieved, mostly on an outdoor basis; throughout the entire period 1850–1914, the total never dropped below 750 000.[38] On the other hand, large sums had been accumulated; for instance in 1908, the Scottish Widows' Mutual Society had a life assurance fund of £19 million, a figure stated in its advertising literature of that year.[39] Yet, even after the First World War, few working-class men or women had much surplus income once the essentials had been taken care of. It is little wonder, therefore, that financial matters, the day-to-day grind of counting coppers, visiting pawnshops or 'tapping up' neighbours needs to be remembered along-side discussions of aspects of self-improvement such as saving and investment, for which the sources are more readily available.[40]

One of the most important of all the workers' concerns was for adequate shelter. Given the varying quality of what landlords had to offer, it is with little surprise that we learn that working-class men found occasions to group together to buy land and to buy or build houses that they themselves could own. A culture which emphasised property own-ership, while the state made so few social provisions for the working-class family, was perhaps bound to encourage collective investment in bricks and mortar. This happened with the emergence in the 1840s of Britain's first building societies.[41]

The building societies involved not so much the labouring class as the upper working class and the minor middle class, including what Samuel Smiles called 'skilled and thrifty working-class men'. This latter group 'set especial store on thrift and respectability' which they felt was 'ideally embodied in house-ownership'.[42] At first building societies were just collections of men who grouped together in order to build homes for themselves or for sale. This way, lower-middle-class tradesmen and specu-lators alike might profit from the sort of venture normally reserved for the larger speculator. First a plot of land would be bought, then houses put on it. In some cases, the members of the society simply moved in and thus ended the venture. In other cases, lots would be drawn, and houses built one at a time. If an individual was lucky, his would be the first house built; but he could also be last in the queue. These terminating building societies, as they were called, had a fixed objective: to put collective capital to work to alleviate individual limitations.[43] Permanent building societies were different; these had a long-term objective of saving and spending, both of which were interlinked. Members made deposits and interest was paid; the stock was then invested in building ventures, or home purchases, through mortgages and so on. As time went by, however, building societies became increasingly savings-orientated and thus more useful to working-class customers: this change can be seen in the fact that between 1880 and 1914 their combined share capital increased from £27.1 million to £46.5 million as their loan capital declined from £25.7 million to £15.9 million. By the inter-war period, reports on the building societies were writing of 'small savers' – individuals for whom building society investment was considered to be a risk-free venture. While it is not clear who were these relatively prosperous individuals, with their savings accounts, own homes, and friendly society insurance policies, Paul Johnson correctly suggests that, even as late as the 1930s, most investors were middle class. As a consequence, 'until 1914 the effect of building societies on the housing market was slight'. Only around ten per cent of houses were owner-occupied in that year, and a 'negligible proportion of these were owned by manual workers'.[44] The great growth period of building societies was between the wars.

Land purchase had been a sharply political issue in the 1840s when Richard Cobden had taken up the 40s freehold movement as a way of gaining votes.[45] Although the Building Societies Act (1836) prevented societies from owning land, the Birmingham Freehold Land Society, led by John Taylor, managed to get round the problem so that they could organise land purchases 'for the purpose of procuring qualifications in the County for the representation of North Warwickshire'. Four further societies were founded in 1847, with 113 in existence by 1853, 69 of which were in the provinces and 44 in the capital. The middle class was prominent in these organisations; Titus Salt was president and W. E. Forster was vice-president of the Bradford Freehold Land and Building Society, established in mid-1849. Like its Birmingham antecedent, this society aimed 'to Improve the Social, Promote the Moral, and Exalt the Political Condition of the Unenfranchised Millions'.[46] The real object was well short of universal suffrage, and the clientele was mostly drawn from the middle ranks of society – the kind of prosperous artisan, small-shopkeeper or clerk for whom £20 in land and the qualification to vote was more than an idle dream.[47] These were, Cobden argued, 'the middle and industrious classes' whom he would trust with as much political power as possible. These societies may have been an assault on landed privilege, but they were also 'a powerful means of converting thrift into consumption'.[48] Membership was also meant to be a distinguishing feature of the industrious as opposed to the dangerous classes. Indeed,

Samuel Smiles was rather smug about the effect that landownership could have upon those of a radical disposition:

> It has been said that Freehold Land Societies, which were established for political objects, had the effect of weaning men from political reform. . . . 'I know both co-operators and Chartists who were loud-mouthed for social and political reform, who now care no more for it than a Whig government; and decline to attend a public meeting on a fine night, while they would crawl like the serpent in Eden, through a gutter in a storm, after a good security. They have tasted land, and the gravel has got into their souls.'[49]

While the great majority of the working people could not afford to own their own homes in 1914, there had always been a few workers who found the money to invest in bricks and mortar. In the case of the Walkley district of Sheffield, for example, a writer noted in 1912:

> it goes without saying that those owning the plots and houses were the more industrious and respectable of the working classes, and this stamp of respectibility and independence is still manifest all over the district, for where the original owner survives [from the 1860s when the project began] he occupies the same house, or otherwise his progeny have taken his place.[50]

If most workers could not stretch to a small house in Walkley, many could still afford to save a little money each week. Hoarding was a common practice among working people; probably more people had money squirrelled away at home than had money in bank accounts, for throughout our period the majority of money deposited by individuals in savings banks was not placed by the working class in their accounts. Even Irish paupers were thought to have gold sovereigns stitched into the linings of their coats. Evidence of hoarding is, however, anecdotal; there is no means of quantifying the extent to which working-class people preferred the mattress or the old tea caddy to the bank or post office. Those who ventured out with their money, looking for a safe berth and a steady yield, might have tried the savings bank and the building society. The Co-operative, which is examined below, and savings clubs offered savings opportunities associated with specific purchases. Savings clubs, for example, were often run by shops, allowing the payment of regular weekly sums in order to buy expensive items. Purchases for

Christmas were often made this way, often through pub-based networks, in something akin to later catalogue shopping, the difference being that goods were not advanced until the last payment was made.

Pawnbroking was one of the most powerful images of credit and debt in the nineteenth century. The pawnshop owner looms large in popular mythology. Whether demonised as the stereotypical 'grasping Jew', or remembered more fondly as the benevolent but business-minded 'uncle' figure, the pawnshop owner evoked dread as well as offering salvation. In 1870 there were nearly 4000 pawnshops operating under licence in Britain; but the peak year was 1914 when the figure was 5087, after which the number declined. Pawnbrokers lent money against goods; wedding rings, fob-watches, furniture and even items of clothing and bedding could be pawned in return for an advance of up to £10, a limit set by an act of 1872, and interest was charged on the loans. Pawnbrokers made more from repeat transactions (where an item was pawned and redeemed every week) than from business that occurred just once over a fixed period. Although pawnbrokers had a reputation for ruthlessness, the strategy adopted by the customer determined the amount of interest accrued, though some had little control over their budgetary needs.[51] For a respectable working-class woman – and it was usually the wife's task – a visit to what was commonly termed the pop-shop was a humiliating experience, but it was a means to obtain immediately a sum of money. Nevertheless, critics felt pawnbroking was the worst form of budgeting a working-class family could indulge in because it invariably led to a spiral of increasing debt. The use of pawnbrokers was also inefficient in the sense that the loans obtained were nowhere near the value of the goods pawned.

For those with money to save – and it must be stressed that, throughout our period, these were a minority of the working class – there was a plethora of small, local banks and building societies. Among the most common banking institutions, which attracted working-class deposits, were the Trustee Savings Banks (TSB), of which there were hundreds of branches. But the most popular, and the safest, destination for small savers was the Post Office Savings Bank (POSB), which paid 2.5 per cent interest on every full pound. Working-class depositors in 1896 included members of many different occupation groups, with children and scholars (20.9 per cent), married women (13.9), artisans and mechanics (11.8) and spinsters (10.9) in the lead. As late as the 1930s, no more than one-third of depositors were weekly-waged earners.[52] Indeed, the whole area of saving and investment, house-buying and mortgages, was beyond the ordinary working man and his family. What little they had was spent, often before it was earned; that is why, for the overwhelming mass of workers, the co-operative was the most important collective self-help intervention in the century before the First World War.

The Co-operative Society

Management of the family budget was notoriously difficult when the balance of income and expenditure could be so fine. Critical factors, including death, unemployment or the birth of a child, could cause chaos for a family already finely attuned to the need for absolute frugality. While credit was something of a dirty word in the working-class argot, it was also a necessity for many. Mothers had to feed their families, and if the money caddy was empty two days before pay day, something had to be done. It is small wonder, then, that in early industrial towns, in the 1830s and early 1840s, prior to the spread of co-operative stores, chandlers' shops were very popular. Advancing goods on credit, these shops provided a bridge between one pay day and the next. Many of the shopkeepers who ran these outfits were unscrupulous; debt held customers in thrall so that short weight and adulteration were accepted with a mixture of reluctance and resignation. The truck system of payment added to working-class woes in this respect. It was estimated that in the early part of this period one-quarter of all earnings were paid in truck – tickets that could be exchanged for goods, particularly food, at the local 'tommy shop'. There was a widespread apprehension among working men that 'tommy shop' food was overpriced and low in quality.[53] This is the system against which the co-operative system was pitched.

Like the friendly societies, co-operation had roots in an earlier period.[54] Co-operation meant different things to different people, from workers' collectives and model communities, on the one hand, to retailing for the common good on the other. The truck system had been roundly condemned before the emergence of the modern co-operative store, not least by socialists such as Robert Owen, who imagined co-operative producers up and down the country working for the collective good. But this form of communitarian co-operation achieved only the barest breath of life in the 1820s and early 1830s, in what one authority described as 'the brief Middle Ages of co-operation'.[55] Efforts to thwart the truck system also saw the advent of co-operative-type shops in these years, but there were significant obstacles to their progress. Employers often opposed such manifestations of working-class independence, and threatened workers who sought to abandon truck stores which the employers themselves often owned. Truck wages were cheaper than money wages and the least well-organised workers were usually those who suffered most by its regimen. Thus women's wages were even more likely to be paid in truck than men's. One female weaver told Lord Ashley's Select Committee that she had received only 1s in cash, and the rest in truck, for a full year's work. Criticism of consumer co-operation also came from the radical wing. Robert Owen, for example, was a noted critic. His utopian socialism was based upon a loftier vision than shopping; he was a socialist, an advocate of communitarianism[56] – model communities working for themselves – and he felt that storekeeping was unworthy of the name 'co-operation'. Owenism embraced the principle of co-operation and rejected the competitive individualism so bound up with early industrialism. Yet the movement still developed away from Owenism – going 'from community building to shopkeeping'[57] – as the century progressed.

The co-operative retailing system emerged in its modern sense in 1844 at Toad Lane in Rochdale, when 28 working men opened their now legendary store. These men were concerned with the issue of working-class consumption – what people ate and what they paid for it. They were inspired by the words of George Jacob Holyoake, who, in an attack on the truck and 'tommy' systems, had captured the essential need for co-operation:

> Anybody can see that the little money you get is half-wasted, because you cannot spend it to advantage. The worst food comes to the poor, which their poverty makes them buy, and their necessity makes them eat. Their stomachs are the waste-baskets of the State. It is their lot to swallow all the adulteration of the market.[58]

The idea of the 'Rochdale Pioneers' was to buy good-quality, simple foodstuffs at wholesale prices, thus cutting out the middleman and obviating adulteration. Cash purchases were vital, because such a modest concern could not provide credit. The idea caught on, and by the 1850s there were scores of similar societies. By the 1860s and 1870s virtually every industrial town had a co-operative store. The store was not exclusively the domain of the labour aristocracy, though its opposition to credit undoubtedly excluded some of the poorer members of the working class. Yet in Cumbria Irish iron-ore miners were among the most fervent of the movement's supporters. The co-operative movement was parti-cularly successful in the North and Midlands. By the end of the century co-operative stores were often the most impressive buildings on the main streets of most northern industrial towns. By this time, the co-operative store had expanded its trade to include coal, furniture and other house-hold goods. A considerable departure had taken place in 1862 with the formation of the Co-operative Wholesale Society, which sought to enable bulk provisioning with even less of a threat from the middleman. There were also other ventures on the production side, such as a biscuit and sweets factory at Crumpsall in Manchester, which was opened in February 1873.

The co-operative retail outlets emphasised both spending and saving, the latter linked to the former. Profit was not a motive, although the co-operative dividend – a payment of society profits – was paid annually to all members in proportion to their expenditure. Many working-class people were able to leave some of these dividends with the society, accu-mulating interest. The Co-operative Wholesale Society inaugurated its own bank in the 1870s, but did not encourage small account holders. By 1914 it had only a few hundred depositors, a tiny number compared to the Post Office Savings Bank, which had more than 8.5 million accounts, almost 80 per cent of which were under £25. By 1919, the figure for co-operative investors had reached 15 516, a still insignficant total.[59]

At the outset, the co-operative decision not to give credit clearly denied the shops certain custom and therefore members. Some of the poorest in society remained chained, if not to the truck shop, then to the independent trader, who granted them credit and held their slate. For these people, it was unlikely that the cycle of debt was ever broken by switching over to the co-operative, and, in times of hardship, the safety net would have been provided by the pawnbroker. Not all co-operative societies, however, remained as unwavering on the question of credit. By the turn of the century, credit was being given in many places, despite protestations from the centre, because the vagaries of the market required as much.

Regional factors also influenced the strengths and weaknesses of the movement. Co-operation was strongest where competition was least. It enjoyed particular support in Lancashire and Yorkshire, where it grew earliest and largest. The North-East of England also had a strong co-operative tradition, especially within the mining villages.[60] Similar observations can be made of the coal and iron regions of Cumbria; in this isolated area there was usually no store other than the co-operative.

In these areas members received a higher dividend, because weak or non-existent competition meant the co-operators could set higher market prices. In London, competition was fierce, margins were tighter, and, therefore, dividend yields were much lower.

Working-class self-help was undoubtedly at its most impressive in the co-operative movement. Friendly societies and the Post Office Savings Bank also had hundreds of thousands of members, but nothing reflected the associational culture of the British working-class like the co-operative movement. Its stores were deeply embedded in the language and lives of millions of ordinary people countrywide. It had travelled some considerable distance from it millenarian roots to arrive at this position, but that does not necessarily mean it acquiesced to the dominant ideologies of the age. Even if its Owenite anti-capitalist phase of the 1820s had passed, this does not represent a blanket acceptance of 'the middle-class embrace'. Indeed, as Peter Gurney argues, co-operative forms seem to have been contested until the First World War.[61] Although co-operation was undoubtedly suffused with the language of middle-class respectability – Samuel Smiles saw it as the 'secret of social development'[62] – it was also a signal of the extent to which a collective vision could deliver something that was independent and of lasting worth. What is more, throughout our period, the co-operative system continued to grow, playing a still greater role in the economic lives of the working class of Britain. It was 18 337-strong in 1864, and had more than 400 000 members by 1883. In the decade that followed, membership numbers doubled, and continued to grow almost as rapidly, reaching nearly 2.3 million in 1913, 3.2 million in 1923 and more than 6 million in 1937.[63]

Drink, Temperance and the Quest for Respectability

For many Victorians, drink defined morality. Abstainers, especially those who joined temperance societies, viewed indulgence in alcohol as a threat to the mortal soul of the individual; families and communities were thought to be threatened by the effects of heavy drinking, although social reformers implicitly acknowledged the problem of low wages when arguing that a balanced working-class budget left no room for significant amounts of drinking. Drink was, therefore, a dangerous luxury: working men were better off without it and women should avoid it altogether. In crusading against drink, the temperance movement underpinned the Smilesian belief in the importance of a clear mind; self-education required restraint and was not aided by the dulling after-effects of intoxicating liquor. Smiles himself saw life as a series of temptations to be rebuffed, drink being one of the worst. He remembered how Hugh Miller, the geologist, had remarked upon the potential hazards:

> Hugh Miller has told how by an act of youthful decision, he saved himself from one of the strong temptations so peculiar to a life of toil. When employed as a mason, it was usual for his fellow-workmen to have an occasional treat of drink, and one day two glasses of whisky fell to his share, which he swallowed. When he reached home, he found, on opening his favourite book – 'Bacon's Essays' – that the letters danced before his eyes so that he could no longer master the sense. 'The condition', he says, 'into which I had brought myself was, I felt, one of degradation. I had sunk, by my own act, for the time, to a lower level of intelligence than that on which it was my privilege to be placed. . . . I in that hour determined that I should never again sacrifice my capacity of intellectual enjoyment to a drinking usage; and, with God's help, I was enabled to hold the determination.'[64]

The message was clear: drinkers and abstainers were as different as masons and geologists; what is more, the drinking mason could never become a great geologist. This link was not lost on those who preached, or those who were persuaded by, the anti-drink message. Evidence suggests, too, that the abstainers were usually a very particular breed of the new working class, with Methodism, trade unionism, Chartism and Co-operative membership often going hand in hand. This was the case even among Britain's infamously heavy-drinking Irish population. Their main religion, Catholicism, threw up one of the century's most influential and hard-working temperance crusaders, Fr Theobald Mathew, who issued the pledge to thousands of (usually short-term) converts at meetings in places as far afield as Dublin, London and New York. Robert Crowe, the Chartist tailor, remembered mixing his radical politics and a commitment to Mathew's temperance cause with support for Daniel O'Connell's home-rule movement.[65]

The abstainer was, as a rule, generally skilled; he and his family sought to make sense of the world through spiritual and moral improvement, education and self-help; by engaging in respectable pastimes and by limiting their expressions of pleasure. Such families were nonconformists in more than just a religious sense. In their commitment to Adam's ale, water, rather than beers and spirits, they were in a minority.

In both 1830 and 1914 the public house remained the focal point of working-class leisure. Towns and cities teemed with pubs; drunkenness and drink-related violence were commonplace. Women who drank in public were often frowned upon by moral reformers and by the more abstemious among their own class. Drink became one of the most criticised aspects of popular culture, and perhaps the dividing point of 'rough' and 'respectable' cultures.[66] Drink may have condemned thousands of families to poverty (as Booth and Rowntree argued in their surveys later in the period) but, by rejecting its appeal, another portion of the working class was able to convince their social superiors that not all members of the same class succumbed to the same temptations. In the rural setting, pubs allowed members of far-flung communities to socialise and to exchange information. The Anglican Church was neither opposed to pubs, nor threatened by them; indeed the two institutions have been described as in some ways complementary, with parsons selling church ales, and publicans favouring the Church of England and supporting the Conservative Party.[67]

The churches were the forefront of the urban campaign against drink. From the 1830s, an evangelical zeal swept the temperance movement along: societies such as the Band of Hope, the Independent Order of Rechabites, the Temperance League, the Order of the Sons of Temperance and the Total Abstinence League sprang up across the country, preaching moral enlightenment and social and moral improvement through the renunciation of 'John Barleycorn', the 'demon drink'. Most of these societies were more than instruments of moral reform and self-education; they also had a friendly dimension attached, registered and protected under the law governing such societies as the Oddfellows, sharing together an abstemious mixture of fruit cordial and life assurance.

Temperance halls were among the earliest and most impressive buildings in the burgeoning industrial towns, but their physical presence and social function were tiny next to that of the scores of public houses that might be found within a square mile or so of most town centres. The ratio of pubs to people was often higher in old towns than in the new. In 1854 the Furness market town of Ulverston had one pub for every 129 inhabitants, whereas in 1866 in the nearby boom town of Barrow, the figure was 1240. The new towns also tended to be more boisterous and drunken, partly because of the high proportion of young males among the population. A local Congregationalist temperance supporter was shocked to note that in 1873 Barrovians had spent £208 000 on drink.[68] Attempts to quantify the number of people making use of the pub simply exacerbated the horrors for the anti-drink lobby. This was certainly the case in 1854 when a study by the Manchester and Salford Temperance Association indicated that over a period of ten Sundays 120 124 men, 71 609 women and 23 585 children entered enumerated pubs.[69]

Drink versus temperance remained a common dividing line during this period and was, as such, an important determinant of the nature and extent of the working-class community. Drunkenness and the related incidence of poverty formed part of the language of moral self-improvement in this age. Although pubs remained deeply embedded in the language of working-class organisation and identity, they were also an aspect of popular culture which moral reformers wished to eradicate.

For temperance crusaders, it was a truism that a man who drank could not serve his family to the best of his abilities. Every drink was a waste of labour and of money; as he drained the glass, he drained his soul as well as the family budget. It also seemed to stand to reason that a man who spent his spare cash in the pub could not at the same time save for old age or death, infirmity or unemployment. While organising land- (and thus vote-) purchasing schemes for the working-class and lower-middle-class men in Warwickshire, the Birmingham radical and reformed drinker, John Taylor, argued that 'every time a man drinks a quart of ale he engulphs at the same time a yard of solid earth'.[70] The term 'respectable', when applied to the working class, meant those who imbibed middle-class values rather than drink.[71]

Summary

The combined effect of these clubs, societies and associations was enormous. Although they are not without earlier precedents, they grew particularly purposefully in the nineteenth century. In different ways, the movements and aspirations discussed in this chapter represent the coming together of a number of requirements of working-class life. First, they suggest a certain degree of accommodation within the overarching system of capitalism, which in turn derives partly from a second factor, the day-to-day needs of ordinary working people. Despite these aspects, however, a third impulse which can be noticed is a general notion of class, or at least of belonging to a status group with shared expectations and experiences. The boom-and-slump nature of industrial capitalism and the vagaries of urban social life had a particularly acute effect on what radicals often called the productive classes; and the need for collective responses to both individual and group problems was emphasised by the practical limitations of laissez-faire and self-help. Friendly societies, trade unions, the co-operative and a plethora of other institutions provided funds for the protection of members; clubs, pubs and neighbours formed an intricate web of mutual support and collective self-help which underpinned the idea of community within working-class lives. Independent identities were not smothered by a system of accommodation and reform; they were enforced and sharpened through the same networks. Clubs and associations entered the social life of the ordinary man and his family, and they provided help for the unemployed, the sick and the widowed.

While a destitute Oddfellow could expect help from his lodge, most of the men and women who experienced the extreme privations of long-term poverty never enjoyed those periods of calm or prosperity which might allow provision to be made for even more acute misfortune than might be ecountered on a daily basis. Thus, when we address the widespread and important phenomenon of associationalism, especially those dimensions beyond the co-operative, we are mainly referring to the prosperous working class – a group who, as Disraeli observed in the 1870s, had achieved a genuine stake in society:

> The hon. Gentleman the member for Birmingham talks of the working classes as if they were paupers ... I protest against that description. The working classes are not paupers; on the contrary, they are a very wealthy class – they are the wealthiest in the country. Their aggregate income is certainly greater than any other class; their accumulations are to be counted by millions; and I am not speaking merely of the deposits in savings banks, but of funds of which I am aware they are in possession, and which are accumulated to meet their trade necessities and to defend their labour and rights, which can also be counted by millions; and therefore I protest against that language ... that the great body of the working classes in this country are in a state of pauperism.[72]

Although Disraeli's argument is specious, given the size of the working class, there is a modicum of truth in what he said: some of the working class – especially better-off male artisans – were indeed displaying their collective financial clout. The networks of mutual help, the need or the impulse for ordinary men and women to collectivise the self-help ethos of the day, did in the end make an indelible mark upon the country.

This mark was partly financial, but it was also a mark made upon the middle-class conscience – an acknowledgement upon the part of Disraeli's class that the class below was not simply a brutalised mass.

Did these things elevate the working class in accordance with bourgeios ideology, or was this an age of achievement delineated by the working man's vision of his own world? Working people followed middle-class directions when the message was palatable; but rejection was soon at hand if the sacrifice seemed to exceed the new-found benefits. This was certainly the experience of the temperance movement. Most working people arrived at the common sense (in both the literal and Gramscian sense) of mutualism by their own twisted route; they did not need the philanthropist or the moral reformer to tell them that associations of like-minded people got along better than unfettered individuals. For the middle class, these movements represented the civilising of society; for workers, the message was one of solidarity and collective empowerment. 'Consumer consciousness and class consciousness', Peter Gurney has persuasively argued of the co-operative movement, 'were intimately bound up with each other.'[73] This was true of a host of organisations in which the working class took the raw materials of a middle-class vision and shaped it to their own ends. In one important sense, therefore, the mechanisms of self-help afforded people space and a little security to think about the world on their own terms. Financial independence could lead to other forms of independence, not least in the arena of politics.

But what difference did building society accounts, club membership and co-operative shopping really make? While mutualism and the culture of associationalism strengthened the group identity of miners, ship-builders, engineers, millworkers, and a whole host of better-paid, skilled workers, it did little for the day labourer or the dockside casual. At the same time, no group, except the very poor, was universally or permanently excluded from the right to self-help or its benefits. In a much wider sense, however, key continuities remained in place. Writing of Britain over 50 years ago, Cole and Postgate argued that: 'two nations confronted each other in 1946, though much less starkly than in the days of Chartists when Disraeli wrote *Sybil*. . . . The great majority of those who died still had almost nothing to leave to their successors.'[74] If this had been the situation immediately after the Second World War it was even more so on the eve of the First. But, without labour's associational and mutalist tendencies, life would have been far bleaker.

6

CONFLICT AND CONCILIATION

Introduction

Man is, in the phrase associated with Aristotle, a political animal. In the wider sense, such is the case. Yet in most societies those active in the politics of parties and organisations have been a small minority. The reasons for this vary, but with regard to Britain in the period between 1830 and 1914, one explanation lies in the narrow franchise. The majority of adult men and all women were excluded from voting in parliamentary elections. Those left outside the political system, preoccupied as they were by the day-to-day concerns of work and family, often lacked the time and energy to challenge the forces of oligarchy. Moreover, the minority who held political power had developed a series of arguments in favour of retaining it. In particular, the rights of property were built into the electoral system. The unelected House of Lords was largely the preserve of substantial landowners, while membership of the Commons depended on the votes of a ratepaying electorate. Further, Members of Parliament tended towards the view, famously expressed by Edmund Burke, that their duty was to advance national, not local, interests. As representatives, rather than delegates, there was no reason why they should heed what they saw as the prejudices of their electors.[1]

This situation led to several vigorous movements to reform Parliament. As we noted in our introduction, the early 1830s were a vital period in the history of labour, with the agitation for parliamentary reform of decisive importance. Indeed, the Reform Act of 1832, which confirmed the exclusion of the working class, strengthened rather than satisfied the demand for a wider franchise. The sense that members of the middle class had exploited the threat of unrest to gain representation

144

for themselves, but had then abandoned those without the new property qualifications, gave impetus to the agitation. In reality, although in 1832 the size of the electorate in England and Wales increased from an estimated 435 000 to 653 000, at a time when the adult male population was above 3.5 million, the existing structure of political power was not drastically changed; the new electorate 'was neither radical nor tory: it was conservative'.[2] Older, aristocratic elites remained powerful in government, while continuing to accommodate representatives of the newer commercial and manufacturing interests. Among the country's rulers, there was a general view that the Reform Act had made a necessary but final adjustment to the electoral system. Such, however, was not the view of radical reformers. In the 1830s and 1840s, much of their fire was directed at the 'shopocrats' and millocrats' who had conspired to deprive the workers of their political rights, and were also exploiting them economically.

These grievances were sharpened, moreover, by the policies of the Whig governments that held office from 1830 to 1834 and 1835 to 1841. Probably the most resented of these was the Poor Law Amendment Act of 1834. This seemed to criminalise poverty: the workhouse – not a new institution, but more generally deployed – was widely identified with the prison. Furthermore, the Anatomy Act of 1832, also inspired by a Benthamite quest for rational efficiency, allowed paupers' corpses to be used for medical dissection. Previously, anatomists had battled with the crowd attending executions to secure the corpses of the hanged – one notorious riot followed the hanging of the celebrated criminal Jack Sheppard.[3] Now, poor law officials were empowered quietly to dispose of dead paupers, thus apparently equating poverty with crime.[4]

Another aspect of the period that antagonised workers was the state's attitude towards collective action. In spite of the repeal of the Combination Acts a decade earlier, there remained widespread hostility among the governing classes towards trade unions. The trial and transportation in 1834 of six agricultural labourers – immortalised as the 'Tolpuddle Martyrs' – did most to create a great outcry. Though upheld by the Whig government, the convictions of poor men who had sought to act together in what they had no doubt was a legal way created a tangible sense of injustice. Petitions to Parliament and other forms of pressure led to free pardons and the return of the six to England. But in 1838 the treatment of five Glasgow cotton spinners, who were also transported, again provoked a sense of injustice.[5] The attempt to organise all sections of workers in the Grand National Consolidated Trades Union during 1834 ended in failure. Only the small craft unions, such as the 'Old Mechanics' (founded as the Journeymen Steam Engine Makers in Manchester in 1826), seemed capable of surviving, and then by taking a conciliatory approach to employers and a 'no politics' position on other questions.

These discontents found some outlet in newspapers that, because they paid no stamp duty, had to be semi-clandestine. Their price, typically 1d, was kept low by owners who refused to pay the duty of 4d per copy. Known as the 'unstamped', these papers vigorously campaigned against abuses of every type. Consequently, the government regarded the radical press as a dangerous force. In December 1819, during a period of disorder, legislation was introduced to curb newspapers 'tending to excite Hatred and Contempt of the Government and Constitution of these realms as by law established, and also vilifying our holy religion'.[6] Magistrates vigorously imprisoned vendors, who were usually too poor to pay fines, while some of the better-known publishers were convicted. William Carpenter, John Cleave, Henry Hetherington and James Watson were all sentenced to spells in prison during the early 1830s. This pressure either to price or prosecute the radical press out of existence became itself another source of grievance, despite the reduction of the stamp duty to 1d in 1836. Together with other forms of resentment and discontent that flourished in the 1830s, it helped to create the best known labour organisation of the period.

Chartism

In 1834 an unstamped working-class newspaper commented on the case of the 'Dorchester Unionists' and the then 'fruitless efforts made for their return'. The lesson was simple:

> the people, *alias* the productive classes, *alias* the Trades' Unions, have no representative in Parliament. . . . The plain fact is, that until the people get represented, they will always be beat on votes by a House which does not represent them. In good earnest, let them pursue what they are now after – let them not neglect this – but let them also add to it universal suffrage and vote by ballot.[7]

Reformers had long called for an extension of the franchise (though many limited this to male suffrage) and 'the ballot', by which was meant voting in secret to reduce the danger of intimidation. Other proposals that attracted radical support by the 1830s were the abolition of a property qualification for MPs, as well as for electors, so that poor men might stand for, as well as vote in, parliamentary elections, and the payment from public funds of MPs' salaries. This latter would not only facilitate the candidature of workers' representatives, it was also intended to give MPs more independence. Radicals saw the legislature as mired in the 'Old Corruption', a spoils system of sinecures, placemen and bribery with the power to compromise even the well-intentioned. Further, it was necessary to sweep away pocket or rotten boroughs where a small number of electors could be bribed or otherwise pressured to vote for a particular candidate. The most notorious of such constituencies had been abolished by the Reform Act, but several small boroughs with fewer than three hundred electors kept their MPs. Equal electoral districts were the reformers' remedy for this imbalance. To ensure greater accountability to the electorate, there was also widespread support for the life of a parliament to be one year (seven years was the constitutional maximum).

These proposals, which had been favoured by reformers for many years, were linked together as the 'six points' of the People's Charter, the mass movement to petition Parliament. The willingness to seek redress by constitutional means is a feature of organisations of labour throughout our period. This was by no means the only approach taken – the level and character of violent agitation will be assessed later in this chapter – but the belief that the House of Commons could accommodate working-class claims remained powerful and pervasive. Even the unreformed Parliament had contained members, such as Sir Francis Burdett, who were prepared to advocate a programme of reform similar to that incorporated into the People's Charter. After 1832 there was a section of the House of Commons, always a minority and only loosely grouped together, that provided at least a voice on matters of concern to the working class. Thomas Wakley, for example, had been prominent in the parliamentary campaign to gain a pardon for the Tolpuddle Martyrs. When millions of signatures had been collected in support of the Charter, there were MPs prepared to present them in the form of a petition.[8]

Moreover, those without sufficient property to qualify for a vote were not without rights. It was accepted that elections were tumultuous affairs. Candidates would court popular support at the hustings as a way of demonstrating their right to go to the poll (sometimes radicals would stand in the early stages, withdrawing on the eve of voting to avoid defeat and having to share the costs of the election). The drunkenness, mud-throwing (literally as well as figuratively) and cheering were regarded as a part of the political process; as a Tory MP told the Commons: 'Cockades and the liberty of huzzaing, were things which every Englishman admired; they contributed to give him an idea of the rights he enjoyed and on the possession of which he prized himself.'[9] Rowdy behaviour long remained a feature of elections – one argument advanced against votes for women was that the 'gentler sex' should not be exposed to such vulgarity – and was generally tolerated by all concerned. However, a more subtle form of pressure could be exerted on shopkeepers and tradesmen who had the vote but depended on working-class customers. Until voting was made secret in 1872, it was possible to keep a record of the manner in which electors cast their votes. These details were often regarded as important enough to be printed in the form of poll books. Through boycotts, or in the phrase of the time, 'exclusive dealing', those without the vote could show their disapproval of tradesmen who had supported reactionary candidates. In Rochdale, for example, a committee of non-electors applied pressure on behalf of radical Liberals. When in the general election of 1841 a shoemaker, Hamlet Nicholson, worked for the Tory candidate, the radicals encouraged two rival shoemakers to set up in the same street. His business was ruined.[10]

However, though in a few towns working men, usually with Liberal Party backing, gained election as councillors, it took many years before representatives with working-class origins were elected to the House of Commons. Until that process began in the late nineteenth century, direct workers' pressure for change was applied from outside Parliament. Only a minority denounced class collaboration, on grounds similar to those of the *London Democrat* of 1 April 1839: 'Whatever the middle classes have ever taken into hand has turned out to the people's cost to be delusive and fraudulent; therefore as the producing classes intend to regenerate their country, they must rely on themselves and themselves alone.'[11] Generally, there was an acceptance, if often guarded, of middle-class men who acted as advocates of the rights of the people. Indeed, some of these spoke with a force and bitterness that matched the most demogogic of working-class radicals. The Revd J. R. Stephens, a Methodist minister, for example, at Newcastle on New Year's Day 1838, described himself as 'a revolutionist by fire . . . a revolutionist by blood, to the knife, to the death' and in another speech declared: 'If the rights of the poor are trampled under foot, then down with the throne, down with the Aristocracy, down with the bishops, down with the clergy, burn the Church, down with all rank, all title, and all dignity.'[12]

Although a detailed account of Chartism is beyond the scope of this chapter, a number of general points have relevance to not only the movement itself but also later labour movements. First among these points is the response of the ruling order. In a well-known sentence in *The Communist Manifesto* (1848), Marx and Engels wrote: 'The executive of the modern State is but a committee for managing the common affairs of the whole bourgeoisie.' Like many of the generalisations in that brilliant tract, it is open to argument, yet the essential insight remains: with regard to the defence of property and the maintenance of law and order, the state almost automatically acted in the interests of the dominant class. Few Chartist leaders escaped spells of imprisonment. For example, J. R. Stephens received an 18-month sentence for sedition in August 1839, when he pleaded he had not been a Chartist though he had supported the Charter. In some respects, he was a Tory demagogue who hated the new industrial system, and, after imprisonment, he was less outspoken. William Lovett and John Collins spent a year in Warwick Gaol, convicted of seditious libel after denouncing the methods of the police in suppressing the Birmingham Bull Ring riots of July 1839. Though prison conditions were harsh, they were able to compose a treatise, published after their release in 1840 and attacked by militant Chartists for its advocacy of co-operation between the middle and working classes for the purpose of 'a just and legal system of education'.[13]

By the standards of the time, the prison sentences imposed on Chartists, if their offences did not go beyond inflammatory language, were not lengthy. However, in the face of violence, the state responded in kind. This was evident whenever Chartists adopted 'physical force' tactics, as in the winter of 1839/40. Within a few months, there were attempted risings in Monmouth, where early in November several thousand Chartists marched on Newport, and in Sheffield in January, when a planned insurrection was forestalled by the authorities. Some 22 deaths occurred in Newport as soldiers fired on Chartists, many of whom were armed, and subsequently the three identified as ringleaders were convicted of treason and sentenced to hanging followed by dismemberment. Shortly before their executions, their sentences were commuted to transportation. Samuel Holberry, the leader of the planned rising in Sheffield, was convicted of lesser charges, for which he received four years in prison; so severe were conditions there, including a spell on the treadmill, that they contributed to his death in 1842.[14]

Similarly, the authorities acted to repress the wave of Chartist activity associated with the agitation for a general strike in 1842. For a number of years, radicals had promoted the idea that as labour was the basis of all wealth, and as the existing system deprived workers of their true rewards, collective action was needed. William Benbow had famously, but not for the first time, made the case in a widely read pamphlet of 1832, *Grand National Holiday and Congress of the Productive Classes*. More militant Chartists sought to deploy the weapon of a general strike, which was sometimes referred to as a 'national holiday' that would last for a 'sacred month'. Some Chartists linked up with strikers who, to resist wage reductions in manufacturing districts, were attacking factories. These actions often took the form of damaging the steam engines that powered the mills (termed the 'plug plot', because boiler-plugs were knocked out). Troops were rapidly deployed, as many as six thousand in Manchester, where two policemen had been killed. Leaders were arrested and put on trial. Yet, again putting the treatment of Chartists in the context of the judicial system as a whole, it has been argued that the state was not draconian. General Sir Charles Napier, who commanded the military forces deployed against rioters, in the view of George Rudé, 'was a humane and intelligent officer who appears to have had a genuine horror of shedding civilian blood'. Some 95 Chartists were transported, but, to put this in perspective, between 1830 and 1868 over 90 000 prisoners were shipped to Australia.[15]

In 1848, when tension again rose in advance of the presentation of the third Chartist petition, the authorities again stood their ground. Not only were special constables sworn in – usually from the propertied middle classes – but the Home Office also carefully monitored the movement of activists. Spies and informers were widely employed, and another wave of trials led to the imprisonment of Chartist leaders. It has been persuasively maintained, for example by Saville, that this aspect of the Chartist agitation, the determination of dominant classes to counter the demands of the exploited, was decisive.[16] In comparison, other explanations carry less conviction. It is nevertheless worth briefly examining two of the most common for the light they throw on working-class politics.

First is the view that Chartism was driven by hunger. Economic hardships undoubtedly help to explain the discontent that was so widely felt in the first half of the nineteenth century, but from this it does not follow that Chartism was simply an expression of physical suffering, that it was a 'knife and fork question...a bread and cheese question', to use the phrase of J. R. Stephens that has been employed by many others since. It is possible to make economic self-interest explain the largely middle-class movement to repeal the Corn Laws in the years to 1846 (a cause that was to produce the misnomer 'the hungry forties'[17]). However, just as the 'Manchester School' was motivated by bourgeois radicalism as well as economic interest, Chartism embodied democratic ideas that were linked with, but not simply a response to, the poverty of working people. Attempts therefore to correlate trade-cycle fluctuations and working-class agitation can lead to oversimplifications which explain the growth and decline of Chartism merely in terms of the standard of living. This is not to deny that economic suffering politicised groups such as handloom weavers and helped to swell the Chartist ranks, but many other activists saw themselves as part of a radical tradition too deeply rooted to be affected by short-term variations in the economy.

A second reason often advanced to explain why the Chartists' six points were not achieved stresses the divided leadership of the move-ment. The attitudes of men such as William Lovett and Joseph Sturge, who disliked the language of class conflict and the threat of physical force, have been regarded as incompatible with those of such fiery figures as Feargus O'Connor and George Julian Harney. The latter, the self-styled Marat of the English Revolution – a revolution that did not happen in his time – told readers of the *Northern Star* that 'our country may be compared to a bedstead full of nasty, filthy, crawling Aristocratic and Shopocratic bugs' and answered those who accused Chartists of wishing to destroy property with the remark 'we will not destroy the bedstead, but *we will annihilate the bugs*'.[18] As Gammage noted, audiences of 'hard-worked, ill-fed, sons of toil' were receptive to inflammatory lan-guage: 'A recommendation to moral force would have been laughed to scorn.'[19] Throughout the years of Chartism, there was much discussion among radicals of the case for physical force as a means of change. Some, often inspired by the French Revolution, believed it would be necessary, though peaceful methods should be tried first. Others advocated moral force only. These latter usually urged on their supporters the case for self-improvement, especially through education and temperance. This position, however, could seem too close to that of the judge who, senten-cing a number of Ashton Chartists, told them that:

> instead of endeavouring to obtain universal suffrage, they ought to endeavour to obtain universal temperance, sobriety and virtue: they should begin at the proper end, become good and virtuous citizens, and political power would come to them – all these advantages must come from themselves.[20]

At first sight, it might appear that Feargus O'Connor's land scheme, based on the idea of peasant proprietorship, fitted in with the ethos of self-improvement.[21] His idea of buying estates in order to divide them into small farms did to some extent meet a deep-seated wish among those who craved economic independence. Moreover, his proposals not only appealed to individualists, they also struck a responsive chord with those who shared a well-established tradition of land radicalism. Aristocratic monopolists were in possession of 'the people's farm'; by one means or another, it should be taken back.[22] Critics of O'Connor, however, maintained that his scheme did harm by diverting effort away from the six points of the Charter and could hope to cater for no more than a tiny proportion of the working class. Moreover, by adding to the number of proprietors, it made more difficult the sweeping remedy of land nationalisation: as Bronterre O'Brien, a fellow Chartist but a leading opponent of O'Connor, averred, 'the only legitimate landlord' were the whole of the people through the state. The land scheme extended 'the hellish principle of Landlordism'.[23] In the outcome, the land company collapsed. It had been run negligently if not dishonestly by O'Connor, who also lost money when it failed.

The various elements, briefly indicated above, to be found among the leaders of Chartism had their counterparts among the followers of the movement. In manufacturing areas, those with 'unshorn chins, blistered hands and fustian jackets', as O'Connor famously addressed his supporters, were attracted by the message that without political rights there would be no remedy for economic grievances. The language of the *Northern Star* and other radical papers reinforced a popular class-consciousness. Similarly, although London, the traditional centre of radical ideas, has been seen as a relatively weak centre, there was militancy, especially among members of trades threatened by technical change.[24] Yet, while the element of class conflict does warrant close attention, there were other features of Chartism. It encouraged the participation of women, if in a secondary role, probably to a greater extent than any earlier political organisation. The movement had important cultural and associational aspects. It also, when the Irish were widely regarded as separate from the workers of the rest of the United Kingdom, involved large numbers of them, often prominantly and in a way that alarmed the authorities in 1848.[25] And just as Chartism was foreshadowed by other popular causes, after the rejection of the third and final petition by the House of Commons in 1848, the influence of the movement did not cease.

The Mid-Victorian Years: An Age of Equipoise?

A comparison has often been drawn between the turbulence of the 1840s and the social calm of the 1850s. According to this approach, the Great Exhibition of 1851 symbolises the change that had occurred in popular attitudes. Some contemporaries had warned, only three years after the Kennington Common demonstration, of the dangers of large numbers assembling in Hyde Park, even for the purpose of viewing the exhibits in the Crystal Palace. Many thousands did travel to London, and the government took the precaution of holding troops and police-men in reserve, but the capital remained tranquil. It was possible, in the words of one modern historian, 'to contemplate "the fustian jackets and unshorn chins of England" enjoying a peaceful picnic on the grass in Hyde Park instead of dreaming of how to overthrow society'.[26] More-over, the Great Exhibition of the Works of Industry of All Nations, to use its full title, has been regarded as celebrating the triumph of both industrial capitalism and free trade. As the products of British factories and workshops poured into the markets of the world, the benefits of prosperity spread more widely than ever before. In line with these developments, it appears that the working class shifted its approach. Chartism had ceased to be relevant. Those who were organised in trade unions were drawn to what the Webbs termed the New Model.[27] This gave labour aristocrats greater security of employment and enhanced their status. But all workers, not just the skilled, were incorporated into the capitalist system. As Engels put it in 1858, 'the English proletariat is actually becoming more and more bourgeois, so that this most bourgeois of all nations is apparently aiming ultimately at the possession of a bour-geois aristocracy and a bourgeois proletariat *as well as* a bourgeoisie'.[28] Many historians have taken a similar view. In, for instance, the oft-quoted words of E. P. Thompson:

> workers having failed to overthrow capitalist society, proceeded to warren it from end to end. . . . The characteristic class institutions of the Labour Movement were built up – trade unions, trade councils, T.U.C., co-ops, and the rest. . . . Each assertion of working-class influence within the bourgeois-democratic state machinery, simultaneously involved them as partners (even if antagonistic partners) in the running of the machine. Even the indices of working-class strength – the financial reserves of trade unions and co-ops – were secure only within the custodianship of capitalist stability.[29]

Undoubtedly, such remarks sum up some of the changes that were taking place as the second half of the nineteenth century progressed. Yet it is possible to overplay the differences between the years both before and after 1850. Politically, Chartism did not die in 1848: led by such as Ernest Jones, it existed, if in a vestigal form, for another twelve years.[30] Economically, as we have sought to show in Chapter 2, workers were not greatly better paid or more securely employed in the 'golden years' of the 1850s. Physical violence continued to be a feature of both political and industrial conflict. On the other hand, the representatives of law and order had more firmly secured their position. Increasingly efficient police forces operated in urban areas; especially after the passing of the County and Borough Police Act in 1856 (which was in part a response to riots in Stockport, Blackburn and Wigan in 1852–3). Despite popular resentment against the 'blue-bottles', from the 1850s anti-police violence 'assumed a more restrictive shape and became (like prosti-tution) a typical component of the undercurrent of everyday Victorian life'.[31] At the national level, political leaders had the confidence to rescind the sentences of transportation imposed in the previous decade. In 1854, for example, John Frost, the leader of the Monmouth rising, received a conditional pardon, which prepared the way for him to return from Tasmania in the following year.[32]

As in the earlier part of the century, after 1850 violent incidents occurred in various parts of the country and in a variety of circum-stances. Religious intolerance had not disappeared, and deaths during sectarian riots were not infrequent. The 'Garibaldi riots' of 1862 involved clashes between Protestants and Catholics, while several notable incid-ents were associated with the itinerant anti-Catholic lecturer William Murphy. The growth of the Orange Order and the activities of Fenians had an influence on outbreaks of violence.[33] Widespread social disorder accompanied the attempts of the Salvation Army to spread its gospel, between 1878 and 1882, when violent scenes occurred in over sixty towns and cities.[34] Elections were still marked by tumultuous behaviour. In Nottingham in 1885, for example, a crowd that had assembled in the market place smashed 'every window within reach' after a police charge which, according to one eyewitness, 'resulted in the laming of a large number of people, and one child ... killed in its mother's arms by a police baton'.[35]

Industrial disputes often involved physical violence. In Barrow, for example, a bricklayer, William Blackburn, who was under pressure for working with non-union men, died in a fracas with fellow workers in

1865, while in Manchester there were numerous instances of the application of force in the brickmaking trade.[36] However, it was Sheffield that attracted the most attention for the violent character of its industrial relations. There, as a last resort, gunpowder was used against those who defied the local trade societies, especially the saw-grinders. At a lower level of intimidation, tools would be stolen or damaged, actions known as 'rattening', but a worker or small employer who continued to ignore pressure risked attack on either his person or his premises. James Linley, a saw-grinder who refused to accept the union's restriction on the number of apprentices he should employ, was shot – by two of his former apprentices – and died of his wounds. In 1866, again in Sheffield, the house of a strikebreaker named Fernehough was blown up, an incident that led to a public outcry and, in 1867, the appointment of a commission of inquiry. It was discovered that William Broadhead, the secretary of the saw-grinders' union, who publicly had offered a reward for information about the Fernehough explosion, was actually the instigator of the various outrages that had occurred.[37] Opponents of trade unionism, who saw its leaders as paid agitators with a vested interest in provoking strikes, called for legal remedies. Such a view seemed to be shared by the Lord Chief Justice, when, in 1867, he and three other judges, in the case of *Hornby* v. *Close*, took the view that trade unions were 'in restraint of trade' and therefore disqualified from the law's protection. This decision, which went against the boilermakers, came at a time when some employers were on the offensive against the trade unions. In the building trade, for example, Alfred Mault, the capable secretary of the General Builders' Association, assembled much damaging evidence of restrictive practices.[38] However, middle-class friends of what were regarded as the reputable trade unions, those stable organisations catering for skilled men, defended the rights of workers to act collectively. Similarly, the leaders of the London-based unions (later given the label 'The Junta' by the Webbs) distanced themselves from the events in Sheffield and joined calls for a royal commission of inquiry.[39]

When, in 1869, the findings of a commission appeared, it was the minority report, friendly to the idea of respectable trade unionism, that influenced the legislation of 1871 and 1875 which removed some of the unions' legal disabilities. Governments were, however, motivated not only by argument but also by an awareness that the second Reform Act of 1867 had widened the franchise. As Walter Bagehot advised the 'higher classes' in 1872, 'they must willingly concede every claim which they can safely concede, in order that they may not have to concede

unwillingly some claim which would impair the safety of the country'.
This was necessary given that in most constituencies the majority of
electors 'now consist of the uneducated poor'.[40] In fact, the Reform Act
had increased the electorate to almost two and a half million, or about
one adult male in three. As with the Reform Act of 1832, the legislation
was the outcome of both pressure from outside Parliament and the calculations of the government, although the latter were not made without
some attention to the state of the country. In particular, the Reform
League demonstration of July 1866, when the crowd barred from entry
to Hyde Park 'burst down the dilapidated railings and three days and
nights of intermittent skirmishing followed', brought home to politicians
the dangers of resisting a substantial extension of the franchise.[41]

However, although the threat and the fear of physical force were
present in the second half of the nineteenth century, the characteristic
leader of labour was a man of outward respectability. He could be
observed, for example, at meetings of the Trades Union Congress,
which, from 1868, met annually in one of the larger towns or cities of the
United Kingdom. The delegates' dress and conduct served to allay the
anxieties of the propertied classes. In the early years of the TUC, it was
mainly the labour aristocrats who were represented, and, just as there
has been a continuing debate about the economic position of these men
(for which see Chapter 2), so too has there about their political role. As a
generalisation, the political attitudes of a group tend to grow out of its
economic status. Some historians have accordingly stressed the separation of the skilled artisan from other workers and have gone on to argue
that the 'aristocrat' also adopted a distinctive political ideology. This
approach draws on the opinions of contemporaries, for instance Marx,
who identified a post-1848 'period of corruption' in which the direction
of the working class had passed into the hands of 'venal trade-union
leaders and professional agitators' to become 'nothing more than the tail
of the Great Liberal Party'.[42]

Indeed, politically the typical trade union leader was a Liberal, and
likely to admire the moral authority of William Gladstone, the long-serving
party leader and four times Prime Minister. In spite of the presence of
an aristocratic Whig element and of employers whose workers were not
well paid, organised labour found a place within the Liberal Party. This
was due in part to the radical wing of the party which at least articulated,
and sometimes agitated for, progressive measures in the 1870s and
1880s. Figures such as Joseph Chamberlain, Charles Bradlaugh, Henry
Labouchere and Charles Dilke showed sympathy with republicanism,

the disestablishment of the Church of England (in religion, most trade union leaders were nonconformists and a few secularists), land reform and a further widening of the franchise.[43] The last came about in 1884 and 1885 with a more than doubling of the electorate to some 5 675 000 men and another redistribution of seats. Even before this extension of the number entitled to vote, in towns with large working-class populations, Liberals with political ambitions had found it necessary to accommodate local interests. As we have argued in earlier chapters, the characteristics of labour were not uniform; in political terms, just as Chartism showed regional variations, so too did later popular issues. Fewer local studies have explored aspects of the post-1850 period, though the emerging picture is one of a 'new trend of socially responsible Liberalism set to attract working-class voters'.[44] Moreover, in the House of Commons, the Liberal Party slowly accommodated a few men whose social origins were working class. Often leaders of the coalminers' unions, these 'Lib-Lab' MPs, as they became known, helped to widen the electoral appeal of Liberalism. However, their numbers were small – in 1874 two miners' leaders, Thomas Burt and Alexander Macdonald, were elected; after the general election of 1900 the 'Lib-Lab' representatives numbered eight.[45]

In considering the nature of politics in an age of a widening franchise, however, it must not be assumed that all working men were Liberals. The Conservative cry 'For Queen and Country!', with its romantic and patriotic connotations, could be more stirring than the Gladstonian intonation 'Peace, Retrenchment and Reform'. Disraeli's 'Tory Democracy', combining elements of imperialism, Protestantism, social reform and anti-temperance, was intended to appeal to the working-class voter, who the Conservative Party became adept at attracting then and subsequently. Although these 'angels in marble' were a relatively small proportion of the electorate, they do serve as a warning against any tendency to overlook either the varied nature of the working-class or the effect of competition between the Conservative and Liberal parties for votes.[46]

Nevertheless, these circumstances did not mean that politically active working men had lost their class-consciousness in comparison with the period of Chartism. Although, after mid-century, the maturing capitalist economy led, as we have shown in Chapter 2, to a modest improvement in the standard of living, this can be no more than part of the analysis. There were immense practical difficulties, of organisation, finance and expertise, that delayed the advent of an independent working-class political party. Moreover, that the existing parties were able to attract the support of workers, it has been argued, shows that class-consciousness

alone is too limited a concept to interpret the character of labour. With
the growth of towns, according to Tholfsen, emerged 'the consensual
foundations of mid-Victorian urban culture' which supported a type of
radicalism that could meet the needs of middle- and working-class ideology. This included a common acceptance of the value of self-improvement
and respectability.[47] But the existence of such shared values need not
deny the urban worker's distinctive culture; the espousal of thrift and
sobriety and the pursuit of literacy and rational recreation were means
of economic survival in a system of bourgeois capitalism. As we saw in the
previous chapter, a strong tradition of working-class self-help existed
alongside similar middle-class ideas, and some historians have posited
the existence of a similarly shared radicalism in the post-1850 decades.

Socialism and Trade Unionism

In the second half of the 1880s, sections of the working class, and those
associated with them, began to exert pressure for more far-reaching
reform.[48] By the end of the decade some observers – including G. J. Harney
and Friedrich Engels – were invoking the spirit of Chartism to describe
the levels of organisation and militancy.[49] Moreover, there was an element
of socialist ideology in the industrial disputes of the late 1880s and early
1890s. Some of this came from the Social Democratic Federation.
Though small in numbers, and often sectarian in its Marxism, the SDF
began to agitate among the London unemployed. In protest against
social and political grievances, mass demonstrations were organised,
some of which ended in violence. After the authorities had prohibited
public meetings in Trafalgar Square, the SDF, the Socialist League and
the Metropolitan Federation of Radical Clubs decided to test the ban
and called for a demonstration against the use of coercion in Ireland
(conditions in 'John Bull's other island' and the number of Irish activists
in Britain often influenced the character of popular politics). The police used considerable force to break up the crowd which gathered on
13 November 1887 – so much so that the event became known as Bloody
Sunday. Two of the leaders, John Burns and R. B. Cunninghame Graham,
were arrested and later sentenced to six weeks' imprisonment. In another
demonstration, on 20 November 1887, a 41-year-old unemployed man,
Alfred Linnell, died, in consequence, the organisers claimed, of a police
charge. A mass funeral was organised at which William Morris's 'Death
Song' was sung, with the refrain:

Not one, not one, nor thousands must they slay,
But one and all if they would dusk the day.[50]

However, as on other occasions, the hopes, or fears, of revolution failed
to materialise. The socialist organisations were numerically small and
most of their leaders belonged to the reformist tradition that agitated to
improve, rather than sweep away, society as it existed. Socialists often
worked to strengthen trade unions, although the rationale of these
bodies was to negotiate with employers to gain relatively modest
improvements in pay and conditions. Similarly, one increasingly popular remedy for unemployment, the eight-hour day, represented a
means of sharing more evenly the available work, while mitigating the
toil of workers. At the same time, even the leaders of the firmly established unions, who were still more Liberal than socialist, were inclined to
be critical of their members' share of the wealth they helped to create.
Moreover, by the later 1880s the level of unemployment had fallen. This
gave workers a stronger position in the labour market, notably in 1889
when a successful strike took place in the London docks. Hitherto, those
casually employed had been regarded as incapable of organisation,
despite the success of the Bryant and May's 'matchgirls' in 1888, who
had been led to a strike victory by the feminist and radical, Annie Besant.
The advent of what was termed 'new' trade unionism revitalised the
labour movement. It also helped to heighten the public awareness of the
conditions of workers and their families who survived on low and often
irregular wages. For a time, expressions of class-consciousness also
became more acute, as those possessing property felt more threatened
by the militancy of strikers. In Leeds in 1890 for example, striking
gasworkers positioned themselves on Wortley Bridge from which they
bombarded blacklegs, along with the police, mayor, magistrates and
militia who were accompanying them. Their leader, Will Thorne, was
presented by Engels with a copy of Marx's *Capital*, inscribed to 'the victor
of the Leeds battle'. The proletariat's 'long winter sleep', Engels exulted,
'is broken at last. The grandchildren of the Old Chartists are entering
the line of battle.'[51]

From another bitter industrial dispute, in Bradford in the winter of
1890–91, can be traced one strand leading to the creation of the Independent Labour Party in January 1893. It was not unknown for some
individuals to belong to both the SDF and the ILP; some socialists were
also members of the Fabian Society, the 'think-tank' of non-Marxist
intellectuals which emphasised the means by which existing institutions

could be adapted to the needs of collectivism. But the ILP tended to be stronger in the industrialised north and to espouse a form of socialism that was ethical (or, according to critics, woolly) and non-revolutionary. Some have found in its moralistic approach to the issues of the time elements of religious nonconformity, and some of its early leaders had moved from a chapel to a political ethos. For instance, Philip Snowden, raised as a Wesleyan, was noted for the 'Come to Jesus' tone of his speeches in the pioneer days of the ILP in the West Riding.[52]

By the early 1890s, some of the membership gains of the new unionism had been lost. Furthermore, the older unions felt under pressure, as several interrelated factors came into operation. Among these were technical changes which reduced the protection that skilled work had enjoyed. Newer production methods allowed machinery to undertake at least some of the work that had been the preserve of the craftsman. In part, these innovations were in response to the anxieties of British capitalists that foreign competition was taking their markets. They could no longer tolerate older methods of production if these put at risk their share of the market. When disputes occurred, employers were prepared to risk embittering the situation by bringing in blacklegs. They also had recourse to the courts, and a number of legal cases – in which the judges were suspected of interpreting the law in the interests of the propertied classes – gave trade union leaders further grounds for concern. Employers of labour improved their own organisation. In engineering, the employers' federation locked out members of the Amalgamated Society of Engineers, perhaps the exemplar of skilled workers, in 1897–98. A spokesman of the employers denied the aim was to destroy the union, but the members of his federation were 'determined to obtain the freedom to manage their own affairs which has proved to be so beneficial to the American manufacturer'.[53] Socialist propaganda, in the press and among trade unionists, emphasised the weaknesses of organised labour. One remedy, urged at the annual Trades Union Congress, was independent labour representation in the House of Commons.

At the 1899 TUC a resolution that a conference should be held to consider the question of labour representation was carried. The voting in favour was fairly narrow – 546 000 to 434 000 – with the big 'Lib-Lab' unions of coal and cotton voting against, but the conference duly took place in February 1900. As well as representatives of the trade unions, the SDF, Fabian Society and ILP were invited (so too were the co-operative societies, which declined to attend). Out of this little-noticed conference came the Labour Representation Committee, the forerunner of the Labour

Party. The LRC was nominally an autonomous body, but, though most of its finance came from the fees of those trade unions that affiliated to it, socialists viewed with 'great expectations' the 'national combination for which we worked and prayed'.[54]

In the autumn of 1900, the government called a general election at which the LRC endorsed candidates in 15 constituencies. Two were elected, Richard Bell, at Derby, and Keir Hardie at Merthyr Tydfil. The two represented characteristic, and differing, traits within the labour movement. Bell was a leader of the railwaymen, elected, in tandem with a Liberal, for a double-member constituency which included many voters employed by the railway companies. He regarded his job as representing his union's interests in the House of Commons, where a large number of MPs were railway company directors. In politics, he remained a Liberal (and by the next general election, in 1906, was one of the two Liberal Party candidates to be returned for Derby). Merthy Tydfil was also a double-member constituency, but there Hardie had been opposed by two Liberal candidates. As the leading personality of the ILP, he was well known for his socialist views and advocacy of an independent working-class political party.

By the general election of January 1906, organised labour had strengthened its position. The number of trade unionists affiliated to the TUC rose from 1 200 000 in 1900 to 1 700 000 in 1906. In part due to concerns about the Taff Vale case (which undermined the legal position of unions and made them responsible for damage done to property during strikes), the number of trade unions affiliated to the LRC also increased (although in 1901 the SDF had withdrawn, finding insufficient commitment to class struggle). A large number of trades councils affiliated to the LRC, thus strengthening its claim to represent labour. Moreover, LRC-sponsored candidates had been successful in three by-elections in 1902 and 1903. Behind the scenes, the secretary of the LRC, Ramsay MacDonald, had, with Hardie's approval, in 1903 negotiated with the Liberal Party an electoral pact to avoid Labour and Liberal candidates opposing each other in certain constituencies. Such an agreement enabled the Liberal Party to show it was not unsympathetic to the claims of Labour at a time when progressive elements were drawing together to oppose the tariff reform proposals of the Conservatives. Liberals also indicated a willingness to restore the legal position of the unions to what it had been before the Taff Vale case had made them liable for damages suffered by an employer during an industrial dispute. When the election came, 29 LRC-endorsed candidates were returned, and soon after, along with one independently elected trade unionist, they took the collective name the Labour Party.

Ideologically, not all of the newly elected 30 Labour MPs regarded themselves as socialists; perhaps about half did. Their backgrounds were invariably working class, but most had left their industrial occupations to become full-time trade union officials, and on a number of issues they held ideas that were unrepresentative of the working class as a whole.[55] Some still saw their role as confined to issues that directly affected labour, though as it happened such matters were prominent in the years that followed. A Trade Disputes Act, reversing the effect of the Taff Vale decision, was soon obtained, and most Labour MPs supported the social reforms of the Liberal government. In the general elections of 1910, the Labour Party kept to the agreement of 1903 to ensure its candidates co-operated with Liberals, to the dismay of some socialists.[56] The party had also increased its size in 1909 after the miners' decision to affiliate, along with their dozen or so previously 'Lib-Lab' MPs. Some contemporaries, whose views have been endorsed by a number of modern historians, regarded the Edwardian Labour Party as positioned to supersede Liberalism. The alliance between trade unions and socialists, operating within an electoral system that had a preponderance of working-class men and able to exploit issues on which the older parties were vulnerable, seemed to make the continued rise of Labour inevitable. On the other hand, successes in the general elections of 1906 and 1910 were held to have revitalised the Liberal Party and given impetus to a series of social reforms that would have kept the party at the head of progressive politics, but for the advent of the Great War. It is a question that has generated an extensive literature, too large to survey here.[57]

In the short term, however, the veterans who sat in the House of Commons for mining constituencies did little to shed their Liberalism. By contrast, in the coalfields the spirit was one of increasing militancy. As discussed in an earlier chapter, the numbers of coal miners employed rose steadily in the early twentieth century. After 1910 syndicalism, with its ideology of workers' control, threatened to overturn the existing system of industrial relations in mining and other key sectors of the economy. At the parliamentary level, Labour MPs often were as unsympathetic towards syndicalist ideas as were members of the older parties. Philip Snowden, for example, drew on the long tradition that put political action above industrial in his book *Socialism and Syndicalism*. He allowed that the syndicalist movement had directed attention to the need to remedy the exploitative nature of capitalism, but the means proposed to do this were 'utterly impracticable and undesirable'.[58] It was therefore the task of the socialist to use political methods to emancipate the worker. Strikes (and syndicalism revived the idea of the general strike, which had been relatively dormant since the 1840s) were regarded as unfortunate occurrences by the leadership of the Labour Party. While the government was strongly criticised by Hardie, MacDonald and others for the way in which the police and military were deployed during industrial disputes – including the events at Tonypandy in 1910 and the despatch of a destroyer to the Mersey during the transport strike of 1911 – Labour called for the amicable settlement of disputes. Most observers, however, paid too much attention to syndicalism as a cause of the unrest and too little to the higher cost of living that had squeezed the real wages of many workers. In August 1914, those who had been dismayed by the apparently selfish class-consciousness of British working men jettisoned their opinions as thousands patriotically volunteered to fight for king and country. The Labour Party, too, though committed to resist a European war, swung, with a few exceptions, behind the government. It is too simplistic to explain this by saying that nationalism was more potent than international socialism, yet, in the crisis of summer 1914, most leaders of the working class were carried along by the currents that led to the Great War.[59]

Summary

In many respects, the political status of labour rose between the beginning of Chartism and the outbreak of the First World War. The franchise had been widened considerably. By 1914 the majority of working men had the vote in parliamentary elections. The redistribution of seats removed the abuses associated with pocket boroughs, while the introduction of the secret ballot in 1872 reduced the intimidatory power of employer and landlord. In 1911, another of the points demanded in the People's Charter of the 1830s and 1840s became law when the royal seal was given to legislation that provided for the payment of MPs. These changes did not come about without pressure and agitation, although the existing parties learnt to manage a mass electorate. As Labour, the party created to further workers' interests, appeared to have a narrow electoral base and be facing problems (so much so that one historian has written of its decline),[60] it could be maintained that the propertied classes had managed with some efficiency the growth of political democracy.

As always, the tempo of political change varied between 1830 and 1914. Yet some of the old formulations perhaps draw contrasts that are too sharp. For various reasons, the eighty-odd years between the Great Reform Act and the Great War have been chopped into sections that are too rigid. To some Marxists, seeking to explain the decline 'from Chartism to labourism', the working class changed in about 1850. In the words of Theodore Rothstein, there was a 'transformation of the British working class movement from revolutionary Chartism to pacifist trade unionism'.[61] Then a Fabian historiographical tradition followed the Webbs, who identified in mid-century a 'New Model Unionism'. The two analyses were partly complementary: skilled workers set up secure trade unions and, as labour aristocrats, were incorporated into mid-Victorian liberalism; they opportunistically (as Rothstein termed it) took the gains that were available while disdaining to associate with the mass of unorganised workers. With the loss of Britain's dominance in world trade in the 1880s, Marxists have pointed to an employers' counter-offensive and the revival of socialist ideas which helped to produce the 'new' unionism and the (ultimately reformist) Labour Party.

Of course, as we have indicated in the main part of this chapter, these and other analyses have been developed with much more subtlety than a very brief summary can convey. Few historians would now portray Chartism simply as a mass movement driven by a militant ideology. Some go as far as to suggest that the sort of class collaboration that is seen as common in the third quarter of the century preceded 1850. However, it has been held that social peace and political quiescence were not the sole or dominant characteristics of the third quarter of the century. The representatives of 'capital' and 'labour' might, in a period of technological change, more often have expressed their mutual interests, but conflict and disorder did not disappear. Again, if too much emphasis is placed on mid-Victorian stability, it is possible, in making a contrast, to overstate the extent of the support for socialism and the novelty of the trade unionism of the late 1880s and 1890s. In the Edwardian period, too, some historians have followed contemporaries and emphasised change at the expense of continuity.

That the years between 1830 and 1914 were times of great change for the working class is not denied. However, the pace of change was steadier than is sometimes suggested. Wages and working conditions did not vary drastically; nor did some of the associated industrial and political features of the period. Most workers were not routinely involved in industrial disputes and also had the opportunity to vote seldom if at all.

But disputes between workers and employers could be felt with the same intensity and harshness at the end of the period as at earlier stages. It is possible also to recognise similar features in the response of the authorities to strikes and demonstrations – that is, elements of both repression and conciliation. Although there is no scale on which to measure the levels of class-consciousness between 1830 and 1914, it seems unlikely that the levels varied greatly over the period.

CONCLUSION

In the early 1870s, Thomas Wright observed that to people in the 'upper and middle ranks of society' the 'working classes must . . . appear not only an unreasonable body, but an incomprehensible one also'. Three and a half decades later, the Liberal politician Charles Masterman echoed this view. 'The Multitude of the People of England', he wrote, 'rarely become articulate . . . [and] can only be observed from outside and very far away.' Many other commentators took a similar approach to what G. K. Chesterton in one of his best-known poems called 'The Secret People' ('We are the people of England; and we have not spoken yet. / Smile at us, pay us, pass us. But do not quite forget.')[1] Some of those who sought to penetrate the life of the working class took with them assumptions that created a distorted image of the culture they sought to portray; others were liable unconsciously to explore themselves and their guilty consciences.[2] The present-day student of the period (as of others) must, therefore, be mindful of the way sources can be coloured by their authors' prejudices.

Nevertheless, there is sufficient evidence to offer some concluding generalisations about the experiences of labour in the years between 1830 and 1914. Perhaps the most telling general observation we can make is that by the end of our period, on the eve of the Great War, an urban proletariat had been created. In the course of a single lifetime (though, admittedly, few of those born in 1830 lived until their mid-eighties) the British population more than doubled in size. The focus of the populace had also shifted physically so that a large majority was to be found in towns and cities. It can also be observed that, despite material hardships, working-class living standards and life expectancy had on average improved, albeit not as dramatically as would occur in the twentieth century. As these changes in the economic experiences of the working class began to work into ordinary people's lives, a distinctive culture emerged. By and large the working class lived among people of their own income group and occupational type. Working-class communities were internally stratified – shipbuilders living in different parts of towns from miners, and so on – and were physically separated from their social superiors, many of whom, taking advantage of railways and trams, chose to live in suburbs, and away from the smoky and congested neighbourhoods where they made their living. Moreover, while there was considerable diversity across regions, working-class culture was far more homogenous in 1914 than it had been in 1830 or 1800. By the end of our period there existed a series of well-established working-class industrial and political institutions. These embodied the gains made by labour; explicit within the ideologies that underpinned them, and within the constitutions that upheld them, was the intention of making further advances. Thus it is necessary to make far fewer qualifications when using the term 'the working class' in 1914 than in earlier periods.

Our discussion began with an introduction that attempted to sketch what we consider to be important and controversial questions in the history of labour. Because the past has gone and is irretrievable – except through the medium of what historians call 'the sources' (historical records, and the like) – there is bound to be discussion and debate about the precise meaning of events and the particular intentions of people. Labour history is no exception in this regard, and we hope some of the problems inherent within any attempt to interpret the past are apparent from our introduction. For there we attempted to look, in a necessarily general way, at the burgeoning literature upon which our study at least partly relies. We also considered key concepts such as class, and sought to explain some of the criticisms levelled at labour history by postmodernists.

Any attempt to write a history of labour (for any given point in the past) must begin with the question of work. Questions relating to the wider significance of work were thus considered in our first two chapters. The varieties of work, its effects and the experiences of the people who performed it, explain much of what was experienced by the ordinary people of the nineteenth century. Work was (and still largely remains) central to the lives of most people, and therefore to labour history itself. The life choices of ordinary men and women were governed first and foremost by the need to earn a living. Nothing else mattered as much; nothing else achieved such primacy in the decision-making that governed an individual's or a family's behaviour.

At the same time, we sought to explain how work covered a bewildering range of job types, that levels of remuneration were varied, and that job security fluctuated across time and trades. Even the census enumerators of the nineteenth century were unable satisfactorily to account for the real degree of this diversity. Our analysis of work types, wage levels, and the wider experiences associated with paid and unpaid labour (what has been called the 'social history of work'[3]), was shaped both by official census materials and by more prosaic personal accounts. Despite the problems of generalising about work, however, we were still able to conclude that, for all this variety, the pursuit of wages, the need for paid employment, connected, rather than separated, all occupational groups.

Our discussion of work was guided by Edward Higgs's reminder that, 'at least until 1891, householders were not asked to indicate the paid economic activity of the members of their household, they were asked to give their "Rank, Profession, or Occupation"'.[4] This revelation thus led us away from the idea that work was some simple statistical expression and towards a belief that what mattered most was the culture and experiences that welled up from work itself. Work was as much a question of status as it was of remunerated toil. It connected men and their wives, women and their families – and indeed whole neighbourhoods – through an additional layer of common experience: that of the craft or skill or day-to-day grind. In some cases this connection could equate simply with higher pay. Thus we note the high wage levels of miners and shipbuilders, the job security and craft-consciousness of skilled craftsmen. Equally, white-collar workers – clerks and the like – might have enjoyed a certain status because they worked with clean hands and wore a collar and tie, but they did not always receive higher pay than the black-faced collier or the oily mechanic.

These early chapters emphasised, in general terms, how change affected the lives of working people: for example, the emergence of large centres of production, such as textile factories, and the widespread penetration of proletarian waged labour. This is important, for social as well as the economic reasons; the relationship between masters and workers, captured in Thomas Carlyle's idea of 'the cash nexus', became much more important in the nineteenth century than at any point before. At the same time, these characteristics were also considered the key continuities in the experience of labour. Readers were reminded of the cogency of Raphael Samuel's observations that traditional small workshops remained important throughout our period, and that hand toil as well as machine production shaped the labour experience.[5] Working people were affected on a daily basis by issues surrounding work. What our early chapters (1 and 2) show perhaps above all else is that work was a human relationship, a daily tug-of-war over leisure time, perks, the intensity of labour, and also a struggle to control the labour process. It is this daily experience, an undeniably materially based set of opposing interests, that shaped class relations as they developed. The consciousness of ordinary men and women cannot be divorced from the work that defined their daily existence. We thus conclude that to privilege anything above the material circumstances of life is to decontextualise them.

The shadow of work thus falls across all the chapters of this book. In chapters 3 and 4 we considered the role played by labour migration both in changing, and in perpetuating, aspects of work and class culture. For many workers, the spectre of unemployment, the diminishing of a particular trade, or the chimerical opportunities elsewhere, led to migration. For a hundred years – at least until the 1860s – labour migrants were the most important single factor in explaining urban growth in Britain's towns and cities, where, because of poor environmental conditions, death-rates outstripped birth-rates. Labour migration created a dynamic population whose movement spread old skills and new ideas as surely as it dispersed people.

Labour migration clearly played a large part in shaping the communities and cultural customs that we examined in Chapter 4. Joanna Bourke has recently argued that historians' perceptions of the working-class community owe much to the sentimental remembrances found in the autobiographies of members of the working class.[6] Many of these people – usually, though not exclusively, men – went on to become trade union officials and Labour Party MPs, and the further away from their roots they went, the more idealised and misty-eyed their memories became.

Despite the truth of what Bourke has argued, it is still possible to see communities in objective, that is 'real', terms. In Chapter 4 we attempted to demonstrate that the community *was* at the heart of working-class life, by describing the sorts of conditions in which people lived, the neighbourhoods they formed, the social relations they pursued, and the types of leisure activity they enjoyed. Although urban life was different in 1830 to what it was to be in 1914, we stressed the continuities that shaped workers' lives throughout this period. Again, we reminded readers that work defined people's lives; it also dictated migratory flows and regulated the pulse of their communities. Communities were formed because of the need to work, the need for shelter, and the desire to interact with other people. These impulses were not, at heart, very different at the beginning than at the end of our period of study.

The link between Chapter 4 and the final two chapters lies in the way that the members of the working-class communities fostered a collectivist economic and political ethos. The Victorians' philosophy of individual moral improvement, we argued in Chapter 5, was deployed by members of working-class communities to the benefit of themselves as much as to indicate an acceptance of the improving ethos of the bourgeoisie. The notion of self-help remained largely in place throughout our period. While there were numerous examples of state involvement in people's lives, social intervention was extremely limited until the early 1900s. Individuals, occupational groups, workers, and communities of working people were very much required to provide their own economic safety nets. Unsurprisingly, perhaps, this philosophy had a dramatic adhesive effect on communities. Groups were stronger than individuals and it was in recognition of that fact that a vigorous associational culture of clubs and societies emerged to dominate working-class organisation in these years.

At the same time, Chapter 5 also suggested something of a schism within the working-class community centred upon those concepts of associationalism and mutualism. Working men's clubs, friendly societies, building societies, savings banks, the Co-operative, and so on, were preponderantly the domain of those employed in skilled or well-paid work. For the day labourer in the large town, the corner shop with its offer of credit, and the pawnbroker with his willingness to lend money against the smallest of low-value belongings, or else friends and family, were the likeliest sources of support in hard times.

If Chapter 5 indicated that many workers struck an accommodation with capitalism in the period 1830 to 1914, Chapter 6 went on to examine the extent to which this was the case in the political sphere. In completing our study with an examination of emergent working-class movements, we sought to demonstrate how both conflict and conciliation were important in this period. Perhaps more than any other aspects of labour history, trade unions and political institutions have been explained in terms of rigid periods and particular moments of energy or atrophy. In Chapter 6, we tried to suggest a more graduated approach, to stress continuities of experience and forms of action. This is not to dismiss a Marxist analysis that stresses the revolutionary 'near misses', such as 1848, nor to understate the extent to which mass platform radicalism in 1830 was different from the moderated aims of the Labour Party in 1914. To stress continuities is not simply to play the postmodernist card, inserting 'people' for 'class' or 'popular politics' for 'class struggle'. History is rarely so obviously dichotomous. Where some have stressed the equipoise of the 1850 to 1880 period, for example, we attempt to cite examples of continuing struggle and resistance. It is worthy of note, for example, that this period – the Webbs' classical phase of new model unions – also saw the 'rattening' and physical violence against workers which gave rise to a lengthy examination, by a royal commission (1867–9), of the role of trade unions in society. Equally, when socialism began to influence the labour movement in Britain, as it did in the 1880s, the extent of that permeation was essentially limited. In most cases, then, we tried to stress that both conflict *and* conciliation governed the activities of the organised working class – and we do stress that, by the end of the nineteenth century, it is possible to write about a working class in the singular rather than the plural.

We hope, too, that our choice of period is justified by what we say here and in the chapters that precede this discussion. For us, the early part of the 1830s was something of a watershed. The successful inculcation of a reformist tradition captured in the 1832 Reform Act; the victory of utilitarianism over humanism, noticeable in the harsh poor law of 1834; and the isolated nature of the 'Swing' Riots – each of these overlapping series of events seemed to offer something of an endorsement of a modified *ancien régime* and of capitalism's seemingly inexorable progress. Just enough was conceded and just enough clawed back to suggest to most people that while reforms could be wrung out of the political elite, there was to be no capitulation by the propertied classes in the face of that awakening Leviathan, the working class.

Though all periodisation is, to some extent, arbitrary, to end this study in 1914 needs less justification than other dates. Britain's declaration of war in August 1914 was to leave few members of the population unaffected. From a variety of motives – of which patriotism was not the least – most workers backed the war effort. Even when the sons of the working class, along with those of their social betters, perished in their thousands, support for the war remained strong. Ironically, as the numbers of dead increased, the war's huge demands for men and munitions brought material benefits for those on the home front. The chronic underemployment that had been a feature of many workers' lives since the Industrial Revolution gave way to shortages of manpower. Labour scarcity did more to drive out the sweater than the pre-war Trades Boards Act which had been intended to improve the wages of some of the most exploited of workers. The government courted organised labour in order to prosecute the war more efficiently. Trade union leaders agreed to suspend the hard-won restrictions on managements' control of the labour process and in 1915 the Labour Party accepted an invitation to join the newly created coalition government. As the length of the war mocked the early prediction that British troops would celebrate the Christmas of 1914 in Berlin, there were shortages of food, coal, clothing and other goods. The working class was clearly affected by these hardships, with certain groups, such as war widows, affected more than most. Then again, for many workers, including women drafted into factories for the war effort, higher earnings and regularity of employment cushioned the impact of price inflation. Moreover, although Lloyd George's promise of 1918 that Britain would become 'a fit country for heroes to live in' was to become a bitter echo in the inter-war years, there were legislative attempts to improve health, housing and education, and gains were made in shortening the length of the working week. There was also the realisation of another demand that went back to the Chartists and beyond when virtually all adult men and women over the age of 30 gained the parliamentary franchise in 1918. Thus, in many respects, 1914 does mark the end of the Victorian age and the advent of a new era.

NOTES

Unless stated otherwise, the place of publication is London.

Introduction: Themes in British Labour History, 1830–1914

1. E. P. Thompson, *The Making of the English Working Class* (1963), esp. part 3, provides one of the most memorable accounts of this period of transition and turmoil in labour history.
2. 'Address of the National Association of Protection of Labour. To the Workmen of the United Kingdom', in M. Morris (ed.), *From Cobbett to Chartism, 1815–48* (1948), p. 82.
3. B. Inglis, *Poverty and the Industrial Revolution* (1972 edn), p. 293.
4. For these riots, see E. J. Hobsbawm and G. Rudé, *Captain Swing* (1969) and J. E. Archer, *By a Flash and a Scare: Arson, Animal Maiming and Poaching in East Anglia, 1815–1870* (Oxford, 1990), pp. 89–101.
5. C. Wilkins, *A History of Merthyr Tydfil* (1867), cited in D. Smith, 'Breaking silence: Gwyn Thomas and the "prehistory" of Welsh working-class fiction', in C. Emsley and J. Walvin (eds), *Artisans, Peasants and Proletarians, 1760–1860: Essays Presented to Gwyn A. Williams* (1985), p. 104.
6. There is some debate over the exact size of the electorate, both before and after reform. See, for example, J. Cannon, *Parliamentary Reform, 1640–1832* (Cambridge, 1972); M. Brock, *The Great Reform Act* (1973); F. O'Gorman, *Voters, Patrons and Parties: The Unreformed Electorate of Hanoverian England, 1734–1832* (Oxford, 1989); and below, ch. 6, pp. 144–5.
7. Quoted in R. G. Gammage, *History of the Chartist Movement, 1837–1854* (1894; repr. 1969), p. 57.
8. D. G. Fraser, *The Evolution of the British Welfare State* (London, 1973), pp. 47–8. See also below, ch. 6, pp. 146–52.
9. P. A. Wood, *Poverty and the Workhouse in Victorian Britain* (Stroud, 1991).
10. Cannon, *Parliamentary Reform, 1640–1832*, pp. 215, 233. Although since its publication research has gone on apace, this book, esp. chs 10–11, offers still the most lucid insight into the immediate events of the reform crisis.
11. De Tocqueville likened the English aristocracy to the Rhine, for, though its source is known, no one knows its end. He also complimented the English for, unlike the French, applying the term 'gentleman' to all well-educated men, irrespective of birth. Thus, he wrote: 'The English aristocracy can

therefore never arouse those violent hatreds felt by the middle and lower classes against the nobility in France where the nobility is an exclusive caste, which while monopolising all privileges and hurting everbody's feelings, offers no hope of ever entering its ranks.' *Journeys to England and Ireland, 1833* (1977 edn), p. 67.

12. This is a central theme of R. Samuel, 'The workshop of the world: steam power and hand technology in mid-Victorian Britain', *History Workshop Journal*, 3 (1977), pp. 6–72.

13. On the handloom weavers, see D. Bythell, *The Handloom Weavers: A Study in the English Cotton Industry* (Cambridge, 1969). A recent reappraisal, in which the author asserts that handloom weaving remained an important trade after 1850, is G. Timmins, *The Last Shift: The Decline of Handloom Weaving in Nineteenth-Century Lancashire* (Manchester, 1993).

14. The term 'take-off' was used by the economic theorist W. W. Rostow in *The Stages of Economic Growth* (1959) to explain the Industrial Revolutions of the late eighteenth and nineteenth centuries in Europe and America. Rostow, whose thesis has, however, been extensively criticised by later writers, argued that vanguard sectors led the rest of the economy to a position of 'take-off' into self-sustained growth.

15. The periodisation is, however, challenged in an important new study. See R. Price, *British Society, 1680–1880: Dynamism, Containment and Change* (Cambridge, 1999), esp. ch. 1, which stresses a combination of gradual change and continuity in the history of British manufacturing.

16. B. R. Mitchell and P. Deane, *Abstract of British Historical Statistics* (Cambridge, 1962), pp. 118–19, 120–1, 147–8.

17. S. and B. Webb, *The History of Trade Unionism* (2nd ed., 1920). The Webbs' place in the historiography of labour has recently been discussed by R. J. Harrison in *The Life and Times of Sidney and Beatrice Webb: The Formative Years* (2000), ch. 6.

18. The acknowledged founding fathers of the Annales tradition were Lucien Febvre and Marc Bloch, who edited the movement's journal, *Annales*, from 1929. Their contribution to the ' history of everyday life' is less noteworthy than that of later disciples, such as Emmanuel Le Roy Ladurie. See P. Burke, *The French Historical Revolution: The Annales School 1929–89* (Oxford, 1990), esp. ch. 4 for the 'third generation', including Ladurie.

19. Webbs, *History of Trade Unionism, passim.*

20. N. Kirk, *Change, Continuity and Class: Labour in British Society, 1850–1920* (Manchester, 1998), p. 6, and *passim.*

21. The British Marxists working on the industrial period include E. P. Thompson, E. J. Hobsbawm and J. Saville, as well as others who were less central.

22. Much of the present debate dates to the publication of G. S. Jones, *Languages of Class: Studies in English Working Class History* (Cambridge, 1983). A recent book by P. Joyce, *Democratic Subjects: The Self and the Social in Nineteenth-Century England* (Cambridge, 1994), took the debate on, as did J. Vernon, *Politics and the People: A Study in English Political Culture, c.1815–1867* (Cambridge, 1993). All three writers deserve to be taken seriously because as practising historians they have at least engaged that which they now question and sometimes reject. Students will find a bewildering number of

debates and arguments over these issues in several journals. Three series in particular provide a good sense of what has been going on. The first, involving Lawrence Stone, Catriona Kelly, Patrick Joyce and Gabrielle Spiegel, can be found in *Past and Present*, 131 (1991), 133 (1991) and 135 (1992). The second included a host of contributors – David Mayfield, Susan Thorne, Jon Lawrence, Miles Taylor, Patrick Joyce, James Vernon and Neville Kirk, Keith Nield and Geoff Eley – and occupied reams of space in the *Journal of Social History*, 16 (1991), 17 (1992), 18 (1993), 19 (1994) and 20 (1995). In the third, in *Journal of Contemporary History*, the main protagonists were Arthur Marwick and Hayden White, before further additional combatants joined the fray: 30 (1995) and much of 31 (1996).

23. On attempts to create 'model' industrial villages, and the impact of them, see S. Pollard, 'The factory village in the Industrial Revolution', *English Historical Review*, 79 (July 1964), pp. 513–31. The 'labour aristocracy' theory has been a subject of some debate. For fuller details of the literature, see pp. 22–4, 156.
24. Webbs, *History of Trade Unionism*, p. 179.
25. A. Toynbee, *Lectures on the Industrial Revolution* (1884; 1919 edn), p. 64.
26. For the standard-of-living debate, see below, ch. 2, pp. 43–5.
27. R. J. Morris, 'Clubs, societies and associations', in F. M. L. Thompson (ed.), *The Cambridge Social History of Britain, 1750–1950*, 3 vols (Cambridge, 1990), II: *People and their Environment* , p. 425. For a more general treatment of the importance of the 1880s as the hinge of modernity, see Price, *British Society 1680–1880, passim*.
28. D. Cannadine, *Class in Britain* (1998).
29. For a selection discussing various approaches to this subject, see K. Jenkins (ed.), *The Post-modern History Reader* (1997).
30. J. Benson, *The Working Class in Britain, 1850–1939* (1988).
31. J. Belchem and N. Kirk (eds), *Languages of Labour* (Aldershot and Brookfield, VT, 1997) for succinct discussions of these issues.
32. Thompson, *Making of the English Working Class*, preface.
33. R. Price, 'Postmodernism as theory and history', in Belchem and Kirk (eds), *Languages of Labour*, p. 13.
34. Patrick Joyce, *Visions of the People: Industrial England and the Question of Class, 1848–1914* (Cambridge, 1991), p. 3.
35. B. Holton, *British Syndicalism, 1900–1914: Myths and Realities* (1976), part 1; G. A. Phillips, 'The Triple Industrial Alliance in 1914', *Economic History Review*, 24:1 (1971), p. 63.
36. Joyce has long recognised that the Irish in Britain, a major settling ethnic group, may hold the key to understanding these multi-layered questions of class. They are, he argues, under-examined 'relative to their importance'. See for example his 'Class', in Thompson, *Cambridge Social History*, II, p. 142.
37. F. Engels, *The Condition of the Working Class in England* (1845; 1987 edn), p. 124 and Engels quoted in G. Davis, *The Irish in Britain, 1815–1914* (Dublin, 1991), p. 159.
38. An excellent discussion of the class-versus-ethnicity debate, focusing on the Irish, is S. Fielding, *Class and Ethnicity: Irish Catholics in England, 1880–1939* (Buckingham, 1992), ch. 1.

39. This is clear from Joyce's 'Return to history: postmodernism and the politics of academic history in Britain', *Past and Present*, 158 (1998).
40. E. J. Hobsbawm, *Labouring Men: Studies in the History of Labour* (1964) and *Worlds of Labour: Further Studies in the History of Labour* (1984). There is a sympathetic critique of the Hobsbawm thesis in N. Kirk, '"Tradition", working-class culture and "the rise of labour": some preliminary questions and observations', *Social History*, 16:2 (1991), esp. pp. 205–11.
41. G. Dangerfield, *The Strange Death of Liberal England* (1935; 1970 edn), p. 21. Dangerfield's retrospective, written many years after events it discusses, provides a brilliant encapsulation of the crisis of Liberalism which, in the view of many, occurred in the late Edwardian years.

1   Varieties of Work

1. Preface to *Abstract of the Answers and Returns . . .* (1844), pp. 7–8.
2. These and other problems are discussed by J. M. Bellamy, 'Occupational statistics in the nineteenth century censuses', in R. Lawton (ed.), *The Census and Social Structure* (1978), pp. 167–73; E. H. Hunt, *Regional Wage Variations in Britain 1850–1914* (Oxford, 1973), pp. 183–96; and E. Higgs, *A Clearer Sense of the Census: The Victorian Census and Historical Research* (1996), *passim*. Higgs has also argued that the census figures substantially underestimate the number of workers, particularly women, employed in agriculture, in 'Occupational censuses and the agricultural workforce in Victorian England and Wales', *Economic History Review*, 48:4 (1995), pp. 700–16. The undercounting of women is also discussed by J. Humphries, ' Women in paid work', in J. Purvis (ed.), *Women's History in Britain, 1850–1945* (1995), pp. 90–8.
3. *General Report* (1893), vol. 4, pp. 35–6. Makers of false teeth, it was noted, were prone to describe themselves as dentists.
4. The table is based on those in B. R. Mitchell and P. Deane, *Abstract of British Historical Statistics* (Cambridge, 1962), p. 60.
5. Bellamy, 'Occupational Statistics', p. 172; cf. G. Routh, *Occupation and Pay in Great Britain, 1906–1960* (Cambridge, 1965), pp. 4–9.
6. H. Braverman, *Labour and Monopoly Capital* (New York, 1974). Compare C. More, *Skill and the English Working Class, 1870–1914* (1980), pp. 21–5 and S. Wood, *The Degradation of Work: Skill, Deskilling and the Labour Process* (1982), *passim*.
7. D. S. Landes, *The Unbound Prometheus: Technological Change and Industrial Development in Western Europe from 1750 to the Present* (Cambridge, 1969), p. 1.
8. R. Samuel, 'The workshop of the world: steam power and hand technology in mid-Victorian Britain', *History Workshop Journal*, 3 (1977), pp. 6–72.
9. Quoted by A. Briggs, 'The language of "mass" and "masses" in nineteenth-century England', in D. E. Martin and D. Rubinstein (eds), *Ideology and the Labour Movement: Essays Presented to John Saville* (1979), p. 67.
10. *Sir James Sexton, Agitator: The Life of the Dockers' M.P.: An Autobiography* (1936), p. 111. Moreover, these distinctions were maintained away from the workplace: in pubs, for example, labourers would use the public bar, while in the saloon bar, as one London publican's daughter put it, 'the uniformed

dock foreman and the tally clerks and skilled mechanics would drink in quiet exclusiveness'. See C. de Banke, *Hand over Hand* (1957), p. 57.

11. T. Wright, *Our New Masters* (1873), p. 6.

12. *Keeling Letters and Recollections* (1918), p. 250.

13. Engels to F. A. Sorge, 7 December 1889, in *Karl Marx and Frederick Engels on Britain* (Moscow, 1962), p. 566.

14. T. Lummis, *The Labour Aristocracy 1851–1914* (Aldershot, 1994), p. xii. This book's bibliography cites the main contributions to the literature on the topic. The use of the concept is vigorously stated in the introduction to the second (1994) edition of R. J. Harrison, *Before the Socialists: Studies in Labour and Politics 1861–1881*, pp. xvii–xxvii.

15. Quoted by M. Savage, 'Women and work in the Lancashire cotton industry, 1890–1939', in J. A. Jowitt and A. J. McIvor (eds), *Employers and Labour in the English Textile Industries, 1850–1939* (1988), p. 206. For examples of skill in agriculture and coal mining, see W. A. Armstrong, *Farmworkers: A Social and Economic History 1770–1980* (1988), p. 245; R. Colls, *The Pitmen of the Northern Coalfield: Work, Culture and Protest, 1790–1850* (Manchester, 1987), pp. 12–13; A. B. Campbell, *The Lanarkshire Miners: A Social History of their Trade Unions, 1775–1974* (Edinburgh, 1979), pp. 38–40.

16. F. Keeling, *Child Labour in the United Kingdom: A Study of the Development and Administration of the Law Relating to the Employment of Children* (1914), p. 8. For a recent survey of the way school replaced work for children up to the age of 12, see E. Hopkins, *Childhood Transformed: Working-Class Children in Nineteenth-Century England* (Manchester, 1994).

17. A. H. D. Acland and H. L. Smith (eds), *Studies in Secondary Education* (1892), p. 182.

18. Quoted in R. A. Bray, *Boy Labour and Apprenticeship* (1912), p. 128.

19. The *Northern Star* (2 December 1842) put the number of prostitutes in London at 80 000: quoted by W. O. Henderson and W. H. Chaloner in their introduction to the 1971 edition of Friedrich Engels's *The Condition of the Working Class in England*, p. xxviii. According to W. Acton, *Prostitution* (1857; 2nd edn, 1968), pp. 32–3, other authorities offered a similar figure, although the chief commissioner of the metropolitan police put the number at 9409.

20. C. Black (ed.), *Married Women's Work* (1915), p. 4.

21. R. Mudie-Smith (ed.), *Sweated Industries, being a Handbook of the "Daily News" Exhibition* (1906), p. 8.

22. For this aspect, and as a useful recent survey of the literature, see S. Blackburn, '"No necessary connection with homework": gender and sweated labour, 1840–1909', in *Social History*, 22:3 (1997), pp. 269–85. The most comprehensive study of poorer women is C. Chinn, *They Worked All Their Lives: Women of the Urban Poor in England, 1880–1939* (Manchester, 1988).

23. See for example, P. J. Perry, *A Geography of 19th-Century Britain* (1975), chs. 3–5; Hunt, *Regional Wage Variations, passim.*

24. Based on B. R. Mitchell and P. Deane, *Abstract of British Historical Statistics* (Cambridge, 1962), pp. 116–19.

25. H. Beynon and T. Austrin, *Masters and Servants: Class and Patronage in the Making of a Labour Organisation* (1994), pp. 77–9, 236.

26. The idea has been discussed in R. Harrison (ed.), *Independent Collier: The Coal Miner as Archetypal Proletarian Reconsidered* (Hassocks, 1978); see also J. Benson, *British Coalminers in the Nineteenth Century: A Social History* (Dublin, 1980), esp. ch. 4, for a corrective of some stereotypical views of miners.

27. C. Dickens, *Hard Times* (1854), p. 75.

28. A. Fowler and T. Wyke (eds), *The Barefoot Aristocrats: A History of the Amalgamated Association of Operative Cotton Spinners* (Littleborough, 1987), p. 63; E. Hopwood, *A History of the Lancashire Cotton Industry and the Amalgamated Weavers' Association* (Manchester, 1969), p. 53.

29. C. Pearce, *The Manningham Mills Strike, Bradford, December 1890–April 1891* (Hull, 1975), pp. vii, 1.

30. E. P. Thompson, 'Homage to Tom Maguire', in A. Briggs and J. Saville (eds), *Essays in Labour History* (1960), p. 285.

31. Mitchell and Deane, *Abstract*, pp. 190, 192–3.

32. Cited by A. Howkins, *Reshaping Rural England: A Social History 1850–1925* (1991), p. 23. Howkins adds that payment in kind 'was merely part of the cement' of the social structure, but compare the discussion of non-wage income in the following chapter.

33. B. S. Rowntree and M. Kendall, *How the Labourer Lives: A Study of the Rural Labour Problem* (1913), p. 192.

34. *Morning Chronicle*, 13 October 1846, cited by D. Martin, *John Stuart Mill and the Land Question* (Hull, 1981), p. 23.

35. G. Edwards, *From Crow-Scaring to Westminster: An Autobiography* (1922), p. 102; R. Groves, *Sharpen the Sickle!: The History of the Farm Workers' Union* (1949), p. 245.

36. Rowntree and Kendall, *How the Labourer Lives*, p. 322.

37. Quoted by C. F. G. Masterman, *The Condition of England* (7th edn, 1912), p. 161.

38. J. Marsh, *Back to the Land: The Pastoral Impulse in England, from 1880 to 1914* (1982), p. 161. For a contribution to the contemporary debate, see J. L. Green, *The Rural Industries of England* (1894), esp. ch. 2. Modern discussions include J. Saville, *Rural Depopulation in England and Wales 1851–1951* (1957), pp. 20–30; G. F. R. Spenceley, 'The Lace Associations: philanthropic movements to preserve the production of hand-made lace in late Victorian and Edwardian England', *Victorian Studies*, 16:4 (1973), pp. 433–52; P. Horn, *The Changing Countryside in Victorian and Edwardian England and Wales* (1984), ch. 5; and the essays in the section on 'Country towns and country industries', in G. E. Mingay (ed.), *The Victorian Countryside* (1981).

39. A. K. Cairncross, *Home and Foreign Investment 1870–1913* (Cambridge, 1953), p. 126. See also S. Pollard and P. Robertson, *The British Shipbuilding Industry 1870–1914* (1979), chs 8–9.

40. Lady Bell, *At the Works: A Study of a Manufacturing Town* (1911 edn), p. 40.

41. J. Mendelson et al., *Sheffield Trades and Labour Council 1858–1958* (Sheffield, [1958]), p. 59.

42. B. Webb, *My Apprenticeship* (1926; 1971 edn), p. 178. See too G. S. Jones, *Outcast London* (1976 edn), p. 12.

43. Bell, *At the Works*, p. 40.

2   Wages and Working Conditions

1.   A. Smith, *Wealth of Nations* (1776), bk 4, ch. 9.
2.   J. S. Mill, *Principles of Political Economy* (1848; Toronto, 1965 edn), p. 754.
3.   For the context of this debate, see M. E. Rose, 'Settlement, removal and the New Poor Law', in D. Fraser (ed.), *The New Poor Law in the Nineteenth Century* (1976).
4.   Quoted in S. Hollander, *The Economics of John Stuart Mill* (Oxford, 1985), p. 25.
5.   T. Carlyle, *Chartism* (1839), ch. 6.
6.   T. L. Peacock, *Headlong Hall* (1816), ch. 7.
7.   For example, P. Kirby, 'Causes of short stature among coal-mining children, 1823–1850', *Economic History Review*, 48:4 (1995) and J. Humphries, 'Short stature among coal-mining children: a comment', *Economic History Review*, 50: 3 (1997).
8.   Mitchell and Deane, *Abstract*, pp. 343–4.
9.   C. H. Feinstein, 'Pessimism perpetuated: real wages and the standard of living in Britain during and after the Industrial Revolution', *Journal of Economic History*, 58:3 (1998), p. 652.
10. A. McLaren, *Birth Control in Nineteenth-Century England* (1978), p. 107.
11. This is one of the themes of S. Szreter, *Fertility, Class and Gender in Britain, 1860–1940* (Cambridge, 1996).
12. This and the following paragraph rely particularly on M. A. Bienefeld, *Working Hours in British Industry: An Economic History* (1972).
13. Quoted by J. T. Ward, 'The Factory Movement', in J. T. Ward (ed.), *Popular Movements c.1830–1850* (1970), p. 72.
14. Perhaps the two outstanding studies of the impact of the factories upon labour are S. Pollard, 'Factory discipline in the Industrial Revolution', *Economic History Review*, 2 (1964), pp. 254–70 and E. P. Thompson, 'Time, work-discipline and industrial capitalism', *Past and Present*, 38 (Dec. 1967), reprinted in E. P. Thompson, *Customs in Common* (1991), pp. 352–403. Important for the later period is P. Joyce, *Work, Society and Politics: The Culture of the Factory in Later Victorian England* (Brighton, 1980).
15. The literature has been surveyed by D. A. Reid in two articles in *Past and Present*, 'The decline of Saint Monday, 1766–1876', 71 (1976), pp. 76–101, and 'Weddings, weekdays, work and leisure in urban England 1791–1911: the decline of Saint Monday revisited', 153 (1996), pp. 135–63.
16. Quoted by J. E. Williams, *The Derbyshire Miners: A Study in Industrial and Social History* (1962), p. 274.
17. C. Booth, *Life and Labour of the People in London. Second Series: Industry*, vol. 5 (1903), p. 73.
18. R. Roberts, *The Classic Slum: Salford Life in the First Quarter of the Century* (1971), p. 61.
19. Quoted by M. Tebbutt, *Making Ends Meet: Pawnbroking and Working-Class Credit* (1983), p. 25.
20. *Sir James Sexton, Agitator: The Life of the Dockers' M.P.: An Autobiography* (1936), p. 69.
21. H. A. Mess, *Casual Labour at the Docks* (1916), p. 44.

22. J. H. Clapham, 'Work and wages', in G. M. Young (ed.), *Early Victorian England 1830–1865* (1934), p. 33.

23. P. King, 'Customary rights and women's earnings: the importance of gleaning to the rural labouring poor, 1750–1850', *Economic History Review*, 44:3 (1991), p. 463.

24. S. Hussey, '"The last survivor of an ancient race": the changing face of Essex gleaning', *Agricultural History Review*, 45:1 (1997), p. 70.

25. J. Greenwood, *The Seven Curses of London* (1869), pp. 169, 171.

26. H. Gosling, *Up and Down Stream* (1927), pp. 39, 42.

27. R. Samuel, *East End Underworld: Chapters in the Life of Arthur Harding* (1981), p. 16.

28. J. Schneer, 'London docks in 1900: nexus of Empire', *Labour History Review*, 59:3 (1994), pp. 24–5; C. Emsley, *Crime and Society in England, 1750–1900* (1996), p. 133. Compare Gosling (p. 39): 'A good waterman would be shocked if he were told that to help himself to a piece of wood or a lump of coal was dishonest. Had he not seen with his own eyes his father, than whom there was none better, and even his grandfather, do likewise?'

29. C. Behagg, 'Narratives of control: informalism and the workplace in Britain, 1800–1900', in O. Ashton, R. Fyson and S. Roberts (eds), *The Duty of Discontent: Essays for Dorothy Thompson* (1995), pp. 135–6.

30. J. Paton, *Proletarian Pilgrimage: An Autobiography* (1935), pp. 213–18.

31. His remark was prompted by the way dog-dung would 'by means of mortar broken away from old walls, and mixed up with the whole mass, which it closely resembles' be adulterated by those who gathered it prior to sale to leather-dressers and tanners. P. Quennell (ed.), *Mayhew's London* (1969 edn), p. 307.

32. For examples, see G. M. Tuckwell and C. Smith, *The Worker's Handbook* (1908), pp. 145–53.

33. P. Gaskell, *The Manufacturing Population of England* (1833), pp. 125–6; M. Turner, 'Drink and illicit distillation in nineteenth-century Manchester', *Manchester Region History Review*, 4:1 (1990), p. 16; B. Taithe, *The Essential Mayhew* (1996), *passim*.

34. F. Willis, *101 Jubilee Road: A Book of London Yesterdays* (1948), pp. 89–92.

35. J. Child, *Industrial Relations in the British Printing Industry: The Quest for Security* (1967), p. 179.

36. J. B. Jefferys, *The Story of the Engineers 1800–1945* (1945), p. 65.

37. Booth, *Life and Labour*, pp. 266, 268.

38. M. Pember Reeves, *Round about a Pound a Week* (1913; 1979 edn), p. 2.

39. P. Snowden, *The Living Wage*, (1912), p. 28.

40. Quoted by R. P. Arnot, *South Wales Miners . . . (1898–1914)* (1967), p. 136.

41. T. Wyke and A. Fowler, *Mirth in the Mill: The Gradely World of Sam Fitton* (Oldham, 1996), pp. 47–9.

42. H. S. Jevons, *The British Coal Trade* (1915), p. 368.

43. F. Brockway, *Socialism over Sixty Years: The Life of Jowett of Bradford (1864–1944)* (1946), pp. 82–6.

44. P. S. Bagwell, *The Railwaymen: The History of the National Union of Railwaymen* (1963), p. 94.

45. Quoted by A. M. Anderson in T. Oliver (ed.), *Dangerous Trades: The Historical, Social, and Legal Aspects of Industrial Occupations as Affecting Health, by a Number of Experts* (1902), p. 24. Anderson was the principal lady inspector of factories. Sir Thomas Oliver had been a member of the Home Office Dangerous Trades Committee which issued a number of reports in the 1890s.
46. B. S. Rowntree, *Poverty: A Study of Town Life* (1910 edn), p. 136.
47. *Report of the Second Annual Conference of the Labour Representation Committee . . .* (1902), p. 17.
48. L. G. Chiozza Money, *Riches and Poverty* (1905; third edn, 1906), p. 311. The point is supported by a more recent historian of wages who has particularly emphasised that by the early 1900s middle-class men had to support families that had 50 per cent fewer children than those of the working class; see E. H. P. Brown, *The Growth of British Industrial Relations: A Study from the Standpoint of 1906–14* (1959), p. 5.
49. Quoted by J. G. Williamson, 'Earnings inequality in nineteenth-century Britain', *Journal of Economic History*, 40:3 (1980), p. 459.

3   Labour Migration

1. Emigration refers to population movement overseas; migration refers to movement *within* the United Kingdom. Hence, in the period of the Act of Union (1801–1922), it was a case of Irish *migration* to Britain, not *immigration*.
2. This observation is made by D. Baines, 'European emigration, 1815–1930: looking at the emigration decision again', *Economic History Review*, 47:3 (1994), p. 525.
3. This is the subject of J. Lucassen, *Migrant Labour in Europe, 1600–1900: The Drift to the North Sea* (1987).
4. E. G. Ravenstein, 'The laws of migration', *Journal of the Statistical Society*, 48 (1885) and his second paper, 52 (1889).
5. B. Thomas, *Migration and Economic Growth: A Study of Great Britain and the Atlantic Economy* (Cambridge, 1954). Charlotte Erickson has also asserted the importance of the urban dimension in, for example, 'Who were the English and Scottish emigrants in the 1880s?', in D. V. Glass and R. Ravelle (eds), *Population and Social Change* (1972) and 'Emigration from the British Isles to the USA in 1831', in *Population Studies*, 35 (1981). By far the best attempt to explain the interconnection between migration and emigration is D. E. Baines, *Migration in a Mature Economy: Emigration and Internal Migration in England and Wales, 1861–1900* (Cambridge, 1985).
6. For Norwegian peasant migration, see J. Gjerde, *From Peasants to Farmers: The Migration from Balestrand Norway to the Upper Middle West* (Cambridge, 1985); and J. Gjerde, 'Chain migration from the west coast of Norway', in R. J. Vecoli and S. M. Sinke (eds), *A Century of European Migrations, 1830–1930* (Urbana and Chicago, 1991).
7. R. Lawton, 'Rural depopulation in nineteenth-century England', in D. R. Mills (ed.), *English Rural Communities* (1973), p. 206. The problems associated with using the census to measure migration are discussed in D. E. Baines, 'Birthplace statistics and the analysis of internal migration', in R. Lawton (ed.),

The Census and Social Structure (1977), pp. 146–64. A fine introduction to the balance between industrialisation, urbanisation and migration can be found in R. Lawton and C. G. Pooley, *Britain, 1740–1950: An Historical Geography* (1992).

8.   There is some debate concerning the origins of overseas emigrants (whether they were urban, rural or rural and then urban). A useful contribution, which reviews the debate before concluding that Scots emigrants were mostly of urban origin, is J. Brock, 'The importance of emigration in Scottish regional population movement, 1861–1911', in T. M. Devine (ed.), *Scottish Emigration and Scottish Society* (Edinburgh, 1992), pp. 104–34.

9.   J. Langton, 'The industrial revolution and the regional geography of England', *Transactions of the Institute of British Geographers*, 9 (1984), p. 157.

10. C. G. Pooley, 'Welsh migration to England in the mid-nineteenth century', *Journal of Historical Geography*, 9:3 (1983), pp. 287–306.

11. We are reminded here of the work of a number urban sociologists, particularly Oscar Lewis, 'The folk-urban ideal type', in P. Hauser and L. Schnore (eds), *The Study of Urbanisation* (New York, 1965) and Herbert Gans's work on urbanised Mexican peasants, *The Urban Villagers* (New York, 1962).

12. The idea of migration as a chaotic uprooting was popular with post-war American writers, particularly Oscar Handlin, *The Uprooted: The Epic Study of the Great Migrants that Made the American People* (Boston, 1951) and has found certain echoes in Irish-American nationalist writings which portray the Irish as reluctant exiles, driven from their homeland by English colonialism, for example, K. A. Miller, *Emigrants and Exiles: Ireland and the Irish Exodus to North America* (Oxford, 1985).

13. P. Cromar, 'Labour migration and suburban expansion in the north of England: Sheffield in the 1860s and 1870s', in P. White and R. Woods (eds), *The Geographical Impact of Migration* (1980), p. 131. One of the main proponents of this argument is J. Saville, *Rural Depopulation in England and Wales, 1851–1951* (1957).

14. Lawton and Pooley, *Britain*, p. 32.

15. Baines, *Migration in a Mature Economy*, pp. 217–19, table 8.1.

16. This suggestion of Highland family migration, to the Lowlands and overseas, is an oft-cited theme of Devine (ed.), *Scottish Emigration*, esp. intro. and ch. 1.

17. These underestimates are reconsidered in C. M. Law, 'The growth of urban population in England and Wales, 1801–1911', *Transactions of the Institute of British Geographers*, 41 (1967).

18. N. McCord and D. J. Rowe, 'Industrialisation and urban growth in north-east England', *International Review of Social History*, 22:1 (1977), p. 31.

19. Langton, 'Regional geography of England', p. 157; R. Fynes, *The Miners of Northumberland and Durham* (1874), pp. 104–8.

20. P. Norris, 'The Irish in Tow Law, County Durham, 1851–71', *Durham County Local History Society*, 33 (1984).

21. J. D. Marshall, *Furness and the Industrial Revolution* (1958; Beckermet, 1981 edn), pp. 354–5.

22. See C. Holmes, 'Cosmopolitan London', in A. J. Kershen (ed.), *London: the Promised Land? The Migrant Experience in a Capital City* (Avebury, 1997).

23. Much of the detail in this paragraph is derived from P. J. Waller, *Town, City and Nation: England 1850–1914* (Oxford, 1983; 1991 edn), ch. 2 (quotation from p. 24).

24. Much of the detail in this paragraph is derived from Devine (ed.), *Scottish Emigration*, esp. Devine's introduction and the essay by Malcolm Gray.
25. See D. M. MacRaild, *Irish Migrants in Modern Britain, 1780–1922* (Basingstoke, 1999), pp. 29–30 for comparisons between Ireland and Scotland.
26. Data from S. Pollard, 'The ethics of the Sheffield outrages', *Transactions of the Hunter Archaeological Society*, 7 (1953–4), p. 122.
27. B. R. Mitchell and P. Deane, *Abstract of British Historical Statistics* (Cambridge, 1962), pp. 24–7.
28. Pooley, 'Welsh migration', pp. 292–7, figs 5, 6; table I; D. M. MacRaild, *Culture, Conflict and Migration: The Irish in Victorian Cumbria* (Liverpool, 1998), p. 51, table 2.8.
29. J. D. Chambers and G. E. Mingay, *The Agricultural Revolution, 1750–1880* (1966), p. 103.
30. Lawton, 'Rural depopulation', pp. 202–3.
31. A. Redford, *Labour Migration in England, 1800–1850* (1926), *passim*; C. J. Withers, 'Highland migration to Dundee, Perth and Stirling, 1753–1891', *Journal of Historical Geography*, 11:4 (1985), pp. 395–418.
32. A. K. Cairncross, 'Internal migration in Victorian England', *Manchester School*, 17 (1949), pp. 67–87; Lawton, 'Rural depopulation', pp. 196–7.
33. This is demonstrated in Saville, *Rural Depopulation, passim*.
34. This point is made in Lawton and Pooley, *Britain*, p. 30.
35. Chambers and Mingay, *Agricultural Revolution*, p. 120.
36. Additionally, the navvy 'must never be confused with the rabble of steady, common labourers, whom they out-worked, out-drank and out-rioted, and despised'. T. Coleman, *The Railway Navvies* (1968 edn), p. 25.
37. C. F. G. Masterman, *The Condition of England* (1909; 7th edn, 1912), p. 160.
38. Chambers and Mingay, *Agricultural Revolution*, pp. 186–9.
39. G. E. Mingay, 'The rural slum', in S. M. Gaskell (ed.), *Slums* (Leicester, 1990), p. 97. For an earlier period, see J. M. Johnston, *British Emigration Policy, 1815–1830: 'Shovelling out Paupers'* (Oxford, 1972).
40. F. G. Heath, *The English Peasantry* (1874), pp. 140–6, 153–6; Chambers and Mingay, *Agricultural Revolution*, pp. 146, 188–9.
41. Chambers and Mingay, *Agricultural Revolution*, p. 197.
42. A. Armstrong, *Farmworkers: A Social and Economic History 1700–1980* (1988), p. 135.
43. Figures from Lawton, 'Rural depopulation', pp. 198–9. But see also the discussion in A. L. Bowley, 'Rural depopulation in England and Wales: a study of the changes of density', *Journal of the Royal Statistical Society*, 77 (1914).
44. Baines, 'Birthplace statistics', *passim*.
45. Marshall, *Furness*, pp. 354–5.
46. MacRaild, *Irish Migrants in Modern Britain*, pp. 22–3.
47. B. M. Kerr, 'Irish seasonal migration to Great Britain, 1800–1838', *Irish Historical Studies*, 3 (1942–3), pp. 370–4; see also A. O'Dowd, *Spalpeens and Tatie Hokers: History and Folklore of the Irish Migratory Agricultural Worker in Britain* (Dublin, 1991).
48. T. M. Devine, 'Highland migration to Lowland Scotland, 1760–1860', *Scottish Historical Review*, 62:2 (1983).
49. T. M. Devine, *The Great Highland Famine: Hunger. Emigration and the Scottish Highlands in the Nineteenth Century* (Edinburgh, 1988), p. 81.

50. D. F. Macdonald. *Scotland's Shifting Population, 1770–1850* (Glasgow, 1937), pp. 132–3, and J. E. Handley, *The Irish in Scotland, 1798–1845* (Cork, 1945), p. 34 suggest that Highlanders were pushed out by the Irish, whereas T. M. Devine, 'Temporary migration and the Scottish Highlands in the nineteenth century', *Economic History Review*, 32:3 (1979), points to the continuing importance of temporary work.

51. An impressive comparative study of British and American economic development, where labour supplies and the role of technology were different, is H. J. Habakkuk, *American and British Technology in the Nineteenth Century* (Cambridge, 1962). Labour shortages encouraged American farmers and capitalists to invest very heavily in technology.

52. W. H. Chaloner, *The Social and Economic Development of Crewe, 1780–1923* (Manchester, 1950), pp. 46–7.

53. J. D. Marshall and J. K. Walton, *The Lake Counties from 1830 to the Mid-Twentieth Century* (Manchester, 1981), pp. 46, 86.

54. For the navvies, see Coleman, *Railway Navvies*; D. Sullivan, *Navvyman* (1983); and D. Brooke, *The Railway Navvies: 'That Despised Race of Men'* (Newton Abbot, 1983).

55. E. J. Hobsbawm, 'The tramping artisan', *Labouring Men: Studies in the History of Labour* (1964), pp. 34–63.

56. H. Southall, 'The tramping artisan revisits: labour mobility and economic distress in early Victorian England', *Economic History Review*, 64:2 (1991), pp. 272–96. R. A. Leeson, *Travelling Brothers* (1979), ch. 10.

57. Baines, *Migration in a Mature Economy*, p. 159; Marshall and Walton, *Lake Counties*, pp. 41, 86; J. Rowe, *The Hard Rock Men: Cornish Migrants and the North American Mining Frontier* (Liverpool, 1974); D. Emmons, *The Butte Irish: Class and Ethnicity in an American Mining Town, 1875–1925* (Urbana and Chicago, 1989).

58. These events are discussed in Pollard, 'Sheffield outrages'.

59. S. Pollard and P. Robertson, *The British Shipbuilding Industry, 1850–1914* (1979), p. 163.

60. *Ibid.*, pp. 156–7, 162–3, 178, 197.

61. MacRaild, *Culture, Conflict and Migration*, pp. 46–7.

62. The idea that all (pre-Famine) Irish labour was ultimately bound for America is considered by R-A. Harris, *The Nearest Place that Wasn't Ireland: Early Nineteenth-Century Labor Migration* (Ames, Iowa, 1994). For a detailed overview of all the main issues, see MacRaild, *Irish Migrants in Modern Britain*, chs 1–2.

63. F. Neal, *Black 47: Britain and the Famine Irish* (Basingstoke, 1997) is a major study of the Famine influx.

64. Withers, 'Highland migration', p. 413; B. Disraeli, *Sybil, Or the Two Nations* (1845; 1985 edn), p. 130; E. Gaskell, *Mary Barton; a Tale of Manchester Life* (1848; 1985 edn), p. 222 and *North and South* (1855; 1994 edn).

65. E. H. Hunt, *Regional Wage Variations in Britain, 1850–1914* (Oxford, 1973); J. G. Williamson, 'The impact of the Irish on British labor markets during the Industrial Revolution', *Journal of Economic History*, 46 (1986), reprinted in R. Swift and S. Gilley (eds), *The Irish in Britain, 1815–1939* (1989).

4   Community

1. P. Gurney, '"Measuring the distance": D. H. Lawrence, Raymond Williams and the quest for "community"', in K . Laybourn (ed.), *Social Conditions, Status and Community, 1860–c.*1920 (Stroud, 1997), p. 160.
2. R. Williams, *Keywords* (1976), pp. 65–6.
3. See introduction to M. Drake (ed.), *Time, Family and Community: Perspectives on Family and Community History* (Oxford, 1994), esp. p. 1.
4. R. Dennis and S. Daniels, '"Community" and the social geography of Victorian cities', in *ibid.*, p. 202.
5. An evocative consideration of community in a de-industrialising age is R. Colls, 'Save our pits and communities', *Labour History Review*, 60:2 (1995), pp. 55–65.
6. Although concerned mostly with an earlier period, J. Rule, *The Labouring Classes in Early Industrial England, 1750–1850* (1986), pp. 155–67 contains an excellent discussion of the idea of community.
7. Gurney, '"Measuring the distance"', p. 160.
8. J. P. Kay Shuttleworth, *Moral and Physical Condition of the Working Classes Employed in the Cotton Manufacture in Manchester* ([1832]; 1970), p. 20.
9. J. D. Chambers and G. E. Mingay, *The Agricultural Revolution, 1750–1880* (1966), p. 197.
10. J. Burnett, *A Social History of Housing, 1815–85* (1978; 1986 edn), pp. 30–1.
11. Cited in J. D. Marshall and J. K. Walton, *The Lake Counties from 1830 to the Mid-Twentieth Century* (Manchester, 1981), pp. 92–3.
12. James Caird, *English Agriculture in 1850–51* (1852), p. 389.
13. G. E. Mingay, 'The rural slum', in S. M. Gaskell (ed.), *Slums* (Leicester, 1990).
14. W. Cobbett, *Tour in Scotland; and in the Four Northern Counties of England: In the Autumn of the Year 1832* (1833), p. 84.
15. M. J. Daunton, 'Housing', in F. M. L. Thompson (ed.), *The Cambridge Social History of Britain, 1750–1950*, 3 vols (Cambridge, 1990), II: *People and Their Environment*, p. 217.
16. Kay Shuttleworth, *Moral and Physical*, p. 21.
17. I. C. Taylor, 'The court and cellar dwelling: the eighteenth-century origins of the Liverpool slum', *Transactions of the Historic Society of Lancashire and Cheshire*, 62 (1970).
18. F. Neal, *Sectarian Violence: The Liverpool Experience, 1819–1914* (Manchester, 1988), p. 4.
19. E. Gauldie, *Cruel Habitations: A History of Working-Class Housing, 1780–1918* (1974), p. 83.
20. For national figures, see, for example, P. Razzell, *The Conquest of Small Pox: The Impact of Innoculation on Smallpox Mortality in Twentieth Century Britain* (Firle, Sussex, 1977). The disease resulted in 540 deaths in 1871–2. These figures were reported in the *Barrow Herald*, 6 July 1872 as part of discussions of a local epidemic.
21. Reported in J. Adshead, *Distress in Manchester: Evidence . . . of the State of the Labouring Classes in 1840–2* (1842), p. 16.
22. Henry Mayhew, *London Labour and the London Poor* (1985 edn) pp. 113–19.

23. *Report of the General Board of Health on a Preliminary Inquiry into Sewerage, Drainage and Supply of Water, and Sanitary Condition of Inhabitants of the Town of Whitehaven* (1849), p. 8.
24. Reprinted in J. Ginswick (ed.), *Labour and the Poor in England and Wales, 1849–1851*, 8 vols (1983); I, p. 78.
25. Burnett, *Housing*, p. 70.
26. Cited in Burnett, *Housing*, p. 70.
27. D. Englander, *Landlord and Tenant in Urban Britain, 1838–1918* (Oxford, 1983). This book is especially concerned with wartime rent strikes, but early discussions do refer to poor housing and a sense of landlords' exploitation.
28. E. Roberts, 'Working-class housing in Barrow and Lancaster, 1880–1930', *Transactions of the Historic Society of Lancashire and Cheshire*, 69 (1977), p. 121.
29. Although not the most recent writing on the subject, M. Anderson, *Approaches to the History of the Western Family, 1500–1914* (1980) is still perhaps the most trenchant. It should be read with Anderson's updated essay cited in the following note.
30. The phrase 'affective individualism' is Lawrence Stone's in *The Family, Sex and Marriage in England, 1500–1800* (New York, 1977). For a discussion of proletarianisation, see D. Levine, 'Industrialisation and the proletarian family in England', *Past and Present*, 107 (1985), *passim*. The best short overview is Anderson, 'What is new about the modern family', in Drake (ed.), *Time, Family and Community*, pp. 67–90.
31. P. Burke, *History and Social Theory* (Oxford, 1992), p. 56.
32. For an introductiory discussion, see J. A. Sharpe, *Early-Modern England: A Social History 1550–1760* (1987), ch. 2.
33. M. Anderson, *Family Structure in Nineteenth Century Lancashire* (Cambridge, 1971), ch. 5.
34. One of the clearest and most accessible evaluations of women's experiences of work in the nineteenth century is J. Saville, 'Working-class women in nineteenth-century Britain', in C. Holmes and A. Booth (eds), *Economy and Society: European Industrialisation and its Social Consequences: Essays Presented to Sidney Pollard* (Leicester, 1991), pp. 141–53. For discussion of a range of women's personal testimonies (often admittedly reminiscences from the twentieth century) relating to the north-east coalfield, but more broadly useful as an insight into past working-class life, see H. Beynon and T. Austrin, *Masters and Servants. Class and Patronage in the Making of a Labour Organisation: The Durham Miners and the English Political Tradition* (1994), ch. 7.
35. R. Roberts, *The Classic Slum* (Manchester, 1971), p. 26.
36. E. Ross, 'Survival networks: women's neighbourhood sharing in London before World War I', *History Workshop*, 15 (1983), p. 5. More detailed accounts are E. Ross, *Love and Toil: Motherhood in Outcast London, 1870–1918* (Oxford, 1993); and C. Chinn, *They Worked All Their Lives: Women of the Urban Poor in England, 1880–1939* (Manchester, 1988).
37. See M. J. Tebbutt, *Women's Talk: A Social History of 'Gossip' in Working-Class Neighbourhoods, 1880–1960* (Aldershot, 1995) for an interesting discussion of this.
38. E. P. Thompson's 'Rough music' represents a scholarly treatment of the subject touched upon by Hardy. See *Customs in Common* (1991), pp. 467–538.

39. S. Fielding, *Class and Ethnicity: Irish Catholics in England, 1880–1939* (Manchester, 1993), p. 60.
40. This is discussed by M. J. Hickman, *Religion, Class and Identity; The State, the Catholic Church and the Education of the Irish in Britain* (Aldershot, 1995), esp. chs 4–5.
41. E. Roberts, 'Working-class standards of living in three Lancashire towns, 1890–1914', *International Review of Social History*, 27 (1982), pp. 50–1, figures from table 4. See also E. Roberts, 'Working-class standards of living in Barrow and Lancaster, 1890–1914', *Economic History Review*, 30 (1977), pp. 314–15 for the more nutritious food served by the wives of Barrow and Lancaster.
42. Saville, 'Working-class women', p. 145.
43. This woman's words were remembered by one of the commissioners, Sidney Webb, who recorded them in his *Story of the Durham Miners* (1921), cited in Saville, 'Working-class women', p. 145.
44. J. Lawson, *A Man's Life* (1932), p. 52. See also Bill Williamson, *Class, Culture and Community: A Biographical Study of Social Change in Mining* (1982), p. 126.
45. J. Burnett, *Destiny Obscure: Autobiographies of Childhood, Education and Family from the 1820s to the 1920s* (1982), p. 219.
46. C. Cookson, *Our Kate: An Autobiography* (1974), p. 26.
47. Saville, 'Working-class women', p. 146.
48. F. G. Heath, *The English Peasantry* (1874), pp. 94–100, 140–5.
49. A. Young, *A Tour in Ireland. With General Observations on the Present State of that Kingdom made in the Years 1776, 1777 and 1778* (Cambridge, 1925 edn), p. 185.
50. Adshead, *Distress in Manchester*, pp. 29–30.
51. *Barrow Advertiser and District Reporter*, 15 October 1868.
52. W. Cooke Taylor, *Notes of a Tour in the Manufacturing Districts of Lancashire* (1842; 1968 edn), p. 132.
53. The best brief introduction to this question is H. Cunningham, 'Leisure and culture', in Thompson (ed.), *Cambridge Social History*, II, pp. 279–340. For the early part of our period, see H. Cunningham, *Leisure in the Industrial Revolution, c.1780–1880* (1980). A useful collection on the subject is J. K. Walton and J. Walvin (eds), *Leisure in Britain, 1780–1939* (Manchester, 1983).
54. J. M. Golby and A. W. Purdue, *The Civilisation of the Crowd: Popular Culture in England, 1750–1900* (1984), p. 201.
55. E. Taplin, *The Dockers' Union: A Study of the National Union of Dock Labourers, 1889–1922* (Leicester, 1985), p. 17.
56. E. P. Thompson, *The Making of the English Working Class* (1963; 1986 edn), p. 74. See D. A. Reid, 'The decline of St Monday, 1766–1876', *Past and Present*, 71 (1976). More recently, Reid has revisited this theme with an assessment of the tradition's decline, based upon an analysis of the day upon which working people chose to marry. The increasing prominence of Saturday suggests that the working week was becoming sacrosanct in our period: 'Weddings, weekends, work and leisure in urban England, 1791–1911: the decline of Saint Monday revisited', *Past and Present*, 153 (1996).
57. R. Hutton, *The Rise and Fall of Merrie England: The Ritual Year, 1400–1700* (Oxford, 1994).
58. R. W. Malcolmson, *Popular Recreation in English Society, 1700–1850* (Cambridge, 1973), p. 57; R. Munting, *An Economic and Social History of Gambling in Britain and the USA* (Manchester, 1996), p. 16.

59. Cunningham, 'Leisure and culture', p. 305.
60. J. Bullock, *Bower's Row: Recollections of a Mining Village* (Wakefield, 1976), pp. 14–16. See also R. W. Malcolmson and S. Mastoris, *The English Pig: A History* (1998), *passim*.
61. E. P. Thompson, 'Time, work-discipline and industrial capitalism', *Past and Present*, 38 (1967), reprinted in E. P. Thompson, *Customs in Common* (1991).
62. Munting, *Gambling in Britain and the USA*, pp. 6–28. See also M. Clapson, *A Bit of a Flutter: Popular Gambling and English Society, c.1823–1961* (1992), chs 2–3; and C. Chinn, *Better Betting with a Decent Feller: Bookmaking, Betting and the British Working Class* (1991).
63. The most up-to-date overview is H. MacLeod, *Religion and Society in England, 1850–1914* (Basingstoke, 1996), which has an excellent bibliography.
64. The various religions are analysed in G. Parsons and J. R. Moore (eds), *Religion in Victorian Britain*, 4 vols (Manchester, 1988).
65. For perspectives on the importance of Catholicism, and on its social dimensions, see D. M. MacRaild, *Irish Migrants in Modern Britain, 1750–1922* (Basingstoke, 1999), ch. 3.
66. J. E. Handley, *The Irish in Modern Scotland* (Cork, 1947), p. 227.
67. Three volumes by D. Birley emphasise the development and importance of modern sport: *Sport and the Making of Britain* (Manchester, 1993), *Land of Sport and Glory: Sport and British Society, 1887–1910* (Manchester, 1994) and *Playing the Game: Sport and British Society, 1910–1945* (Manchester, 1995).
68. G. S. Jones, *Languages of Class: Studies in English Working Class History, 1832–1982* (Cambridge, 1983), p. 225. For a more popular treatment of the theme, see C. MacInnes, *Sweet Saturday Night* (1967).
69. Cunningham, 'Leisure and culture', pp. 309, 314; A. Metcalfe, 'Organised sports in the mining communities of south Northumberland, 1800–1889', *Victorian Studies*, 25 (1982), p. 479.
70. *Barrow Herald*, 24 June 1871.
71. *Ibid.*, 13 February 1875.
72. R. J. Morris, 'Clubs, societies and associations', in F. M. L. Thompson (ed.), *Cambridge Social History of Britain, 1750–1950*, 3 vols (Cambridge, 1990), II, pp. 426–8. See too C. Waters, *British Socialists and the Politics of Popular Culture, 1884–1914* (Manchester, 1990), *passim*.
73. Birley, *Playing the Game*, p. 1.
74. A. Freeman, *Boy Life and Labour: The Manufacture of Inefficiency* (1914), p. 152. For street life, see also H. Hendrick, *Images of Youth: Age, Class and the Male Youth Problem, 1880–1920* (Oxford, 1991), pp. 129–31.
75. A. F. Winnington Ingram, *Work in Great Cities: Six Lectures on Pastoral Theology* (1895), p. 13.

5   Self-Help and Associationalism

1. The author who posited these three possibilities prefers the latter: M. Chase, 'Out of radicalism: the mid-Victorian freehold land movement', *English Historical Review*, 56 (1991), p. 325.

2. Prominent among those applying the 'linguistic turn' to labour history are Patrick Joyce and James Vernon. However, a more traditional study, J. Benson, *The Working Class in Britain, 1850–1939* (1988), also questions the applicability of an homogenous notion of class. These authors and the question of class are discussed in our introduction, above, pp. 11–14.

3. R. N. Price, 'The working men's club movement and Victorian social reform ideology', *Victorian Studies*, 15:2 (1971), p. 117.

4. R. J. Morris, 'Clubs, societies and associations', in F. M. L. Thompson (ed.), *Cambridge Social History of Britain, 1750–1950*, 3 vols (Cambridge, 1990), II.

5. A recent discussion can be found in A. J. Kidd, *State, Society and the Poor in Nineteenth Century England* (1999).

6. E. Burke, 'Thoughts and details on scarcity', in *The Works and Correspondence of the Right Honourable Edmund Burke*, 8 vols (1852), V, p. 190; see also J. R. Poynter, *Society and Pauperism: English Ideas on Poor Relief, 1795–1834* (1969), pp. 52–5.

7. D. Fraser, *The Evolution of the Welfare State* (1973), pp. 33–4.

8. This line of thinking remained prominent into the mid-Victorian years, and informed opinion on both sides of the Atlantic. Thus see, for example, James Bryce, 'The American experience in the relief of the poor', *Macmillan's Magazine*, 25 (1871–2).

9. S. Smiles, *Self-Help; with Illustrations of Conduct and Perseverance* (1886 edn), p. 1.

10. S. Smiles, *Thrift: A Book of Domestic Counsel* (1875; 1908 edn), p. 121.

11. Cited in J. Benson, *The Penny Capitalists: A Study of Nineteenth-Century Working-Class Entrepreneurs* (Dublin, 1988), p. 139.

12. Fraser, *Welfare State*, p. 96.

13. T. Koditschek, *Class Formation and Urban–Industrial Society: Bradford 1750–1850* (Cambridge, 1990), p. 460.

14. Useful studies of the contribution of press campaigns to social reform include G. R. Searle, *The Quest for National Efficiency* (Oxford, 1971); B. B. Gilbert, *The Evolution of National Insurance* (1966); J. R. Hay, *The Origins of the Liberal Welfare Reforms, 1906–1914* (1975).

15. E. Royle, *Modern Britain: A Social History, 1750–1985* (1987), p. 186.

16. Benson, *Penny Capitalists*. Two important essays on this aspect of working-class life are E. Roberts, 'Working-class standards of living in three Lancashire towns, 1890–1914', *International Review of Social History*, 27:1 (1982), and E. Roberts, 'Working-class standards of living in Barrow and Lancaster, 1890–1914', *Economic History Review*, 30:2 (1977). For pawnshops, see M. Tebbutt, *Making Ends Meet: Pawnbroking and Working-Class Credit* (Leicester, 1983), *passim*.

17. J. M. Golby and A. W. Purdue, *The Civilisation of the Crowd: Popular Culture in England, 1750–1900* (1984), p. 185.

18. F. D. Maurice, *Learning and Working*, edited with an introduction by W. E. Styler (1855; Hull, 1968 edn), p. 132.

19. Quoted in G. D. H. Cole and R. Postgate, *The Common People, 1746–1946* (1966 edn), p. 379.

20. Price, 'Working men's club', p. 133.

21.   G. Tremlett, *Clubmen: History of the Working Men's Club and Institute Union* (1987), p. 21.

22.   *The Coal Question: An Inquiry Concerning the Progress of the Nation, and the Probable Exhaustion of our Coal-mines* (1866; New York, 1965), pp. xlvii–viii. The real target of Jevons's ire, however, was child labour: 'A worse premium upon improvidence and future wretchedness could not be imagined.'

23.   J. R. Leifchild, *Our Coal and our Coal-pits; The People in Them and the Scenes around Them. By a Traveller Underground* (1856), p. 224.

24.   *Ibid.*, p. 225.

25.   D. Vincent, *Literacy and Popular Culture: England, 1750–1914* (Cambridge, 1989).

26.   In contrast, John Benson has argued that 'The majority of the better off found their consolation, not in the education of their children but in the material benefits of the new consumerism': *The Working Class in Britain, 1850–1939* (1994 edn), p. 146.

27.   Morris, 'Clubs, societies and associations', pp. 396–405.

28.   P. H. J. H. Gosden, *The Friendly Societies in England, 1815–1875* (Manchester, 1961); G. Crossick, *An Artisan Elite in Victorian Society: Kentish London, 1840–80* (1978), esp. ch. 9.

29.   Words from the act, 33rd Geo. III, c. 54, quoted in R. W. Moffrey, *A Century of Oddfellowship. Being a Brief Record of the Rise and Progress of the Manchester Unity* . . . (Manchester, 1910), p. 197, appendix II.

30.   Gosden, *Friendly Societies*, pp. 10, 11, 13.

31.   Moffrey, *Century of Oddfellowship*, pp. 11–13.

32.   Gosden, *Friendly Societies*, pp. 30–1.

33.   Moffrey, *Century of Oddfellowship*, p. 196.

34.   Gosden, *Friendly Societies*, p. 46.

35.   Quoted by Ben Turner, *About Myself* (1930), p. 55.

36.   A Journeyman Engineer [Thomas Wright], *Some Habits and Customs of the Working* Classes (1867), p. 74.

37.   For the Catholic Church's attitude towards trade unions and politics and its self-help alternatives, see J. H. Treble, 'The attitude of the Roman Catholic church towards trade unionism in the north of England', *Northern History*, 5 (1970) and G. P. Connolly, 'The Catholic church and the first Manchester and Salford trade unions in the age of the Industrial Revolution', *Transactions of the Lancashire and Cheshire Antiquarian Society*, 135 (1985). The only comprehensive treatment of Ribbonism is John Belchem, '"Freedom and Friendship to Ireland": Ribbonism in early nineteenth-century Liverpool', *International Review of Social History*, 39 (1994).

38.   See M. E. Rose, *The Relief of Poverty, 1834–1914* (1972), p. 53 appendix A.

39.   Advertisement in *Barrow and District Year Book* (1908), p. 3.

40.   Tebbutt, *Making Ends Meet*, *passim*.

41.   There are numerous studies of the building societies. Detailed histories of the movement can be found in S. M. Price, *Building Societies: Their Origin and History* (1958); E. J. Cleary, *The Building Society Movement* (1965); and M. Body, *The Building Societies* (1980). See also several references in J. Burnett, *A Social History of Housing, 1815–1970* (1980).

42. F. M. L. Thompson, *The Rise of Respectable Society: A Social History of Victorian Britain, 1830–1900* (1988), p. 168.
43. This movement is discussed by Chase, 'Out of radicalism', pp. 319–45.
44. P. Johnson, *Saving and Spending: The Working-Class Economy in Britain, 1870–1939* (Oxford, 1985), pp. 116–18; also p. 119, table 4.6.
45. See D. E. Martin, 'Land reform', in P. Hollis (ed.), *Pressure from Without in Early Victorian England* (1974), esp. pp. 150–2.
46. Ezra Naylor, *Bradford Building Societies from 1823* (Bradford, 1908), p. 66.
47. The class basis of these societies is illustrated in S. D. Chapman and J. N. Bartlett, 'The contribution of building clubs and freehold land societies to working-class housing in Birmingham', in S. D. Chapman (ed.), *The History of Working-Class Housing: A Symposium* (Newton Abbot, 1971).
48. Chase, 'Out of radicalism', p. 319.
49. Smiles, *Thrift*, p. 122. Smiles was quoting G. J. Holyoake.
50. G. Hobson, 'Walkley: a fifty year old workingman's garden suburb', *The Town Planning Review*, 3:1 (1912), p. 42.
51. Johnson, *Saving and Spending*, pp. 165–9.
52. *Ibid.*, pp. 87–96.
53. J. Burnett, *Plenty and Want: A Social History of Diet in England from 1815 to the Present Day* (1979 edn), p. 55.
54. The literature on co-operation is substantial but often unscholarly. A perceptive discussion of the movement's historiography can be found in P. Gurney, 'Heads, hands and the co-operative utopia: an essay in historiography', *North West Labour History*, 19 (1994/5), pp. 3–23. Gurney, *Co-operation, Culture and the Politics of Consumption in England, 1870–1939* (Manchester, 1996) is by far the best full-scale analysis of the movement's golden age.
55. P. Redfern, *The New History of the Co-operative Wholesale Society* (1938), pp. 10–11.
56. R. G. Garnett, *Co-operation and the Owenite Socialist Communities in Britain, 1825–45* (Manchester, 1972), ch. 1. See also J. F. C. Harrison, *Robert Owen and the Owenites in Britain and America: The Quest for the New Moral World* (1969); G. Claeys, *Machinery, Money and the Millennium: The New Moral Economy of Owenite Socialism, 1815–67* (1987).
57. S. Pollard, 'Nineteenth-century co-operation: community building to shop-keeping', in A. Briggs and J. Saville (eds), *Essays in Labour History* (1960).
58. G. J. Holyoake, *The History of Co-operation* (1908), pp. 270–1.
59. Redfern, *Co-operative*, p. 404; Johnson, *Saving and Spending*, p. 101, table 4.3.
60. L. McCullough Thew, *The Pit Village and the Store* (1985); K. Brown, 'The lodges of the Durham Miners' Association', *Northern History*, 23 (1987).
61. P. Gurney, 'The middle-class embrace: language, representation, and the contest over co-operative forms in Britain, c.1860–1914', *Victorian Studies*, 37 (1994).
62. Smiles, *Thrift*, p. 110.
63. Data derived from Redfern, *Co-operative*, table on p. 532.
64. Smiles, *Self-Help*, pp. 303–4.
65. See E. Malcolm, *'Ireland Sober, Ireland Free': Drink and Temperance in Nineteenth-Century Ireland* (New York and Dublin, 1986), ch. 3; and for Crowe, see D. Thompson, 'Ireland and the Irish in English Radicalism before

1850', in D. Thompson and J. Epstein (eds), *The Chartist Experience: Studies in Working-Class Radicalism and Culture, 1830–1860* (1982).

66. Still the best study of Victorian attitudes to drink (though concentrating on the temperance crusade) is B. Harrison, *Drink and the Victorians: The Temperance Question in England, 1815–1872* (1971).

67. B. Harrison, 'Pubs', in H. J. Dyos and M. Woolf (eds), *The Victorian City: Images and Reality* (1973), p. 161.

68. J. D. Marshall, *Furness and the Industrial Revolution* (1958; Beckermet, 1981 edn), p. 327; *Barrow Herald*, 6 September 1871.

69. W. J. Lowe, *The Irish in Mid-Victorian Lancashire: The Shaping of a Working-Class Community* (New York, 1989), p. 37.

70. W. E. Ritchie, *Freehold Land Societies: Their History, Present Position, and Claims* (1853), p. 19.

71. The connections between these aspects of 'respectability' are discussed in Harrison, *Drink and the Victorians*.

72. Speech in the House of Commons (Election Bill), 31 July 1871, *Hansard's Parliamentary Debates, Third Series*, vol. 208, cols 588–9.

73. Gurney, 'Middle-class embrace', p. 279.

74. G. D. H. Cole and R. Postgate, *The Common People, 1746–1946* (1966 edn), p. 688.

6   Conflict and Conciliation

1. For Burke's position, stated in his address to the electors of Bristol, see B. W. Hill (ed.), *Edmund Burke on Government, Politics and Society* (1975), pp. 156–8.

2. M. Brock, *The Great Reform Act* (1973), p. 319. The figures are taken from C. Cook and B. Keith, *British Historical Facts 1830–1900* (1975), p. 116, although other authorities offer different calculations.

3. P. Linebaugh, *The London Hanged: Crime and Civil Society in the Eighteenth Century* (1991), p. 39.

4. The fullest analysis of the Anatomy Act is R. Richardson, *Death, Dissection and the Destitute* (1988), while among discussions of the hostility created by the new poor law are M. E. Rose, 'The anti-Poor Law agitation', in J. T. Ward (ed.), *Popular Movements c.1830–1850* (1970); N. C. Edsall, *The Anti-Poor Law Movement, 1834–44* (1971); and J. Knott, *Popular Opposition to the 1834 Poor Law* (1986).

5. S. and B. Webb, *The History of Trade Unionism* (1911 edn), pp. 153–4. For an assessment of the strike of 1837 during which a blackleg was murdered, and the trial of 1838, see W. H. Fraser, 'The Glasgow Spinners, 1837', in J. Butt and J. T. Ward (eds), *Scottish Themes* (Edinburgh, 1976).

6. Quoted in J. H. Wiener, *The War of the Unstamped: The Movement to Repeal the British Newspaper Tax, 1830–1836* (1969), p. 3. The newspaper tax, first introduced in 1712, was raised to 4d in 1815. That its function was to suppress sedition rather than raise revenue was indicated by the £20 penalty for publishing or selling an unstamped paper. See also P. Hollis, *The Pauper Press: A Study of Working-Class Radicalism of the 1830s* (Oxford, 1970).

7. *Poor Man's Guardian*, 21 June 1834.
8. For Wakley's role, see S. S. Sprigge, *The Life and Times of Thomas Wakley* (1897), ch. 29. There is a useful survey of radical issues and personalities in D. Nicholls, 'Friends of the people: parliamentary supporters of popular radicalism, 1832–1849', *Labour History Review*, 62:2 (1997), pp. 127–46.
9. Quoted by E. Halévy, *England in 1815* (1924; 1961 edn), p. 151.
10. J. Vincent, *The Formation of the Liberal Party 1857–1868* (1966), p. 102.
11. Quoted by T. Rothstein, *From Chartism to Labourism: Historical Sketches of the English Working Class Movement* (1929), p. 46.
12. Quoted by R. G. Gammage, *History of the Chartist Movement 1837–1854* (1894; 1969 edn), pp. 56, 59.
13. W. Lovett and J. Collins, *Chartism; A New Organization of the People* (1840; reprinted with an introduction by A. Briggs, Leicester, 1969), p. vi.
14. D. Thompson, *The Chartists: Popular Politics in the Industrial Revolution* (1984), pp. 79–86, 280–1.
15. G. Rudé, 'Protest and punishment in nineteenth-century Britain', *Albion*, 5:1 (1973), pp. 18–19.
16. J. Saville, *The Consolidation of the Capitalist State, 1800–1850* (1994), p. 81.
17. According to W. H. Chaloner, *The Hungry Forties: A Re-examination* (1957), p. 6, the phrase did not come into currency until 1904, when it was coined as part of the free-trade campaign against tariff reform.
18. *Northern Star*, 9 February 1839, quoted by A. R. Schoyen, *The Chartist Challenge: A Portrait of George Julian Harney* (1958), p. 49.
19. Gammage, *Chartist Movement*, p. 97.
20. *The Annual Register . . . 1848* (1849), p. 166.
21. O'Connor owned property in Ireland and his scheme can be linked to projects advocating spade husbandry to remedy Irish poverty. See D. Read and E. Glasgow, *Feargus O'Connor: Irishman and Chartist* (1961), pp. 108–9.
22. M. Chase, *'The People's Farm': English Radical Agrarianism 1775–1840* (Oxford, 1988), *passim*.
23. A. Plummer, *Bronterre: A Political Biography of Bronterre O'Brien 1804–1864* (1971), p. 181; J. MacAskill, 'The Chartist Land Plan', in A. Briggs (ed.), *Chartist Studies* (1959), p. 339.
24. D. Goodway, *London Chartism 1838–1848* (Cambridge, 1982), p. 225.
25. D. Jones, 'Women and Chartism', *History*, 68 (1983); Thompson, *The Chartists*, ch. 7; J. Schwarzkopf, *Women in the Chartist Movement* (1991); O. Ashton et al. (eds), *The Chartist Legacy* (1999); D. M. MacRaild, *Irish Immigrants in Modern Britain, 1750–1922* (1999), pp. 131–8.
26. F. Bédarida, *A Social History of England 1851–1975* (1979), p. 5.
27. Webb, *Trade Unionism*, ch. 4. See, however, W. H. Fraser, *A History of British Trade Unionism, 1700–1998* (1999), p. 1 for a recent critique of the Webbs' categorisation.
28. Engels to Marx, 7 October 1858, in *Karl Marx and Frederick Engels on Britain* (Moscow, 1962), pp. 537–8.
29. E. P. Thompson, 'The peculiarities of the English', in R. Miliband and J. Saville (eds), *The Socialist Register 1965* (1965), pp. 343–4. Reprinted in E. P. Thompson, *The Poverty of Theory and Other Essays* (1978). Thompson

was commenting on the argument of Perry Anderson that the 'shattering fiasco of Chartism' broke the morale of the proletariat and led to the working class becoming 'the most numbed and docile' in Europe.

30. J. Saville, *Ernest Jones: Chartist* (1952), p. 73; M. Finn, *After Chartism: Class and Nation in English Radical Politics, 1848–1974* (Cambridge, 1993), esp. chs 3–4. Compare M. Taylor, *The Decline of British Radicalism, 1847–1860* (Oxford, 1995), *passim*.

31. R. D. Storch, 'The plague of the blue locusts: police reform and popular resistance in northern England, 1840–57', *International Review of Social History*, 20:1 (1975), p. 89. See too D. Taylor, *The New Police in Nineteenth-Century England: Crime, Conflict and Control* (Manchester, 1997), p. 37 and R. D. Storch, 'The policeman as domestic missionary: urban discipline and popular culture in nothern England, 1950–1980', *Journal of Social History*, 9:4 (1976), pp. 481–509.

32. D. Williams, *John Frost: A Study in Chartism* (Cardiff, 1939), pp. 314–15, which links Frost's pardon to that of William Smith O'Brien, the leader of the Irish rebellion of 1848.

33. F. Neal, *Sectarian Violence, The Liverpool Experience, 1819–1914: An Aspect of Anglo-Irish History* (Manchester, 1988), chs 5–9; S. Gilley, 'The Garibaldi riots of 1862', *Historical Journal*, 16:4 (1973); for Murphy, see MacRaild, *Irish Immigrants*, pp. 176–8, and the sources there cited.

34. V. Bailey, 'Salvation Army riots, the "Skeleton Army" and legal authority in the provincial town', in A. P. Donajgrodzki (ed.), *Social Control in Nineteenth Century Britain* (1977), p. 234.

35. J. H. Linforth, *Leaves from an Agent's Diary: Being Reminiscences of Thirty Years' Work as a Liberal Agent* (Leeds, 1911), p. 93; for a general discussion of violence associated with elections, see D. C. Richter, *Riotous Victorians* (1981), ch. 5.

36. J. D. Marshall, *Furness in the Industrial Revolution* (1958), p. 316; R. N. Price, 'The other face of respectability: violence in the Manchester brickmaking trade 1859–1870', *Past and Present*, 66 (1974), esp. pp. 123–9.

37. G. I. H. Lloyd, *The Cutlery Trades: An Historical Essay in the Economics of Small-Scale Production* (1913), ch. 11; S. Pollard, 'The ethics of the Sheffield outrages', *Transactions of the Hunter Archaelogical Society*, 7 (1953–4), pp. 118–39.

38. W. H. Fraser, *Trade Unions and Society: The Struggle for Acceptance 1850–1880* (1974), pp. 187–8; R. Price, *Masters, Unions and Men: Work Control in Building and the Rise of Labour* (Cambridge, 1980), p. 61.

39. Webb, *Trade Unionism*, ch. 5.

40. W. Bagehot, *The English Constitution* (1872; 1963 edn), pp. 278, 281.

41. R. J. Harrison, *Before the Socialists: Studies in Labour and Politics 1861–1881* (1965), p. 82; see too Richter, *Riotous Victorians*, ch. 4.

42. Marx to Liebknecht, 11 February 1878, in *Marx and Engels on Britain*, pp. 554–5. Compare H. F. Moorhouse, 'The Marxist theory of the labour aristocracy', *Social History*, 3:1 (1978), p. 62.

43. E. Royle, *Radicals, Secularists and Republicans: Popular Freethought in Britain, 1866–1915* (Manchester, 1980), ch. 11; F. A. D'Arcy, 'Charles Bradlaugh and the English republican movement, 1868–1878', *Historical Journal*, 25:2 (1982); E. F. Biagini, *Liberty, Retrenchment and Reform: Popular Liberalism in the Age of Gladstone, 1860–1880* (Cambridge, 1992), *passim*.

44. S. Pollard, *Labour History and the Labour Movement* (Aldershot, 1999), p. 37, referring to Sheffield in 1868. For examples of other studies, see J. Foster, *Class Struggle and the Industrial Revolution* (1974), ch. 7, for Oldham; D. Smith, *Conflict and Compromise: Class Formation in English Society, 1830–1914, a Comparative Study of Birmingham and Sheffield* (1982); J. Garrard, *Leadership and Power in Victorian Industrial Towns 1830–80* (Manchester, 1983) for Rochdale, Salford and Bolton; T. Koditschek, *Class Formation and Urban–Industrial Society: Bradford, 1750–1850* (Cambridge, 1990), ch. 18; M. Hewitt, *The Emergence of Stability in the Industrial City: Manchester 1832–67* (Aldershot, 1996).

45. J. Shepherd, 'Labour and Parliament: the Lib-Labs as the first working-class MPs, 1885–1906', in E. F. Biagini and A. J. Reid (eds), *Currents of Radicalism: Popular Radicalism, Organised Labour and Party Politics in Britain, 1850–1914* (Cambridge, 1991), pp. 189–90.

46. R. McKenzie and A. Silver, *Angels in Marble: Working-Class Conservatives in Urban England* (1968), p. ii for the comment of *The Times* that Disraeli discerned among the urban population the Conservative working man as a sculptor perceives angels in a block of marble. The literature on this topic includes P. Smith, *Disraelian Conservatism and Social Reform* (1967); A. J. Lee, 'Conservatism, traditionalism and the British working class, 1880–1914', in D. E. Martin and D. Rubinstein (eds), *Ideology and the Labour Movement: Essays Presented to John Saville* (1979); and M. Pugh, *The Tories and the People 1880–1935* (Oxford, 1985), *passim*.

47. T. Tholfsen, *Working Class Radicalism in Mid-Victorian England* (1976), p. 159. For discussions of respectability in the north-west cotton district and in Edinburgh, see N. Kirk, *The Growth of Working Class Radicalism in Mid-Victorian England* (1985), ch. 5 and R. Q. Gray, *The Labour Aristocracy in Victorian Edinburgh* (Oxford, 1976), ch. 7.

48. See K. Laybourn, *The Rise of Socialism in Britain, 1881–1951* (Stroud, 1997) and K. Laybourn and D. Murphy, *Under the Red Flag: Communism in Britain, 1849–1981* (Stroud, 1999).

49. E. J. Hobsbawm, *Labour's Turning Point 1880–1900* (1948), p. 85; *Marx and Engels on Britain*, p. 527.

50. Quoted by G. D. H. Cole and R. Postgate, *The Common People 1746–1946* (1961 edn), p. 422, where Linnell is described as 'the first English Socialist martyr'.

51. Quoted in G. and L. Radice, *Will Thorne, Constructive Militant: A Study in New Unionism and New Politics* (1974), pp. 39–40.

52. P. Snowden, *An Autobiography: Volume One 1864–1919* (1934), p. 82.

53. *The Times*, 5 September 1897, quoted by H. A. Clegg et al., *A History of British Trade Unions since 1889: Volume I: 1889–1910* (Oxford, 1964), p. 164. For the courts' decisions affecting the legal status of the unions, see J. Saville, 'Trade unions and free labour: the background to the Taff Vale decision', in A. Briggs and J. Saville (eds), *Essays in Labour History* (1960).

54. *I. L. P. News*, March 1900, quoted in P. P. Poirier, *The Advent of the Labour Party* (1958), p. 89. See also F. Bealey and H. Pelling, *Labour and Politics 1900–1906: A History of the Labour Representation Committee* (1958), *passim*.

55. For discussions see D. E. Martin, '"The instruments of the people"?: the Parliamentary Labour Party in 1906', in Martin and Rubinstein, *Ideology*

and the Labour Movement, and K. D. Brown (ed.), The First Labour Party 1906–
1914 (1985), introduction and ch. 1.

56.   W. Kendall, The Revolutionary Movement in Britain 1900–21 (1969), p. 36; see
      also K. Laybourn, 'The failure of socialist unity in Britain c.1893–1914',
      Transactions of the Royal Historical Society, 6th ser., 4 (1994), p. 169.

57.   Much of it is discussed by K. Laybourn, 'The rise of Labour and the decline
      of Liberalism: the state of the debate', History, 80 (1995), pp. 207–26.

58.   P. Snowden, Socialism and Syndicalism (1913), p. 242.

59.   J. N. Horne, Labour at War: France and Britain, 1914–1918 (Oxford, 1991),
      pp. 42–7.

60.   R. Douglas, 'Labour in decline, 1910–14', in K. D. Brown (ed.), Essays in
      Anti-Labour History: Responses to the Rise of Labour in Britain (1974).

61.   Rothstein, From Chartism to Labourism, p. 218.

Conclusion

1.   T. Wright, Our New Masters (1873), p. 1; C. F. G. Masterman, The Condition of
      England (1909; 1911 edn), p. 85; The Collected Poems of G. K. Chesterton (1942
      edn), p. 176.

 2.   P. Keating (ed.), Into Unknown England 1866-1913: Selections from the Social
      Explorers (1976), p. 29; S. Meacham, A Life Apart: The English Working Class
      1890–1914 (1977), p. 7.

 3.   See J. Zeitlin, 'From labour history to the history of industrial relations',
      Economic History Review, 40:2 (1987), p. 159, for a critical appreciation (and,
      ultimately, a rejection) of 'struggle between employers and workers for
      control of the labour process' as the defining feature of labour's past. The
      most notable historian of the labour process is Richard Price. See his Labour
      in British Society: An Interpretative History (1986), esp. introduction.

 4.   E. Higgs, A Clearer Sense of the Census: The Victorian Censuses and Historical
      Research (1996), p. 94.

 5.   R. Samuel, 'The workshop of the world: steam power and hand technology
      in mid-Victorian Britain', History Workshop Journal, 3 (1977), pp. 6–72.

 6.   J. Bourke, Working-Class Cultures in Britain, 1890–1960 (1994), pp. 136–51.

BIBLIOGRAPHICAL ESSAY

This bibliographical essay aims to indicate those books, rather than articles, a reader might consult for a fuller treatment or a differing emphasis than our text. It does not duplicate everything in the endnotes, nor is it other than a partial – in perhaps more than one sense of the word – selection from the existing literature.

No serious student of labour history should be unfamiliar with a number of classic studies. A. Toynbee, *Lectures on the Industrial Revolution* (1884), J. Thorold Rogers, *Six Centuries of Work and Wages* (1884), S. and B. Webb, *The History of Trade Unionism* (1894; 2nd edn 1920) and the trilogy by J. L. and B. Hammond on the period 1760–1832 – *The Village Labourer* (1912), *The Town Labourer* (1917) and *The Skilled Labourer* (1920) – though corrected and amplified by later historians, provide radical liberal or socialist perspectives of the impact of the Industrial Revolution on the labouring population. In a similar tradition is G. D. H. Cole and R. Postgate, *The Common People, 1746–1946* (1946) and Cole's *A Short History of the British Working Class Movement 1789–1947* (1948). Since then, the most influential left-of-centre contribution remains E. P. Thompson, *The Making of the English Working Class* (1963); though it focuses on an earlier period than ours, it is nevertheless a starting point for any consideration of labour in the long nineteenth century. Two volumes of collected essays by E. J. Hobsbawm – *Labouring Men: Studies in the History of Labour* (1964) and *Worlds of Labour: Further Studies in the History of Labour* (1984) – offer some fine expositions of labour history. Some currents in more recent social and labour history can be discerned in the essays of R. Samuel, *Theatres of Memory*, 2 vols (1994–8).

Then there are numerous excellent syntheses which include material relevant to this book: John Rule's *The Labouring Classes in Early Industrial England, 1750–1850* (1986) is the best discussion of the period preceding that covered in our volume. E. H. Hunt, *British Labour History, 1815–1914* (1981) is particularly useful for the impact of economic changes on the labour force. One of the most original studies is R. Price, *Labour in British Society: An Interpretative History* (1986), which has a brilliant introductory chapter on the (then) most important developments in labour and trade union history. A short book from a Marxist viewpoint, J. Saville, *The Consolidation of the Capitalist State, 1800–1850* (1994), stresses the way labour was 'disciplined' by the process of industrialisation and it might be read in conjunction with N. Kirk, *Change, Continuity and Class: Labour in British Society, 1850–1920* (Manchester, 1998). Quite different is J. Benson, *The Working Class in Britain, 1850–1939* (1988), which plays down the significance of class. Closer to E. P. Thompson's emphasis on class formation, as their title implies, is the short interpretative study by A. Miles and M. Savage, *The Remaking of the British Working Class 1840–1940* (1994). There is a critical treatment of the history of the working class, with a particular emphasis on social and political developments, in J. Belchem's stimulating and characteristically readable study, *Industrialization and the Working Class: The English Experience 1750–1900* (1990). A few historians have attempted comparative studies; a good example is N. Kirk, *Labour and Society in Britain and the USA* (Aldershot, 1994), which in two volumes covers the period 1780–1939.

Many of the essays in the three volumes of F. M. L. Thompson (ed.), *The Cambridge Social History of Britain, 1750–1950* (Cambridge, 1990) provide useful background for those with an interest in labour history, as do volumes one and two of R. Floud and D. McCloskey (eds), *The Economic History of Britain since 1700* (2nd edn, Cambridge, 1994). P. Mathias, *The First Industrial Nation: The Economic History of Britain, 1700–1914* (1983 edn) provides steerage through the important economic issues of the period. M. J. Daunton, *Progress and Poverty: An Economic and Social History of Britain, 1700–1850* (Oxford, 1995) is excellent on the earlier period, and his projected companion volume, covering the years to 1939, is keenly awaited.

Reliable data on wages, prices, the length and intensity of labour and similar indices of working-class living standards are notoriously difficult to come by, although B. R. Mitchell and P. Deane, *Abstract of British Historical Statistics* (Cambridge, 1962) provides many useful examples. J. Thorold Rogers, *Six Centuries of Work and Wages* (1884) offers an interesting insight into nineteenth-century writings on the subject, with many data on the the nineteenth century to be found in the last two chapters (18 and 19). E. H. Hunt, *Regional Wage Variations in Britain, 1850–1914* (Oxford, 1973) is a path-breaking study. For discussions of the problems of utilising the census in studies of employment, see R. Lawton (ed.), *The Census and Social Structure* (1978) and E. Higgs, *A Clearer Sense of the Census: The Victorian Census and Historical Research* (1996). J. Benson, *The Penny Capitalists: A Study of Nineteenth-Century Working-Class Entrepreneurs* (Dublin, 1988) shows the different ways in which people made their livings (thus suggesting, perhaps inadvertently, the even greater difficulty of measuring wages with any degree of accuracy). There is a useful survey of the length of the working week in various occupations in M. A. Bienefeld, *Working Hours in British Industry: An Economic History* (1972).

The extent to which such data are problematical is demonstrated by the vigorous nature of the long-running 'standard of living debate'. The *Economic History Review* has for decades been the site of a seemingly endless discussion of wages, prices, health, heights and nutritional status. It was a debate that began before the Industrial Revolution had run its course with, for example, Frederick Engels's *The Condition of the Working Class in England* (1845; later edns), which remains an evocative and widely quoted source. In their scholarly form, these debates have involved some of the leading figures of economic history – J. H. Clapham, T. S. Ashton, J. D. Chambers, R. M. Hartwell, E. J. Hobsbawm, C. H. Feinstein, and so on. There are helpful introductions to the issues in A. J. Taylor (ed.), *The Standard of Living in Britain in the Industrial Revolution* (1975) and P. Hudson, *The Industrial Revolution* (1992). An essay by C. H. Feinstein, 'Pessimism perpetuated: real wages and the standard of living during and after the Industrial Revolution', *Journal of Economic History*, 58:3 (1998) reaffirms a bleaker view of working-class experiences. One of the most pungent modern contributions to the literature on the standard of living – a book which belongs in the 'pessimist' tradition with Engels, Toynbee and the Webbs – is B. Inglis, *Poverty and the Industrial Revolution* (1971). The 'free-market' Institute of Economic Affairs has entered the controversy with a collection of essays, *The Long Debate on Poverty* (1974 edn). Housing, in the form of rent, consumed a high proportion of working-class budgets in the nineteenth century and its quality, character and location impacted heavily upon the sorts of communities that industrialism shaped. The best analyses of these issues are still E. Gauldie, *Cruel Habitations: A History of Working-Class Housing, 1780–1918* (1974) and J. Burnett, *A Social History of Housing, 1815–85* (1978; 2nd edn 1986). Food took up an even greater part of these budgets and J. Burnett, *Plenty and Want: A Social History of Diet in England from 1815 to the Present Day* (1978) provides a good starting point for the student wishing to study this aspect.

On the issue of labour migration, see J. Lucassen, *Migrant Labour in Europe, 1600–1900: The Drift to the North Sea* (1987), B. Thomas, *Migration and Economic Growth: A Study of Great Britain and the Atlantic Economy* (Cambridge, 1954) and D. Baines, *Migration in a Mature Economy: Emigration and Internal Migration in England and Wales, 1861–1900* (Cambridge, 1985). Scotland is considered in an excellent set of conference papers: T. M. Devine (ed.), *Scottish Emigration and Scottish Society* (Edinburgh, 1992), and Welsh migrations are analysed in C. G. Pooley, 'Welsh migration to England in the mid-nineteenth century', *Journal of Historical Geography*, 9:3 (1983). For the link between urbanisation and labour migration, see C. M. Law, 'The growth of urban population in England and Wales, 1801–1911', *Transactions of the Institute of British Geographers*, 41 (1967). The best single study, though one relating to the earlier period, is still the classic A. Redford, *Labour Migration in England, 1800–1850* (1926). Rural depletion is discussed by A. L. Bowley, 'Rural depopulation in England and Wales: a study of the changes of density', *Journal of the Royal Statistical Society*, 77 (1914). The largest ethnic migrant labour force, the Irish, have attracted particular attention from scholars. For a discussion of this group, see G. Davis, *The Irish in Britain, 1815–1914* (Dublin, 1991) which provides an effective introduction to writings on the Irish migrants in Britain. A more recent study is D. M. MacRaild, *Irish Migrants in Modern Britain, 1750–1922* (1999) which contains an up-to-date bibliography of related interest.

Students wishing to write longer studies on the creed of self-help and associationalism will need to consult the Victorian prophet on these matters. In particular, S. Smiles, *Self-Help; With Illustrations of Conduct and Perseverance* (1859) and *Thrift: A Book of Domestic Counsel* (1875). M. Chase, 'Out of radicalism: the mid-Victorian freehold land movement', *English Historical Review*, 56 (1991) provides a stimulating discussion of the early building-society movement, a theme which is treated more fully in E. J. Cleary, *The Building Society Movement* (1965), S. M. Price, *Building Societies: Their Origin and History* (1958) and M. Body, *The Building Societies* (1980). R. N. Price makes a critical appraisal of one important institution in 'The working men's club movement and Victorian social reform ideology', *Victorian Studies*, 15:2 (1971). A broader-based study of the world of which the CIU was one part is R. J. Morris, 'Clubs, societies and associations', in Thompson (ed.), *Cambridge Social History of Britain*, volume 2. The best work on friendly societies is still P. H. J. H. Gosden, *The Friendly Societies in England, 1815–1875* (Manchester, 1961) while the same author's *Self-Help: Voluntary Associations in the 19th Century* (1973) surveys

co-operative and building societies and savings banks. For the importance of
working-class credit networks see M. Tebbutt, *Making Ends Meet: Pawnbroking
and Working-Class Credit* (Leicester, 1983). The literature on co-operation is huge,
and cannot be recounted here in full. P. Gurney, *Co-operation, Culture and the
Politics of Consumption in England, 1870–1939* (Manchester, 1996) is by far the best
full-scale analysis of the movement's golden age, while R. G. Garnett, *Co-operation
and the Owenite Socialist Communities in Britain, 1825–45* (Manchester, 1972), J. F. C.
Harrison, *Robert Owen and the Owenites in Britain and America: The Quest for the New
Moral World* (1969) and G. Claeys, *Machinery, Money and the Millennium: The New
Moral Economy of Owenite Socialism, 1815–67* (1987) provide the clearest pathways
through the early years. S. Pollard's essay, 'Nineteenth-century co-operation:
community building to shopkeeping', in A. Briggs and J. Saville (eds), *Essays in
Labour History* (1960), argues that the Owenite vision of a new world evolved into
the retailing outfit of the later Victorian period. Overall, the best dicussion of
working-class economic strategies is P. Johnson, *Saving and Spending: The Working-
Class Economy in Britain, 1870–1939* (Oxford, 1985), although important contexts
are found in discussions of laissez-faire, welfarism and state intervention, for
which see D. Fraser, *The Evolution of the British Welfare State* (1973) and K. Laybourn,
The Evolution of British Social Policy and the Welfare State c.1800–1993 (Keele, 1995).

The best brief introduction to 'leisure and culture' is H. Cunningham's essay
of that title in Thompson (ed.), *Cambridge Social History*, volume 2. For the early
part of our period, see Cunningham's *Leisure in the Industrial Revolution, c.1780–
1880* (1980). A useful collection on the subject is J. K. Walton and J. Walvin (eds),
Leisure in Britain, 1780–1939 (Manchester, 1983), while J. M. Golby and A. W.
Purdue, *The Civilisation of the Crowd: Popular Culture in England, 1750–1900* (1984)
provide an analysis which eschews the notion that industrialisation created a
watershed in popular cultural history and instead argue for continuities between
'primitive' and 'later' forms of recreation. For the rural dimension, which Golby
and Purdue also stress, see R. W. Malcolmson, *Popular Recreation in English Society, 1700–1850* (Cambridge, 1973). For religious observance, or otherwise, among
the working class, one writer has done more than any other: his most recent
offering is H. MacLeod, *Religion and Society in England, 1850–1914* (Basingstoke,
1996) which has an excellent bibliography.

Just as there are pitfalls when making generalisations about the impact of
industrialisation on the whole of the working population, so there are too in
dealing with various sections. There is debate about the extent of 'deskilling'
caused by mass production; a good introduction to it is C. More, *Skill and the English Working Class, 1870–1914* (1980). The impact of economic change on women
has been more widely discussed (see the next but one paragraph below). The
'depressed trades' provide a counterpoint to the advances in other spheres. On
one of the most impoverished groups, see D. Bythell, *The Handloom Weavers:
A Study in the English Cotton Industry* (Cambridge, 1969) and (though qualifying
some of the gloomier accounts) G. Timmins, *The Last Shift: The Decline of Handloom Weaving in Nineteenth-Century Lancashire* (Manchester, 1993). Good economic
and social histories are still lacking for many Victorian occupations. For one of
the largest, coal mining, where workers faced a demand for their labour that was
growing, but often very erratically, there is a good survey by J. Benson, *British
Coalminers in the Nineteenth Century: A Social History* (Dublin, 1980). A similarly

dangerous occupation, fishing, has been studied by T. Lummis, *Occupation and Society: The East Anglian Fishermen 1880–1914* (Cambridge, 1985). Several historians have examined the farm labourer, whose wages were often scanty, including K. D. M. Snell, *Annals of the Labouring Poor: Social Change and Agrarian England 1660–1900* (Cambridge, 1985), A. Armstrong, *Farmworkers: An Economic and Social History 1770–1980* (1988) and A. Howkins, *Reshaping Rural England: A Social History 1850–1925* (1991). F. McKenna, *The Railway Workers 1840–1970* (1980) discusses a group that had relative security of employment but very long working hours, while the insecurities affecting those who built the railways is brought out by D. Sullivan in *Navvyman* (1983). For many other occupations – engineering and metalworkers, domestic servants, the various types of employment in building and in textiles – the interested reader has to search out essay-length studies and local histories.

In contrast, though reflecting the tendency to study institutions, the history of organised labour has generated a good deal of interest. No undergraduate disser-tation on the subject would be complete without some reference to the genesis study, S. and B. Webb, *The History of Trade Unionism* (1894, 2nd edn, 1920) if not to what the Webbs termed their 'scientific analysis' of trade unionism, *Industrial Democracy* (1897). The earlier period is covered with customary aplomb by J. Rule, *British Trade Unionism 1750–1850* (1988). H. Pelling, *A History of British Trade Uni-onism* (1992 edn) provides a lucid overview, as do J. Lovell, *British Trade Unions, 1875–1933* (1977), A. E. Musson, *British Trade Unions 1800–1875* (1982) and K. Laybourn, *A History of British Trade Unionism* (1992). There is a detailed study of the 1889–1910 period in H. A. Clegg, A. Fox and A. F. Thompson, *A History of British Trade Unions since 1889* (1964) while some of the essays in C. J. Wrigley (ed.), *A History of British Industrial Relations, 1875–1914* (Brighton, 1982) are valu-able. These, like E. H. P. Brown, *The Growth of British Industrial Relations: A Study from the Standpoint of 1906–14* (1959), focus on formal industrial relations, rather than the 'labour process' or the 'social history of work', as the focal point of labour activity. Later labour militancy is discussed by B. Holton, *British Syndicalism, 1900–1914: Myths and Realities* (1976). A useful comparative study is W. J. Mommsen and H-G. Husung (eds), *The Development of Trade Unionism in Great Britain and Germany, 1880–1914* (1985). For women and the trade union movement, see S. Lewenhak, *Women and Trade Unions* (1977) and S. Boston, *Women Workers and Trade Unions* (1987). The most recent and up-to-date study – one which stresses continuities rather than watersheds in the development of modern trade unions – is W. H. Fraser, *A History of British Trade Unionism, 1700–1998* (1999).

There is now sizeable body of writing on women and labour. S. Rowbotham, *Hidden from History* (1972) continues to be an important polemical introduction, but see also S. Walby, *Patriarchy at Work: Patriarchal and Capitalist Relations in Employment* (1986). I. Pinchbeck, *Women Workers and the Industrial Revolution, 1750–1850* (1930; 3rd edn 1981) remains an important study of the early period. The best short study of women's experiences of work in the nineteenth century is J. Saville, 'Working-class women in nineteenth-century Britain', in C. Holmes and A. Booth (eds), *Economy and Society: European Industrialisation and its Social Consequences: Essays Presented to Sidney Pollard* (Leicester, 1991). Fuller analyses of this arena include A. V. John (ed.), *Unequal Opportunities: Women's Employment in England, 1800–1918* (1986) and E. Roberts, *Women's Work 1840–1940* (Cambridge,

1995). For working-class women's political experiences, see J. Liddington, *One Hand Tied Behind Us: The Rise of the Women's Suffrage Movement* (1978). E. Ross, *Love and Toil: Motherhood in Outcast London, 1870–1918* (Oxford, 1993), C. Chinn, *They Worked all Their Lives: Women of the Urban Poor in England, 1880–1939* (Manchester, 1988) and M. Tebbutt, *Women's Talk: A Social History of 'Gossip' in Working-Class Neighbourhoods, 1880–1960* (Aldershot, 1995) each discuss important aspects of the 'woman's domain'.

While the empiricists and the polemicists have expended huge quantities of energy on the 'standard of living debate', theorists have usually been occupied with concepts such as class and ethnicity. More recently, postmodernism has attempted to challenge Marxism's hegemonic control of the citadels of labour history. The works on British Marxist historians such as E. P. Thompson, E. J. Hobsbawm and J. Saville (cited elsewhere in this essay) provide an important springboard to any attempt to understand labour history and the question of class. Postmodern discourse has begun to exert a considerable influence on British social history, not least in the area of labour history and in particular on the question of class. One of the foundational texts for students wishing to learn more about the 'linguistic turn' (wherein language is granted privileged constitutive powers in shaping the actions and ideas of past peoples) is G. S. Jones, *Languages of Class: Studies in English Working Class History* (Cambridge, 1983). Among other studies that find class an inadequate approach to understanding the historical process are two books by P. Joyce, *Visions of the People: Industrial England and the Question of Class, 1848–1914* (Cambridge, 1991) and *Democratic Subjects: The Self and the Social in Nineteenth-Century England* (Cambridge, 1994), J. Vernon, *Politics and the People: A Study in English Political Culture, c.1815–1867* (Cambridge, 1993), M. Taylor, *The Decline of Radicalism, 1847–1860* (Oxford, 1995), J. Lawrence, *Speaking for the People: Party, Language and Popular Politics in England, 1867–1914* (Cambridge, 1998) and E. F. Biagini, *Liberty, Retrenchment and Reform: Popular Liberalism in the Age of Gladstone, 1860–1880* (Cambridge, 1992). A recent study denies that class should be a credo but instead attempts to rehabilitate the concept as a 'prism' for refracting our explanations of social relations: D. Cannadine, *Class in Britain* (1998), while various critiques of the 'linguistic turn' can be found in a collection of essays edited by J. Belchem and N. Kirk, *Languages of Labour* (Aldershot, 1997). One of the most trenchant discussions of the seemingly dichotomous position of class and ethnicty can be found in the early chapters of S. Fielding, *Class and Ethnicity: Irish Catholics in England, 1880–1939* (Buckingham, 1992).

Studies of social unrest and of popular radicalism usually, by extension if not directly, come under the umbrella of labour history. Only the merest sketch can be afforded here, and readers will wish to turn to specialist general works such as J. Belchem's *Popular Radicalism in Nineteenth-Century Britain* (1996). The social unrest of the 1830s has generated a number of important works. Foremost among these is E. J. Hobsbawm and G. Rudé's analysis of discontent in the rural south-east, *Captain Swing* (1969). A regional study which brings out the persistence of incendiarism and other methods of protest (which were probably employed more widely than has been recognised) is J. E. Archer, *By a Flash and a Scare: Arson, Animal Maiming and Poaching in East Anglia, 1815–1870* (Oxford, 1990). Opposition to the new Poor Law has been studied by, among others, J. Knott, *Popular Opposition to the 1834 Poor Law* (1986), and M. Rose in J. T. Ward (ed.),

Popular Movements c.1830–1850 (1970), a volume that also deals with other working-class issues. The Chartist movement has attracted massive interest from historians. First stops in the search for further reading are J. F. C. Harrison and D. Thompson, *Bibliography of the Chartist Movement, 1837–1976* (Hassocks, 1976) and O. Ashton et al., *The Chartist Movement: A New Annotated Bibliography* (1995). D. Thompson, *The Chartists: Popular Politics in the Industrial Revolution* (1984) is probably the best single-volume study. M. C. Finn, *After Chartism: Class and Nation in English Radical Politics, 1848–1874* (Cambridge, 1993) discusses the issues taken up by radicals in the third quarter of the century. A useful new short study is J. Walton, *Chartism* (1999).

The role of those workers who were male, skilled, relatively well-paid and able to exert an element of control over the terms of their employment has been much debated. The concept of a mid-Victorian 'labour aristocracy', which Hobsbawm in particular has explored (see *Labouring Men* and *Worlds of Labour*), has generated a literature too copious to detail. However, much of it is surveyed, if sceptically, by T. Lummis, *The Labour Aristocracy 1851–1914* (Aldershot, 1994); in a lengthy introduction to the second edition his *Before the Socialists: Studies in Labour and Politics 1861–1881* (Aldershot, 1994), R. J. Harrison makes a spirited defence of the concept. Not all historians have avoided the sort of teleological approach which discusses the working-class politics of the 1880s in a way that constantly looks forward to the 'rise of labour'. Some of the essays in E. F. Biagini and A. J. Reid (eds), *Currents of Radicalism: Popular Radicalism, Organised Labour and Party Politics in Britain, 1850–1914* (Cambridge, 1991) are a useful corrective to this approach.

Nevertheless, the rise to government of the Labour Party in the post-1918 years has helped to ensure an extensive literature on its pre-1914 period. For many years, the standard account was H. Pelling, *A Short History of the Labour Party* (1961; 11th edn 1996), although the same author's *The Origins of the Labour Party, 1880–1900* (Oxford, 1965) is more relevant to our period. In addition to their valuable earlier chapters, K. Laybourn, *The Rise of Socialism in Britain c.1881–1951* (Stroud, 1997) and A. Thorpe, *A History of the British Labour Party* (1997) include good bibliographical surveys of the early Labour Party, while D. Tanner, *Political Change and the Labour Party, 1900–1918* (Cambridge, 1990) brings out its uneven geographical development. For the ILP, see D. Howell, *British Workers and the Independent Labour Party, 1888–1906* (Manchester, 1983); for the SDF, M. Crick, *The History of the Social Democratic Federation* (Keele, 1994); and for the Fabians, A. M. McBriar, *Fabian Socialism and English Politics, 1884–1918* (Cambridge, 1962). Also useful on the background to Labour's emergence, and related currents, are C. Waters, *British Socialists and the Politics of Popular Culture, 1884–1914* (Manchester, 1990) and L. Barrow and I. Bullock, *Democratic Ideas and the British Labour Movement, 1880–1914* (Cambridge, 1996). D. E. Martin and D. Rubinstein (eds), *Ideology and the Labour Movement: Essays Presented to John Saville* (1979) includes essays on aspects of the period.

The biographical literature is too extensive to list. For most of the individuals mentioned in our text there are biographies. A few left autobiographies. The volumes of J. M. Bellamy and J. Saville (eds), *Dictionary of Labour Biography* (1972–) and volumes two and three of J. O. Baylen and N. J. Gossman (eds), *Biographical Dictionary of Modern British Radicals* (Brighton, 1984, 1988) are useful starting points, as are the three volumes edited by J. Burnett et al., *The Autobiography of the Working Class: An Annotated Critical Bibliography 1790–1945* (Brighton, 1984–9).

Historians ought to encourage their readers to go beyond the secondary literature and into the primary sources. There are several documentary collections, including G. D. H. Cole and A. W. Filson, *British Working Class Movements: Select Documents 1789–1875* (1951) and E. J. Hobsbawm, *Labour's Turning Point 1880–1900* (2nd edn, Hassocks, 1974). It should, however, be borne in mind that records tended to be kept by leaders of organisations such as trade unions or observers of the working population such as Henry Mayhew; first-hand accounts of the experiences of ordinary workers are relatively rare, though there are some examples in two books by J. Burnett: *Useful Toil: Autobiographies of Working People from the 1820s to the 1920s* (1974) and *Destiny Obscure: Autobiographies of Childhood, Education and Family from the 1820s to the 1920s* (1982).

Finally, it cannot be denied that all historical works are, sooner or later, superseded. The assiduous student will seek to monitor the flow of books and articles by consulting the scholarly journals; some, including the *Labour History Review* and the *Economic History Review*, provide annual bibliographies that list new publications. Also useful is the Royal Historical Society's *Annual Bibliography of British and Irish History*, which has appeared since 1975, and R. C. Richardson and W. H. Chaloner, *British Economic and Social History: A Bibliographical Guide* (1976; 2nd edn 1996), which contains numerous useful references for labour historians.

INDEX

Abercrombie, Patrick, 38
Aberdeen, 81
Acts of Parliament, *see under
individual titles*
Adshead, Joseph, 103
agricultural depression, 74
agricultural labourers, *see*
farmworkers
agriculture, 77, 106
allotment system, 50–1, 107
Alton Locke (Kingsley), 28
Anatomy Act (1832), 145
Anglicanism, *see* Church of England
animals, cruelty to, 106, 108
Annales school of history, 10, 174
anthrax, 58
apprenticeships, 41, 54, 74, 101–2
see also child labour
Arch, Joseph, 34
aristocracy, 144, 145, 148, 152
Tocqueville on, 6, 173–4
aristocracy of labour, *see* skilled
workers
Artisans' Dwellings Act (1875), 95
Ashington, 71
Ashley, Lord, 136
Ashton, 151
associationalism, 114–43
Australia, emigration to, 62, 70
Ayrshire, 82

Bacup, co-op and chapel in, 38
Baden Powell, R. S., 111
Bagehot, Walter, 155
Band of Hope, 140
Barnard Castle, 71
Barrow-in-Furness, 110, 154

migrants to, 67, 81
pubs and clubs in, 122, 140
shipbuilding in, 36, 80, 81
Barrow Shipbuilding and Iron
Company, 55
basket making, 35
Batley, wool trade in, 33
Baxter, Dudley, 59
Bedfont, Middlesex, incendiarism
at, 3
beggars, 38, 49
Belfast, shipbuilding in, 8, 36, 80, 81
Bell, Richard, 161
Bell, Lady Florence, 39
Benbow, William, 150
Bentham, Jeremy, 116
Besant, Annie, 159
Birkenhead, shipbuilding in, 8
Birmingham, 15, 125
building societies in, 132
growth of, 64, 70
housing in, 92, 94
migration to, 72
Black Country, nail and chain
making in, 27
Blackburn
cotton weaving in, 32
riot in, 154
Blackpool, holiday resort, 109
Blatchford, Robert, 110
Boer War, 18, 57, 119
boilermakers, 36, 155
Boilermakers, United Society of, 59
Bolton
cotton spinning in, 32
growth of, 65, 71
women cotton workers in, 24

205